Shepheards Devises

Shepheards Devises

Edmund Spenser's
Shepheardes Calender
and the Institutions
of Elizabethan Society

ROBERT LANE

The University of Georgia Press
ATHENS & LONDON

© 1993 by the University of Georgia Press
Athens, Georgia 30602
All rights reserved
Designed by Kathi L. Dailey
Set in 9.5 on 13 Trump Medieval by
  Tseng Information Systems, Inc.
Printed and bound by Thomson-Shore
The paper in this book meets the guidelines for
permanence and durability of the Committee on
Production Guidelines for Book Longevity of the
Council on Library Resources.

Printed in the United States of America

97 96 95 94 93 C 5 4 3 2 1

Library of Congress Cataloging in Publication Data

Lane, Robert, 1946–
    Shepheards devises : Edmund Spenser's Shepheardes
calender and the institutions of Elizabethan society /
Robert Lane.
      p.   cm.
    Includes bibliographical references and index.
    ISBN 0–8203–1514–1 (alk. paper)
    1. Spenser, Edmund, 1552?–1599. Shepheardes
calender.   2. Literature and society—England—
History—16th century.   3. Pastoral poetry, English—
History and criticism.   4. Social institutions in
literature.   I. Title.
PR2359.L36   1993
821'.3—dc20   92–27594
                                        CIP

British Library Cataloging in Publication Data available

Woodcuts from Edmund Spenser's *Shepheardes Calender*,
1579, are reproduced by permission of The Huntington
Library, San Marino, California. *Queen Elizabeth
Attended by Three Goddesses*, © Her Majesty Queen
Elizabeth II, is reproduced by permission of the Royal
Collection, St. James's Palace. *Elizabeth I's Arms* is
reproduced with permission of John R. Phillips.

To Judith

and to the

**Raleigh/Wake Coalition
For the Homeless**

Expose thyself to feel what wretches feel,
That thou mayst shake the superflux to them,
And show the heavens more just.

Contents

Acknowledgments

This is the place where, while rendering sincere thanks for real debts, we construct lineages for our work. Appropriately enough, those lineages usually focus heavily on graduate school teachers or on those who contributed to the specific project, though in my case, and I suspect in most others, there are powerful influences outside these that my work brings to the surface.

For me those influences may go back as far as the preacher in the Deep South church in which I grew up during the 1950s and 1960s who confided to the youth group that, while he did not "preach civil rights," if the members of the congregation did not hear that theme in his sermons, "they just aren't listening." That is only the earliest experience I can recall of encoded speech in a situation markedly like patronage (where the audience paid the salary). It, of course, suffered from all the ambivalence to which such speech is heir, though my memory of the preacher and his sermons suggests that the point, however belatedly, got through to some.

Later George Pickering, Jr., led me to see how the language that organizes our public life can be infused and animated with moral concern. Other important influences include Frank Bliss and Allen Grossman, who, at two very different points in my life, showed me how enriching, important, and exhilarating reading poetry could be.

I received concrete support from Duke University in the form of a Lievsay Dissertation Fellowship to work on this project. Less immediate, but no less vital to many of us privileged to experience it, was the vibrant intellectual atmosphere in the Duke English Department, which raised our spirits and sharpened our sense of the potential for our profession.

The most direct support came from my dissertation committee: Leigh DeNeef, Stanley Fish, Darryl Gless, Bruce Payne, and my director, Annabel Patterson. They not only drew my attention to what I had not done but also encouraged me to see what I had and what could be done. A special word of heartfelt thanks is owed to Annabel Patterson, whose support and encouragement went beyond the perfunctory, expressed in the copious time and scrupulous attention she gave to this project. It has been a privilege to work with someone who is not only an articulate, thoughtful critic but a simply superb teacher as well.

The anonymous reader for the University of Georgia Press lent valuable advice, and Arthur Marotti's encouragement gave much needed and much appreciated stimulus. Nancy Grayson Holmes of the press shepherded this project faithfully, and always cheerfully, through the publication process. With her thoughtful attention Angela Ray helped make the text more readable.

I am also very grateful to the other members of the Raleigh/Wake Coalition For the Homeless, who generously, if unwittingly, gave me an experience that enriched my understanding of the works I discuss here by magnifying my sense of the possibilities for affinity and compassion.

Finally, it is conventional to express gratitude for the unstinting, even heroic, tolerance of loved ones while the author was "distracted" with the project that lies before the reader. Far from tolerating a project that took me away from our life together, Judith Ferster has an abiding genius for making our intellectual work an integral part of that life, energizing all of it. That is only one among the many evidences of her love, expansive in its scope and breathtaking in its steadfastness. Her presence graces my life.

The final aim of art is to reclaim the
world by revealing it as it is, but as if it
had its source in human liberty.

—Jean-Paul Sartre

Take the Commons part, for they did
intend a Commonwealth.

—English priest to his parishioners
during the 1536 uprising

Introduction

Literature and Society

If you goe nye,
Fewe chymneis reeking you shall espye:
The fatte Oxe, that wont ligge in the stal,
Is nowe fast stalled in her crumenall [purse].
Thus chatten the people in theyr steads,
Ylike as a Monster of many heads.
But they that shooten neerest the pricke,
Sayne, other the fat from their beards doen lick.
For bigge Bulles *of Basan* brace hem about.

These remarkable lines from the September eclogue of *The Shepheardes Calender* (116–24) open up a wealth of issues that modern criticism has ignored.[1] Immediately striking is their reference to social conditions that are readily available to the speaker's audience: "If you goe nye . . ." This poetry is presented, not as an expression of psychological states, but as a description of a public world. Its character thus cannot be adequately described by criticism that divorces poetry from social conditions, either perceiving it as the portrayal of an essential human nature or celebrating the insularity of its "language as such."[2]

Equally striking is that the conditions referred to here involved a revolution in Elizabethan society: the changing structure of agrarian relations. The elements incorporated into this passage—missing chimneys and livestock converted into cash—evoke the issues that arose from the

1

transformation of the countryside by the commercialization of agriculture. Enclosures, the erosion of common rights, and the rural depopulation that turned peasant farmers into landless laborers or transients were the subjects of complaint and intense debate in sixteenth-century political discussion. Finding those issues in a serious work of poetry requires us to reevaluate and reshape the critical accounts we give of that poetry, to include rather than to exclude this material.

The complaints themselves are intriguing, first because the speaker *reports* them: "Thus chatten the people in theyr steads." This poetry is not offered as the product of the author's single voice, marking his personality or genius, but it is multifaceted, plurivocal. In particular, it incorporates the voices of those we do not expect to find in poetry— "the people," the nonelite of Elizabethan society. Their presence here disturbs any simple identification between serious poetry and a courtly elite or an aristocratic perspective. To be sure, that perspective does get into this passage, in the epithet commonly used by the elite to refer to the people: "Ylike as a Monster of many heads." Far from simply affirming this outlook, however, the placement of the insult, in the midst of cogent complaints voiced by those whom, by convention, it renders monstrous, signals the text's interrogation of class relations in society. It marks the class hostility of the period by bringing into focus the issue around which that hostility revolved: the political status and capacity of the nonelite in society.

Though the poetry is offered as a report, its relationship to these questions is not that of a removed survey. Rather, the lines take a part in the social and political debates they evoke, affirming the view of those "that shooten neerest the pricke." The proverbial phrase "other the fat from their beards doen lick" declares the exploitation that was involved in the changing agrarian patterns and, through the allusion to the biblical "Bulles *of Basan*," enlists religious authority on behalf of those oppressed by that restructuring.[3] This polemical stance cannot be accounted for by criticism that identifies "literature" with an Olympian perspective that resolves (or dissolves) contention into harmony.

Modern criticism often forges that harmony out of the opposition between the "aesthetic" and the "political," positing, either tacitly or explicitly, a zero-sum relationship in which more of either element necessarily means less of the other. But the *Calender* confounds critical aestheticization premised on an "excellence" purchased at the expense of the social and political world. That world is integral to this poetry, engraved into the cup that is the traditional emblem of pastoral art:

A mazer ywrought of the Maple warre:
Wherein is enchased many a fayre sight
Of Beres and Tygres, that maken fiers warre:
And over them spred a goodly wild vine,
Entrailed with a wanton Yvie twine.

Thereby is a Lambe in the Wolves jawes:
But see, how fast renneth the shepheard swayne,
To save the innocent from the beastes pawes:
And here with his shepehooke hath him slayne.
(August 26–34)

The aesthetic value of the artist's craft (the "wanton Yvie twine" echoing similar details on Virgil's and Theocritus's cups) is integrated with social conflict ("fiers warre"), especially the exploitation endemic to it (the "Lambe in the Wolves jawes").[4] Incorporating that exploitation, the poet—the "shepheard swayne"—plays a decisive role in the struggle to alleviate it, running "to save the innocent from the beastes pawes."[5]

This poetry's partisan character has been disregarded by the predominant tradition of literary criticism with its essentialist perspective, organized around transcendent categories of human nature and aesthetics that exclude social and political dimensions from their purview. Some recent critics, however, have articulated a critique of that tradition, its formal aesthetics and its more ordinary reading practices. Edward Said has complained of criticism's divorce from "the human and the circumstantial," demoting history in favor of a realm that embodies the stability and security history lacks. Frank Lentricchia has similarly protested the "denial of history" that has sapped criticism of any constructive social or political function, discrediting society as either an important matter for reflection or a fulfilling arena for action. And in their different ways Annabel Patterson and Terry Eagleton have reinstated the concept of social function that was once central to the literary idea and was certainly central to Spenser.[6] Yet while the general critique has advanced to the point where we might even perceive a paradigm shift, in Spenser studies we have a long way to go.

Because of the long-standing recognition that the *Calender* refers in some way to political circumstances, criticism of this work should, one would think, be a particularly fertile field for tracking the negations and negotiations of history.[7] Much recent criticism continues to adopt the essentialist perspective in locating the subject of Spenser's poetry in a universal human nature, beyond and antagonistic to historical circumstance. Michael Murrin, for example, sees allegory, Spenser's characteristic mode, as "the essential human speech because it alone expresses human nature." This truth confers a transcendence that frees personality from "the chains of contingency."[8] Human nature is also central to Spenser's pastorals in Nancy Jo Hoffman's view: the pastoral singer, "the image of representative man," expresses "archetypal human experience." This investment in the universal character of human nature devalues specificity and individuality.[9]

Hoffman acknowledges her debt to Paul Alpers, whose work on the pastoral, while more nuanced, remains committed to an insular aesthetic authority, that of the poetic singer. His essay "Pastoral and the Domain of Lyric in Spenser's *Shepheardes Calender*" is striking because it tries to rebut the historicist objection that those critics who discuss Spenser's aesthetics ignore the historical dimension of his work. Alpers attempts to meet this criticism by the nominalist act of identifying Spenser's "historical aim" as an aesthetic one, calling his project the creation of a "domain of lyric." While Alpers says he believes that the historicist charge cannot be answered by "oppos[ing] the historical and the aesthetic," he does just that. The literary authority he invokes is defined by its capacity to establish "a qualified but nonetheless genuine independence," free of social constraints and political responsibility. The literary principles that engender this independence rest on the self-sufficiency of both the text and the figure of Colin Clout. For Alpers, Colin's "lyric authority" culminates in the final two eclogues, where it is conceived as residing in a detached, mastering self, validated by "the feeling of lyric presence" and rendered autonomous of social dynamics through art.[10]

Despite its antisocial orientation, essentialist criticism embodies important social and political claims. Hoffman's work, for example, is introduced by anxieties over class that her criticism works to allay. She applauds pastoral's "democratizing power" but quickly quarantines this impulse from any intercourse with the social world.[11] The impulse pastoral evokes toward affinity across divisive social lines is cast as an illusion, a phantom that "cannot tolerate much by way of fact." The aesthetic value of the *Calender* rests on this segregation, "dismissing the hurly-burly of politics for the enduring patterns of human life." Pastoral fails precisely when it allows the social world to "intrude."[12] For Hoffman the democratizing impulse is finally presented as a hypocritical "delusion": it is "the paradox of the upper-middle-class egalitarian impulse, which may be more self-pleasing than altruistic." Presented as hardheaded, her perspective is, in fact, comfortably reassuring. She relieves us—her audience of middle- and upper middle–class intellectuals—of any social responsibility that includes questions of class, and she anoints as given and irremediable an undefined class structure, with any impulse toward community across class lines relegated solely to the "safe playfulness" of a wholly fictional realm.[13]

Murrin's criticism also involves class issues, since only a privileged few can apprehend the transcendent truth that allegory expresses. As the vehicle for identifying the "aristocratic and academic" elite, this literary mode "separat[es] the many from the few."[14] While Murrin does not spell out the political implications, privileging this elite as the locus of both superior wisdom and moral value in society certifies its members as the most qualified to govern and justifies their governing in a way that preserves their privileged status.

The essentialist orientation of these critics on the local issue of Spenser is paralleled with striking fidelity in Allan Bloom's *The Closing of the American Mind*, a work that aims at cultural critique of the broadest kind, encompassing canonical principles, a theory of reading, and a program for higher education, all set in the frame of a deeply conservative account of post-Enlightenment world history and sanctioned by Platonic idealism. Bloom's views are also premised on an "essential" self opposed to history and society. He despairs that "we feel ourselves too dependent on history and culture." For him historical situatedness, the implication of the individual in social dynamics, is the chief threat to the self, whose fulfillment can be achieved only by "escaping the bonds [of] civil society's conventions." As with the literary critics, the route out of the social cave is the reading of certain "classic" texts and doing so in a certain way.[15] Directed as it is toward the "essential"—the decisively antisocial—self, reading must be unhistorical, even antihistorical.

Yet the nakedly functionalist agenda of Bloom's work makes explicit what is merely implicit in the work of the literary critics: that although literature is supposed to be innocent of politics, those who recycle it today are not. Trying to mobilize anxieties over "loss of values," Bloom enlists the humanities and the universities in a political and social program that promotes a hierarchy crowned with those who possess the "truth," while devaluing the differences that pluralism embodies and celebrates. Central to that program is the aristocracy of privileged readers Murrin hints at, modeled on Plato's philosopher-kings. Resolutely antidemocratic, Bloom's intellectual aristocracy is the preferred political model, in contrast to democracy, the rule of inferiors.[16] He calls on the university to undo the harm democracy has done and to restore the aristocracy's preeminence, providing a "better education for the best people" through reading "the classics." Those texts, regarded as embodying the final truth about "nature and man's place in it," should be allowed "to legislate" for the world, through the agency of those who are capable of seeing that truth. And like the philosophers of antiquity, "none [of whom] believed it feasible or salutary to change the relations between rich and poor in a fundamental or permanently progressive way," Bloom's aristocracy of the intellect clearly depends on one of the bank account.[17]

Opposed in every way to the idealist view of literature is historicism, whose subject is society itself. Although *historicism* as a term has had different referents, I use it here to denote an analysis that values historical knowledge not only for itself but also as a vital means of understanding the social order. As the Soviet historian Yuri Afanasiev put it: "As amnesia—loss of memory—destroys the individual personality of man, so amnesia of history damages social consciousness, barbarizes and makes no sense of the life of the society."[18] Reading literature historically—as part of its society rather than above or beyond it—makes that society more accessible to us. Putting literature back into the social conversation from which it emerged can enhance our understanding of social practices and institutions both then and now and of selves fashioned within those dynamics rather than against them.

There have, of course, been accounts of *The Shepheardes Calender*, and Renaissance literature in general, that invoke Elizabethan history and society. Yet in offering a different historicist view, I implicitly define such attempts as inadequate. While the historical impulse is welcome, however it has manifested itself, it is important to define those shortcomings. Some accounts, for instance, were constrained by a narrowly biographical conception of literary criticism. Thus, Paul McLane sought the meaning of the *Calender* in a rigorous equation between its figures and Spenser's personal life.[19] Though the *Calender* does allude to historical figures, its meaning is only initiated, not exhausted, by this reference. Critics like McLane fail to ask what the broader social significance of such allusion is, what social practices the figures refer to or represent, and why they are present where they are in the *Calender*. This failure produces an atomized history, constituted exclusively by individuals and their action, and a debilitated poetry, reduced to editorial comment on persons or incidents isolated from more comprehensive social patterns. Such "coterie history" constricts the interaction between history and literature by ignoring the role of social practices and institutions both in the production of literature and as its subject.

On the other hand, new historicists like Louis Montrose have attempted to remedy the shortcomings of what they call the "old historicism" by emphasizing "the *historicity of texts*," that is, "the social embedment . . . of all modes of writing." They situate literature "among the multiple forms of writing, and in relation to the non-discursive practices and institutions" of society.[20] Some new historicist work, however, invests those practices with a status that elides human initiation, rendering social phenomena as the impersonal operation of social or linguistic entities such as "power" or "discursive fields" and society itself, finally, as a monolithic structure in which all differences (especially political resistance) turn out to be only incidental variants of a single imperative.[21] While this conception has been justifiably criticized for supplanting human agency, emphasis on the sociopolitical dimension need not entail the disappearance of human agents.[22] My work emphasizes social and political institutions and practices because their elucidation is necessary for an understanding of the *Calender*, but those dynamics were registered and mediated—whether wholly consciously or not—by a writer we know as Edmund Spenser. None of that social experience, or the cultural resources he brought to bear on it in this poem, originated with him, but he perceived it, worked to understand it, and responded to it, crafting its articulation in order to communicate it—to represent it—in a particular way, all with a view toward reshaping the society of which those dynamics were constituent elements.[23]

Criticizing earlier historicism for reading literature as the reflection of a presumed stable body of "facts," new historicist critics also emphasize "the textuality of history," in Montrose's terms, "the unavailability of a full and authentic past . . . not already . . . mediated by the surviving texts of the society in question." Because social and political practices are indeed incarnated in linguistic formations, this application can produce valuable insights into such practices.[24] There is a risk, however, that "textualizing" history—the record of events and workings of institutions—will vitiate our capacity to articulate the character of the society that is the object of our study. Acknowledging as a *theoretical* premise the indeterminacy of historical knowledge may be a wise precaution, but to extend that epistemological doubt so as to nullify any claims we might make about the past seems a peculiarly self-denying ordinance. The real distinctions among historicists finally rest on the character of the claims they make, not (after all the disclaimers are in) between those who claim to discern the shape of the past and those who deny themselves that capability.

On a less theoretical plane, "textualizing" history may well engender a complacency about our obligation to give a responsible account of the historical material available to us, an accountability without which the label of *historicism* is empty. While no historicist account of a past society can be definitive in a final sense, no historicist interpretation of that society's literature can aspire to coherence unless it conscientiously engages that material in describing both the general themes and the broad motifs of the literary work, as well as the possible referents of specific words and phrases. This is not simply because these works "allude to" historical phenomena, though they do, but because they themselves are embedded in the social dynamics and matrices they register. One need not resort to the naive reflectionism of some earlier historicist work as the sole account of that registration or, returning to essentialism through the back door, privilege the literary text as alone providing the key to the elemental character of a society. Indeed, one of our current tasks is to expand the repertoire of ways in which we can describe the mutual implication of social dynamics and textual forms.[25] If we take seriously the social dimension of literature axiomatic to historicism, then the description will unavoidably imply some understanding of the society in which that literature was written, an understanding that cannot credibly be based on literary texts alone.

In the case of my own work, the interpretation of the *Calender* expressed here proceeds to some extent in the same manner as its own internal commentator, E.K., did, incompletely and evasively: glossing words, phrases, and images whose resonance has now become obscure.

Where he would short-circuit the critical potential of the text, however, I attempt to reconstruct the interplay between text and society available to Spenser's original audience. The detailed historical reading of the kind I am providing is uniquely capable of drawing out that resonance, especially the text's political valence.[26]

An important example of how literature and social dynamics are mutually entangled is the claim many new historicists make that Renaissance poetry was a thoroughly aristocratic phenomenon.[27] This view rests on the premise of the court's hegemony—a prestige and influence that so saturated Elizabethan society that genuine opposition was impossible—transmitted into cultural practice primarily through patronage, an exchange in which material support dictated poetic output.[28] The poetry produced by this exchange is seen as thoroughly colonized by the court, reduced to an "instrument of state" that "sanctifies political power"—in a word, "civic propaganda"—its authors rendered as "self-consciously the regime's servant[s]."[29] In this model, literature becomes monovocal through the ventriloquism of power; however much literary texts may differ, they converge in celebration of the court. Even the possibility of conflict within the dominant class, between patrons (the kind of conflict that arose over Queen Elizabeth's proposed marriage to the duc d'Alençon), is elided by the Crown's hegemony.

Louis Montrose has recently departed somewhat from his earlier focus on the unilateral influence of patronage, underscoring the reciprocal relationship of poet and queen that allows some room for contesting orthodox representations. Instead of the single relationship of patronage, he emphasizes the "*segmentary* or *sectional* character of power relations," which produce divergent, even "contradictory interests and pressures" that may "divide individuals or groups within themselves."[30] This pluralistic view provides a salutary avenue toward a more nuanced account of the poet's place than exclusive attention to patronage allows. Even in this essay, however, Montrose focuses exclusively on the relationship between poet and queen, restricting the political arena in which poetry operates to representations of the prince and excluding other important political actors from the scene. By locating the challenge to the monarchy in the poet's role as laureate authorial persona (in the *Calender*) or as the masculine, upper-class subject of Petrarchan discourse (in *The Faerie Queene*), unlinked to any vision of society, Montrose narrows the political potential of culture in much the same way the definitive role accorded patronage does. Poetry is denied any meaningful role in examining social and political issues.[31] Instead, criticism of elite culture or practices is relegated to the poet's unconscious, traced only in the suppressed and repressed meanings of his art.[32] There is no room for intentionally "oppositional" poetry or any meaningful acknowledgment of the public debate in which poetry took part. The critical force of poetry is instead blunted, contained by the court culture. "Anticourtliness" itself remains for Montrose "an aspect of courtly or aristocratic culture . . . an authorized mode of discontent."[33]

This view closely identifies poetic practice with the social and political elite of society. However much new historicists may regret this alignment between culture and political power, their emphasis on the political colonization of writing leads them to view it as fundamentally inescapable.[34] This attitude may result from the effort to counter essentialism by depriving literature of the political innocence that perspective implies. Or it may derive partly from a neo-Marxist theory of ideology, as mediated through Althusser. Or it may grow out of the constraints these critics feel in their own situation, a consciousness of their meagre influence on pivotal questions.[35] Whatever the motivation, although new historicism's attitude toward the alignment between political and cultural power differs from the essentialists', its perspective echoes theirs in viewing culture as a fundamentally aristocratic phenomenon.[36]

In affirming the aristocratic paradigm, both essentialist and historicist interpretations of the *Calender* have ignored the critical function of Renaissance culture so central to Spenser's poem. For that culture not only celebrated political power, prospering in the protective shade of an autocratic regime, but also played a signal role in interrogating and critiquing that power. Its challenge was not confined to the absences or latent tensions in its work but was often explicit, as explicit as the regime of censorship would allow, and at times more so.

In their emphasis on the elite, both interpretive perspectives have also overlooked the importance of "the low" in the text and the society, the culture and voice of the nonelite. This dimension of the *Calender* is pervasive, prominently introduced in E.K.'s introductory commentary. It was an essential element in the pastoral tradition Spenser drew on and is closely associated with religious values prominent in the text. This material was integral to the composition of the work: it was from popular culture that Spenser drew many of the resources he used in the composition of the *Calender*, including the woodcuts, calendar format, fables, proverbs, and colloquial, archaic, and dialectal language. These forms were not decorative, but rather constitutive of the text's meaning, incorporating the perspective of the nonelite as a central element in the poem's critique. Although popular culture was recognizably native to Elizabethan England, the view Spenser molded from its elements in the *Calender* is one "furre estraunged" from orthodox representations, reflecting Spenser's own marginal position.[37] Often pitting a spokesman for this view against a representative of the politico-religious establishment, Spenser was able to examine the authority of these institutions and practices, to test the claims made for them. While the *Calender* does not wholly reject these institutions, the pressure of its critique is toward significant reform, in the direction of a more balanced and inclusive social order.

While my work risks the charge of "narrowness" because it focuses on a single sixteenth-century work, the *Calender*'s breadth allows, indeed requires, that the historicist critic become equipped to understand the fundamental issues the work engages: the relationship between church, the repository of moral authority, and Crown, the bearer of political power; the relationship between the social and political leadership and the people; the class structure; the economic organization; and the role of culture in shaping and reshaping these social patterns. These institutions formed the anatomy of the body of Elizabethan society, organizing its political and social relationships, channeling the energies of its members, and fashioning its moral atmosphere. It was in the articulation and resolution of these issues that the society's "identity" at this historical moment would be established.

In order to flesh out the ways that these issues took shape in Spenser's society and the pervasive manner in which the *Calender* registers them, it is necessary to bring to bear on the text some of the wealth of historical material concerning Elizabethan social and political dynamics. Previous criticism has failed to do this, either by suppressing the political altogether, as we have seen, in favor of universal human nature, or, as in the case of new historicism, by confining its reading to the apparently celebratory tone of the April eclogue. Criticism of the September eclogue provides an instructive example. Surprisingly, given new historicists' professed interest in the interactions between culture and power, there is no new historicist treatment of this poem (virtually none of any of the politically charged moral eclogues), despite the issues it takes up. On the other side, Hoffman, in a fashion typical of essentialist criticism, dismisses the social dimension of the eclogue altogether. These questions deflect her analysis away from the suffering imposed by exploitation, shifting it to the "dehumanizing effect" on the oppressors themselves.[38] The social matrix of exploitation that the eclogue explores is wholly neglected.

In similar fashion, Patrick Cullen acknowledges that the eclogue "contains the most open and vehement satire in the *Calender*," but he blunts the satire by censuring its spokesman, Diggon Davie, as "wild-eyed [Cullen uses the word four times in referring to Diggon], irrational; and sometimes incoherent," uttering "unrestrained protests" and guilty of "typical impracticality and intransigence."[39] By focusing on Diggon's "character" rather than on the institutional abuses he is admittedly attacking, Cullen discredits, not just Diggon's particular complaints, but the impulse for social reform itself.[40]

In contrast to these approaches, taking seriously Diggon's social status as a wanderer (cited by both E.K. and Hobbinol) opens up the complex political dimension of the eclogue. In a society in which staying in one's place was a political, social, and geographic imperative, *wandering* had a sharply pejorative sense. Diggon's wandering makes him, by Elizabethan legal definition, a vagrant, a controversial figure in society. Considered by the government "a menace to public order," vagrants were the subject of repeated regulation during Elizabeth's reign.[41] Since most were unemployed and poor, this perceived threat was entwined with economic issues. Reading the eclogue in light of the junctions between vagrancy, poverty, and order reveals how pervasively the *Calender* engages such issues.

At the same time, the eclogue's repeated emphasis on whether and how to speak draws attention to and problematizes the text's own participation—and that of poetry itself—in public debate. Such participation was itself a central political issue, with the Crown utilizing its formidable resources, especially the alignment between religious and political authority, to assert its prerogative to control public discussion. In particular, it excluded from that discussion all except "men of authority, learning, and wisdom."[42] The result was an ominous shrinkage of the space for public deliberation of important issues. While that constriction made joining the debate all the more urgent, it also made it dangerous.

The *Calender* must be seen in this context if its efforts to protect itself while negotiating that hazardous terrain are to be fully understood. Too often past criticism has taken the text's protective veil for its meaning, misreading its representation of orthodoxy as its last word.

That orthodoxy provided an important context for this poem. Its political constituents, the ideologies of uniformity and hierarchy, were consolidated and protected from discussion and challenge by the Crown's strategy of governing speech. Also working against any challenge from the realm of culture were the courtly affiliations of much Elizabethan poetry, against which a socially responsive and responsible cultural practice had to fashion itself. These elements, which constituted the "situation" of this poem, together with the distinctive ways that Spenser fashioned his poem against them, are described in chapter 2.

The strategies Spenser used both to veil and to empower the text's pointed engagement of controversial issues are the subject of chapters 3 and 4. The risk of retaliation is minimized by a number of textual devices, such as political allegory, the debate form, and a commentator in the text who operates at once authoritatively and disingenuously. Further, to sanction the text's speaking on these sensitive issues Spenser drew on authoritative cultural resources—from literature, religion, and popular culture.

Chapter 5 focuses on the heart of the *Calender*'s political engagement: its interrogation of the fundamental institutions in Elizabethan society—primarily Crown, church, and class—carried on in the debates of the "moral" eclogues (February, May, July, and September). Through similar debates in June and October, discussed in chapter 6, the text critically examines the affiliations and social functions of a public poetry committed to and characterized, like the *Calender*, by its project of reform.

1 Historicisms and 1579

The decade of the 1570s witnessed a debate over public affairs whose persistence and intensity matched or even exceeded that of the reign of Elizabeth's brother, Edward VI. Despite the vigilant and rigorous policy of the government to stifle that debate and enforce an orthodoxy congruent with its goals, challenge to that orthodoxy came from every important sector of society, especially the clergy. The challenge at times focused on seemingly local, discrete questions but in almost every instance had far broader implications for the social order.[1] Politics was a much more unsettled affair than it had been in Mary's reign or than it would be later in Elizabeth's, characterized by a striking vitality and visibility of other actors and movements besides the Crown and ruling elite. This character is important as both the occasion for *The Shepheardes Calender* and the stage on which it made its entrance. Soon after 1579 this stage was altered in important ways, primarily by a government-sponsored crackdown on public dissent, consisting of restrictions or outright proscriptions of public speech, including a 1581 statute "against sedicious Wordes and Rumors uttered againste the Queenes moste excellent Majestie" (the so-called Statute of Silence); a 1581 loyalty oath for students at Oxford; royal proclamations in 1583 and 1584 suppressing books by specific religious dissenters as well as all others that tend "to the defacing of true religion and . . . to slander the present . . . government" (the latter proclamation was apparently occasioned by Catholic works, but by no means was it so limited in its terms);

a royal proclamation in 1582 pronouncing all Jesuits and seminary students traitors based on their status alone, without any requirement of overt act or speech; and the censoring of Holinshed's *Chronicles* in 1587.[2]

The single most important element in this repression was the appointment of John Whitgift as archbishop of Canterbury in 1583, which "set the seal on the policy of reaction."[3] Whitgift believed that "lenity . . . hath bred this schism in the Church . . . after so long liberty and lack of discipline," and he set about immediately taking steps to achieve his goal of "reduc[ing] all the ministers [of the Church of England] to uniformity, and due obedience." He drew up articles, approved by the queen, to serve as "touchstones of orthodoxy," requiring all ecclesiastical officers to submit a loyalty oath affirming not only the queen's supremacy in ecclesiastical matters but also the conformity of the church's theological creed (the Thirty-nine Articles) and ritual (*The Book of Common Prayer*)—an important target for the reformers—to the Word of God. The following year he empowered the Ecclesiastical High Commission to subject any clergyman to a comprehensive, searching inquiry into any aspect of his professional conduct over any period, a procedure so chilling that even the conservative William Cecil, Lord Burghley, protested, comparing it to the Spanish Inquisition. Patrick Collinson summarized the impact of Whitgift's policies: "The onslaught which [he] mounted against puritanism within months of assuming the primacy made a watershed in English church history."[4]

During Whitgift's tenure the repression also intensified against those who protested these policies. The Crown's verbal attacks against parliamentary protests in 1584 escalated in 1586 to imprisoning the sponsors of a legislative proposal to reform church organization.[5] In 1586 Whitgift engineered the notorious Star Chamber decree, centralizing the administration of censorship of all printed material under him and the bishop of London. The appointment of Richard Bancroft to the High Commission the next year signaled the continuation of this severe policy, initially in the campaign against "Martin Marprelate" (using methods Collinson compares to those of Joseph McCarthy) and culminating in the lengthy imprisonment of some Puritan leaders, including Thomas Cartwright, in 1589 and executions of other religious dissenters in the early 1590s, some for "seditious words" alone.[6]

The repression took its toll. Reinforced by its successes against Spain, which enhanced its prestige and reduced the fear of papism (which had fueled public support for Puritanism), the regime had by the early 1590s forced religious dissent, its most formidable opposition, underground, out of the public eye and hearing. Even then the government did not relent, however, but pushed for the conventicle act, punishing (even by death) the failure to attend established church services and only those services.[7]

It is important to keep in mind that the *Calender* was published before the regime overwhelmed the impulse to contest royal policy so palpable in the 1570s and virtually eliminated the leverage of those who initiated such debate. Our view of the *Calender*'s critique—how central and comprehensive it is—cannot be separated from our assumptions about the possibilities for critical discourse in English society at that time. Those possibilities narrowed considerably after the 1580s, while the thoroughgoing character of the *Calender*'s critique is consonant with, even emblematic of, the different temper of the 1570s.

The work's critical posture is exemplified by its relationship to the cult of Elizabeth. The pattern of celebration of the queen in literature, portraiture, and civic pageantry that constituted this cult began to take shape early in Elizabeth's reign, becoming recognizable by the 1570s.[8] After 1580, however, as the cult came increasingly under state control, it became more elaborate—evidenced by the more frequent tilts in the second half of the reign and what Roy Strong describes as the "new extremes" in state festivals after the defeat of the Armada—and more of a centerpiece in the government's self-presentation to the people. It came to dominate the cultural terrain in a way it had not in the 1570s.[9] At the same time, the queen, earlier clothed with quasi-divine status as her cult substituted for the outlawed veneration of the Virgin Mary, was, through this "liturgy of state," invested with an increasingly intense religious aura, her image becoming a kind of cultural holy ground, not unlike the flag as the repository of patriotic feeling in this country.[10]

It is tempting to speculate on the connection between the government's repression and its promulgation of Elizabeth's image as but two facets of an authoritarian dominion it worked to establish, a historical instance of what Roberto Unger describes as "the eternal dream of power[,] to rule by a reverential fear that systematically confuses prudence and piety as motives for obedience."[11] Both law and cult celebrated the plenary authority of the Crown while betraying, through their insistent repression—of dissent on the one hand and, as we shall see, of aspects of Elizabeth's person on the other—anxiety over its durability.

Regardless of whether the cult was a part of such a comprehensive program, however, its political effects were substantial. Throughout the reign it linked public emotions to Elizabeth's person, solidifying the regime's power by engendering an attitude of devotion in the subjects, reverence for the person of the queen that created a reservoir of deference for the institution she embodied and the policies it promulgated.[12] The emotional investment in the Crown could dull the sharp edges of social conflict by blurring political and economic differences among its subjects. During the upheavals of the 1590s the cult was especially important in serving to divert attention from the ever more visible strains in the social fabric and to palliate the anxiety generated by an aging, childless monarch and the impending transition to a new, as yet undetermined regime.[13] The *Calender* was enlisted in this effort when Colin's song from the April eclogue praising Eliza was excerpted in *Englands Helicon* (1600). Extracting the song from its place in the eclogue and in the poem as a whole insulated it from the disturbances of its ostensible praise triggered by these contexts, allowing for its presentation as straightforward celebration of the queen.

Montrose echoes the device of *Englands Helicon* by reading the *Calender* through the lens of the April eclogue alone, tending to situate the poem in the historical moment of the anthology.[14] While his descriptions of the praise in Colin's song are nuanced, this isolation substantially narrows the *Calender*'s political thrust in a way that is more consonant with the post-Armada period, when the cult of Elizabeth had greater relative prominence in the realm of political discourse. As important as negotiation over representations of the queen was during Elizabeth's reign, it did not fix the boundaries of that discourse, especially during the earlier decade. And the *Calender*'s reflection on the role of culture cannot be encompassed by the single relationship of poet and monarch. Reading the eclogue from the perspective of the earlier period, putting it back into its proper historical moment as well as its contexts in the poem as a whole, enriches our notion not only of this eclogue but also of the way the whole poem works to critique power.

"Niobe's Sorrow" and April's Praise

The framework of poet and queen in Montrose's analysis of April becomes a contest over rival subjectivities, inhibiting consideration of the processes of royal representation themselves that the *Calender* interrogates, both through the allusion in the eclogue to the story of Niobe and through the recontextualization of this eclogue's praise in others, especially November.

At the center of Colin's song in April is his reference to Niobe, a strikingly puzzling passage that exists in uneasy tension with the celebratory tone of the rest of the song. In it Colin repudiates doing exactly what he has just finished doing, comparing Elizabeth to Phoebus and Cynthia:

> But I will not match her with *Latonaes* seede,
> Such follie great sorow to *Niobe* did breede.
>> Now she is a stone,
>> And makes dayly mone,
> Warning all other to take heede.
>> (86–90)

According to Golding's *Ovid*, Niobe was the queen of Phrygia who arrogantly compared herself to the gods, ordering her subjects to cease worshiping Latona.[15] In retaliation, Latona's children, Phoebus and Cynthia, took revenge by gruesomely murdering Niobe's own children. In grief Niobe turned into a stone that endlessly wept.

Recent critics have sensed the discordant note this passage injects but have not adequately traced its implications.[16] Montrose, for example, tries to explain it away by a forced analogy between Niobe and the poet, whereby "Colin constructs his relationship to Elisa as that of parent and child." But the more natural, and more troubling, analogy is between the female ruler in Ovid's story and Elizabeth herself. Niobe's combined role as mother and political ruler has affinities with that other metaphor so familiar to Spenser's readers, of the queen as mother of England and its people as her children (a central element of the May eclogue).[17]

Further, the Niobe story highlights royal rhetoric: Golding's *Ovid* tells us at the outset that Niobe's fault was that she could not learn "to use discreter kinde of talke" (*Met.* 6.187).[18] The crux of her misconduct lay in appropriating divine status to bolster her position, boasting of herself as "my most sacred Majestie" (6.217) and declaring, "Right well I know I doe deserve a Goddesse for to be" (6.233). By 1579 the allusion to Elizabeth's divinity was common, especially the elevation of the queen into something close to divinity through the Crown's substitution of Elizabeth for the Virgin Mary, "successfully fill[ing] the void left by the

Queen Elizabeth Attended by Three Goddesses
(Royal Collection, St. James's Palace).

Catholic image cult now discredited."[19] The pageant presented to the queen on her arrival at Kenilworth in 1575, for example, proclaimed her

> No worldly wight no doubt,
> some soveraigne Goddes sure.[20]

Jean Wilson sees this event as "signal[ing] the beginning of the cult of Elizabeth as supernatural being," but important examples of flattering comparisons with goddesses can be found as early as 1569. In that year the portrait of *Queen Elizabeth Attended by Three Goddesses* altered the well-known story of the judgment of Paris in a striking way, awarding the golden apple not to Juno, Minerva, or Venus, but to Elizabeth, visually elevated above the level of all three goddesses, who, like Phoebus and Cynthia in Colin's song, shrink from her glory.[21] This painting portrays the relationship between Elizabeth and the deities in the same competitive terms as the Niobe story—in which the queen asks rhetorically, "How dare ye then prefer to me Latona" (*Met.* 6.237)—and the

April eclogue itself, where Cynthia and Phoebus are "dasht" and "over-thrown" by Elisa's glory. Despite the disclaimer in Colin's song, she is their "match."

It will be objected that the April eclogue is itself complicit with this cultural practice, somewhere between hyperbole and blasphemy. After all, Colin speaks of Elisa as his "goddesse plaine" (97), and Hobbinol's emblem, *O dea certe* (from the *Aeneid*), echoes the Kenilworth pageant. And Colin's combination of "that blessed wight" and "the flowre of Virgins" (47–48) "follows the convention," according to Thomas Cain, "which transferred attributes of the Virgin to the Virgin Queen."[22] Yet by prompting reflection on royal rhetoric, the Niobe story evokes doubts about the status of such representations of power, including the eclogue's own.[23] Self-reference here becomes a mode of interrogation.[24] The Niobe story, "warning all other to take heede" (90), includes the April eclogue but is directed at the dangers inherent in the representational strategy itself. Niobe's arrogance, grounded in her self-deification—she would not "to the Gods . . . yeelde in humble wise" (*Met.* 6.188)—evokes the prospect that the Crown's representation might encourage arbitrary rule, embodying as it did the claim that, in Montrose's words, Elizabeth "now differed [from her subjects] not merely in degree but in kind."[25] Such an apotheosis would remove the queen from accountability to any moral authority by which her person and administration could be evaluated. The eclogue's self-critical thrust critiques the political role of the cult as warrant or compensation for the regime's policies.

Though the poet is included within the warning implicit in Niobe's story, the eclogue also bears traces, in E.K.'s allusion to Stesichorus, of the formidable political pressures that weighed on him to join in lauding the monarch. According to E.K., Stesichorus scorned Helen's beauty in favor of that of Himera, "for which his præsumptuous and unheedie hardinesse, he is sayde by vengeaunce of the Gods, thereat being offended, to have lost both his eyes" (433).[26] Stesichorus's sight was restored after he published a palpably false version of Helen's story, his "recantation" or "palinode," which began: "False is that word of mine—the truth is that thou didst not embark in ships, nor ever go to the walls of Troy."[27] With E.K.'s disparagement of Stesichorus's "præsumptuous and unheedie hardinesse" casting a moral justification over what is a naked exercise of power, the story serves as a graphic warning—not to say threat—to poets of the risks entailed in depicting the powerful (significantly, a female queen) in any but the most positive light.

The woodcut from the April eclogue
(Huntington Library).

The self-referential quality of April's eclogue declares the poet's implication in matrices of power and the representational system integral to them but also affirms his capacity for critical reflection on those relations and that system. His practice is not entirely colonized by a power that insinuates itself through the writer's desire for material advancement. Rather, his position is depicted in April's woodcut, in which the singer figure stands by himself off to the side, outside the circle gathered around the royal figure.

The praise of the April eclogue for the royal figure of Elisa is further disturbed when juxtaposed with other eclogues. In June Hobbinol extols the "pleasaunt syte" (1) he hopes to persuade Colin to settle in by borrowing the same cultural apparatus used to celebrate the queen in April. June prominently features, as did the earlier eclogue, nymphs and Graces gracefully dancing to the music of the Muses, with special emphasis on Calliope, the Muse of heroic poetry, all presided over by Phoebe, to whom the April song had compared Elisa.[28] These echoes render Colin's rejection of this *locus amoenus* a further commentary on the cultural practice April represents, an especially pointed one as Colin himself was the author of the earlier song.[29] The interplay between these eclogues reveals a self-critical dimension in the *Calender* overlooked by criticism that isolates April's praise.

"Now Is Time to Dye"

The most explicit challenge to the celebratory tone of April comes in November, whose eclogue at first glance seems simply to extend it. But this poem deftly challenges the deification of Elizabeth by dwelling on her mortality, apparently praising her while actually burying her. A political system so heavily invested in the person of the queen was especially vulnerable to her mortality. The cult of Elizabeth intensified that investment even while it worked, through her deification, to deny her human condition. Anxiety over the threat that mortality represented to existing political arrangements prompted the effort to remove it from public consciousness altogether by the 1571 Crown-sponsored treason statute forbidding anyone to "compasse imagyn invent [or] devyse . . . the Deathe . . . or any bodely harme . . . [to] the Royall Person of . . . our Soveraigne Ladye Queene Elizabeth." The November eclogue falls squarely within this statutory prohibition.[30]

Playing off the legal doctrine of the queen's two bodies, which functioned to immunize the institution of monarchy against mortality, the eclogue works to challenge the implied claim of Elizabeth's cult, embedded in her motto *Semper eadem* (Always the same), that "her triumph even extended over Time and Death."[31] Niobe's pretension to divine status carried with it the claim of having escaped the uncertainty and contingency of history:

> I am greater than that frowarde fortune may
> Empeache me. For although she should pull many things away,
> Yet should she leave me many more. My state is out of feare.
> > (*Met.* 6.248–50)

The oblique warning of the Niobe narrative, a warning central to November, is that no state is "out of feare." Reading April and November together reveals, not the simple sanctification-through-praise of the queen and monarchy, but a complex exploration of the Crown's divine image and the reality of the queen's all-too-human condition.

November makes explicit its link with April:[32]

> Sing now ye shepheards daughters, sing no moe
> The songs that *Colin* made in her prayse.
> > (77–78)

The echoes of April go a long way toward identifying Dido, the subject of Colin's November song, with Elizabeth, although, given the legal implications of that identification, E.K. is understandably coy about it. His reticence is commonly associated with political overtones in the text.[33] The full impact of the queen's presence, and anticipated absence, in this eclogue is revealed when we examine the political significance of the death of the queen that is the eclogue's focus. The significance of that event goes beyond the "death" of Dido as a metaphor for Elizabeth's misguided policies or as a prediction of the literal outcome of the queen's marriage with the duc d'Alençon.[34]

The disruption and discontinuity the prince's death would impose (especially severe in view of Elizabeth's childless state) impelled the development of an important legal tradition to minimize its effects: the doctrine of the prince's two bodies. Constructing a decisive difference between the "natural Body" of the prince and the "Body politic," this legal fiction was designed and utilized to insulate the latter from the former, even while the two were temporarily joined in the physical body of the reigning monarch:

> [The] Body natural . . . is a Body mortal, subject to all Infirmities that come by Nature or Accident, to the Imbecility of Infancy or old Age, and to the like Defects that happen to the natural Bodies of other People. But [the prince's] Body politic is a Body that cannot be seen or handled, consisting of Policy and Government, and constituted for the Direction of the People, and the Management of the public weal, and this Body is utterly void of Infancy, and old Age, and other natural Defects and Imbecilities, which the Body natural is subject to, and for this Cause, what the King does in his Body politic, cannot be invalidated or frustrated by any Disability in his natural Body.[35]

While this doctrine had numerous, potentially conflicting applications and was used by some Catholics to promote Mary Stuart's claim to the throne, the incarnation of the "Body politic" *in* the prince enhanced the prestige of the monarch (and that of the monarchy), folding the prince's mortal condition into an "immortal" institution. Collapsing the two in effect nullified the "Defects" of the natural body, purging the Crown of the contamination of the temporal and giving it "all the Properties, Qualities, and Degrees of the Body politic which is the greater and more worthy."[36] The doctrine thus bestowed on the Crown the quasi-religious sanction of political "immortality," operating as the legal analogue to the cultural deification of the queen.[37] Elizabeth herself seized the privileged status the doctrine conferred, in one instance citing it to remind her Privy Council that her age and gender—subordinate to theirs in Elizabethan codes of power—were more than offset by her royal status: "As I am but one bodye naturallye considered though by [God's] permission a bodye politique to governe, so I shall desyre yow all my Lordes . . . to bee assistant to me."[38]

The doctrine of the two bodies worked to immunize the political institution against death, the most dramatic "Defect" of the prince's natural body, through the constructive immortality of the "Body politic," for, in the words of a 1560 judicial opinion, "King is a name of Continuance. . . . In this Name the King never dies."[39] The legal fiction could not efface the real anxiety over the prince's death, however.[40] This anxiety fueled the intense political debate between Elizabeth and the Commons over the question of succession, a continuing focus for discontent, raising as it did constitutional questions about the respective prerogatives of Crown and Parliament.[41]

The November eclogue registers these anxieties even as it accents the Niobe warning struck in April. Its reflection on mortality produces an indirect challenge to the kind of audacious complacency Niobe displayed ("My state is out of feare"), in lines that have no counterpart in Spenser's model, Marot:

O trustlesse state of earthly things, and slipper hope
Of mortal men, that swincke and sweate for nought,
And shooting wide, doe misse the marked scope:
Now have I learnd (a lesson derely bought)
That nys on earth assuraunce to be sought.
                    (153–57)

Further challenge to Niobe-like claims can be found in the subtle but definitive shift in Dido's status when she dies, embedded in the emphatic past tense used to describe her earthly existence—"while she was, (that was, a woful word to sayne)" (93)—and highlighted by the contrast between that past life and her present state, the *whilome* and *now* of the poem respectively. However complimentary Colin's song is about her life, her divine status is subtly but definitively reserved for her death:

The woodcut from the November eclogue
(Huntington Library).

She raignes a goddesse *now* emong the saintes,
That *whilome* was the saynt of shepheards light:
And is enstalled *nowe* in heavens hight.

. . . .

The honor *now* of highest gods she is,
    That *whilome* was poore shepheards pryde,
    While here on earth she did abyde.
        (175–77, 197–99; my emphasis)

The eclogue's careful segregation of the two bodies of signifiers, mortal and immortal, implicitly critiques the cultural deification of the living queen.[42]

The anticipation of her death could also have served as a personal appeal to the queen, for the proximity and unpredictability of death provided incentive to reform. The reminder of mortality was frequently used for this purpose in Elizabethan popular literature. Perhaps the most striking example of those works that included a call for repentance based on the prospect of death—a common feature of almanacs of the period—is *The Kalender of Shepherdes*, an important forebear of the *Calender*. Its meditation on November advises all persons to "lyve ryght as they wolde dye."[43] The subversive political potential of what was a common moral maxim is revealed by Archbishop Edmund Grindal's incorporation of just such an appeal to Elizabeth in his letter disobeying her command to suppress certain forms of preaching in the church: "Remember, Madam, that you are a mortal creature. Look not only (as was said to Theodosius) upon the purple and princely array, wherewith ye are apparelled; but consider withal what is that that is covered therewith. Is it not flesh and blood? Is it not dust and ashes? Is it not a corruptible body, which must return to his earth again, God knoweth how soon?"[44] Grindal's reminder removes the cosmetic accoutrements of power (its clothing) and (like the eclogue's pronouncement that Dido is "into dust ygoe" [76]) exposes it to its underlying condition.

Finally, November elaborates April's reflection on the relationship between the prince and the poet described by Montrose. The poet here appropriates a pivotal event in the royal biography: Accession Day, November 17. The celebration of this anniversary was "a major state festival" —by 1576 "under official control"—"designed to glorify the monarchy and its policies." Colin transforms this national "paean in praise of the virgin of reform" to "carefull verse."[45] As in April, the reader's attention is here drawn to the importance of the poet: Thenot's response is again to the craft of Colin's song rather than to its subject. Here, however, unlike April's recital of his song, the poet sings personally.[46] And he has moved to a more important position, featured in the center of the woodcut, larger than the royal scene, and crowned for his work. This eclogue thus reverses April's alignment of the queen as present and central and the poet as absent, marginal. Most important, the apotheosis of the queen here is plainly a function of the poet's craft, a reminder of his cultural power.[47] As E.K. so tellingly puts it, "Elysian fieldes . . . be devised of Poetes" (463).

The *Calender*'s critique of the queen's image (encapsulated as "warning") is more penetrating than the cult of which that image is the central icon would seem to allow. These eclogues reveal poetry's potential for reshaping the political landscape, further realized in the balance of the work. Just as April and November re-form the queen's image with verse, using carefully crafted modulations of familiar cultural forms (panegyric and pastoral elegy), other eclogues bring familiar cultural resources to bear on the fundamental institutions of Elizabethan society, subjecting them to the poet's cunning "devises," representing them in order to re-form them as well.

2

"Emongste the Meaner Sorte"

The Social Orientation
of the *Calender*

Modern criticism has generally treated
Elizabethan poetry as a thoroughly aristocratic practice, oriented toward
if not originating in the court. Such criticism responds both to the common distinction made by Elizabethan writers between "true Poetry" and
popular cultural practice and to the importance for the aspiring courtier
of poetry as a rhetorical strategy. Much, though by no means all, Elizabethan discussion of poetics was conducted by courtiers or would-be
courtiers, those with a weather eye out for connections at court. With
notable exceptions like Sir Philip Sidney, their writing was congruent
with court structure and dynamics, their audience the elite. They saw
themselves as allies of power, not its critics, and their work as an instrument of rule, helping, as one writer put it, to "preserve and governe
[kingdoms]."[1] In its tendency, however, to read all Elizabethan poetics
in the frame of court affiliation, modern criticism has elided the sharp
differences that did exist between writers, even those close to court, over
the character of poetic practice, its sanction and social function.

Publication of the *Calender* itself, diverging from the gentlemanly
model of circulating poems in manuscript, signifies its appeal to a
broader audience beyond the aristocratic elite. Advertising its aim to
"goe but a lowly gate emongste the meaner sorte" (467), the text asserts the existence within Elizabethan culture of the lower classes and
their participation, through reading, in public affairs. The debate form,
itself a symbol of deliberative rather than dictatorial process, is used

in the "moral" eclogues to interrogate central institutions of the Elizabethan political landscape, encouraging the text's enlarged audience to "argue and determine" matters of public concern.[2] And E.K.'s learned intervention acutely registers and dramatizes the tension between such broader dissemination and the reservation of critical judgment to the few. The *Calender* takes up the question of who will be a part of that world, who will participate in the contentious conversation over those issues, by enacting the participation of those customarily excluded, drastically altering the shape of the conversation by giving them a voice in it. The sociopolitical apostasy this stance represented can only be fully measured against the prevailing ideologies of hierarchy and uniformity.

"Degrees Descending": The Ideology of Hierarchy and the Political Exclusion of the Low

"We in England Divide our People." Thus began William Harrison's discussion "Of Degrees of People," examining the institution of hierarchy. Foremost among the divisions that defined the social structure was that between gentry and commons, elite and nonelite. "All the people which be in our countrie," Richard Mulcaster stated, "be either *gentlemen* or of the *commonalty*."[3] This class demarcation, resting largely on lineage, embodied overlapping patterns of social status, political power, and, to a lesser but by no means insignificant extent, economic wealth, a convergence that made class a central feature of Elizabethan society, especially its politics.

Social and political institutions come embedded in a symbolic medium that gives them origin, history, purpose, sanction—"meaning" and "value." This dimension is not just a trapping added to their formal, legal constitution, but is integral to their identity; shaping their language, grounding and rationing their authority, directing the energy of their members, and charting their future development. The shorthand term for this medium is *ideology*.

The salient features of ideology are its claim to coherence and its imperative force. It embodies "a sense of reality" that "define[s] the real and the possible," while prescribing roles for the various actors on the social scene. Louis Montrose's description of the function of texts is applicable here: "By representing the world in discourse" ideology is "engaged in constructing the world" and accommodating its audience "to positions within it."[4] It establishes the decorum and sets the limits for the behavior of that audience. In particular, it proscribes behavior that would alter the social structure ideology sanctions, representing that structure as given and necessary, "natural," rather than the product of, or subject to change by, human agency.

The sanction of necessity is frequently mustered by describing political institutions in nonpolitical terms, removing them from the circumstances of human deliberation and choice. This feature, according to Hannah Arendt, is characteristic of authoritarian regimes: "The source of authority in authoritarian government is always a force external and superior to its own power; it is always this source, this external force which transcends the political realm, from which the authorities derive their 'authority,' that is, their legitimacy, and against which their power can be checked." Extant institutions are thus moralized—identified as a realm of "peace" and "order" whose status and durability exceed contingency—and any oppositional voice is cast as a disruptive threat to that quiet harmony.[5] In Elizabethan England religion was the language used to confer this sanction and to define deviance.

The Elizabethan hierarchy, a resolutely top-down model of power, began with the queen at the apex, ruling over "all the estates of the realm." The Act of Supremacy established Elizabeth as "the only supreme governor of this realm . . . as well in all spiritual or ecclesiastical things or causes as temporal." Her political authority rested heavily on religious sanction. Elizabeth's elevation to prince rested on divine ground: "ELIZABETH BY THE GRACE OF GOD QUEENE." Her anointing by God was part of the general investiture recited by the *Homilies* that all "kings, queens and other princes . . . are ordained of God."[6] But Elizabeth's proclamation emphasized the divine action in her particular case: she was queen "because it hath pleased Almighty God . . . to dispose and bestow upon us . . . the Crown."[7] God's installation gave Elizabeth the power of what Reinhard Bendix calls "sanctified command."[8]

Her sanction was fueled by the antipapal feeling (in part a reaction against Mary's regime) that engendered support for Elizabeth's supremacy as a necessary defense against the return of Roman Catholicism. Based on the model of Constantine and developed into the organizing principle of John Foxe's encyclopedic work, the principle of a single ruler over both church and state became a salient part of the established faith and the nation's identity, embodied in both political and ecclesiastical doctrine, the Act of Supremacy and the Thirty-nine Articles.[9] Whatever misgivings Protestant reformers may have had, they traded their support of the Crown's supremacy over the church for Elizabeth's advocacy of a Protestant program, a bargain that curtailed their incentive and latitude for criticizing the regime.[10]

One of the primary "causes" in which the queen's power was "chief" was the social hierarchy, inextricably interfused with the political one. While Elizabeth did not initiate this structure, her regime, incorporating and allying with the wealthy and powerful families of the realm, promoted its status and authority. The upper reaches of this structure were the creation of the queen herself: she bestowed royal titles. This position as "arbiter of social rank" was, of course, a valuable source of patronage.[11] The zeal with which Elizabeth protected this authority is revealed in the story of the queen's rebuke to Philip Sidney for insulting the earl of Oxford (in the "tennis court episode"): "The Queen . . . lays before him the difference in degree between Earls, and Gentlemen; the respect inferiors ought to their superiors; and the necessity in Princes to maintain their own creations, as degrees descending between the peoples licentiousness, and the anoynted Soveraignty of Crowns: how the Gentlemans neglect of the Nobility taught the Peasant to insult upon both."[12]

The queen's personal interest in this incident reflects the significance of degree in Elizabethan society. Its fundamental status was secured by religious means, the *Homilies* rendering it as a part of the natural order created by God: "Almighty God hath created and appointed all things, in heaven, earth, and waters, in a most excellent and perfect order . . . . Every degree of people, in their vocation, calling, and office, hath appointed to them their duty and order. Some are in high degree, some in low." Hierarchy's divine ordination produced the moral imperative to stay in one's place, embodied in the doctrine of vocation announced by the *Homilies*, enjoining subjects to "take in good part our estate and condition, and content ourselves with that which God sendeth, whether it be much or little . . . that every man behold and consider his own vocation, inasmuch as God hath appointed every man his degree and office, within the limits whereof it behoveth him to keep himself." Efforts to rise above one's place, proceeding as they do from "the unlawful and restless desire in men to be of higher estate than God hath given or appointed unto them," violate God's ordinance.[13]

Such ambition was not only sinful but also politically subversive: it "stirreth up many men's minds to rebellion." Since the lower classes had the most to gain from ascending in the hierarchy, it is not surprising they were considered an especially fertile breeding ground for such rebellion. According to Whitgift, the subversive impulse was inflamed by "flattering" the people, for it "moveth them not to be content with their state and calling, but to aspire to greater dignity, and to take those things in hand which commonly turn to their ruin and destruction."[14] The common association of the lower classes with rebellion is revealed in a 1569 memo of Cecil's on how to respond to the Northern Rebellion. Though the revolt was clearly instigated by noblemen, according to Cecil "the vulgar people are to be taught how this rebellion was prejudicial to the realm, and against the honour of God." The primary form that lesson took was execution: the queen ordered seven hundred commoners killed (though perhaps "only" five hundred were).[15]

The church underwrote degree by incorporating it into its organization and architecture.[16] Ecclesiastical hierarchy was considered a part of the church's creed, integral to its identity.[17] The Puritans' attack on this tenet produced a sharp response by the regime, its vehemence largely attributable to the anxiety over the political implications of that attack. Whitgift bluntly acknowledged as much in replying to Cartwright: "Do you not still secretly push at the authority of the civil magistrate under the pretence of speaking against the state ecclesiastical? . . . [I]n reasoning against the government of the church you lay the grounds of confounding, or, at the least, of changing the state of the commonwealth. . . . The self-same reasons overthrow the civil magistrate that overthroweth the ecclesiastical. And therefore the fire kindled against the one must needs be very dangerous for the other." The effects of such "contamination" would, in his view, be disastrous. The equality he believed the Puritans advocated was "the cause of schisms, sects, contentions, seditions, tumults, murders, confusion of churches and commonweals," the end of civil order altogether.[18]

Though premised on the importance of differences in social status and political power, the hierarchical structure was conceived as a single, monolithic entity. When the queen admonished Sidney that "the Gentlemans neglect of the Nobility taught the Peasant to insult upon both," the deference she commanded was not just an example for his inferiors but part of the glue that held the entire social fabric together. Authority at all levels was seen as mutually supportive, analogous, even in some sense identical, so that its failure anywhere threatened its efficacy everywhere.[19] This attitude allowed civic duties of loyalty and submission to be readily incorporated into the Fifth Commandment (Honor thy father and thy mother) in the official catechism: "Although the very words seem to ['extend only to parents by nature']; yet we must understand that all those to whom any authority is given . . . be our superiors, are contained under the name of fathers; because the authority both of them and of fathers come out of one fountain."[20] That foundation is "the holy decree of the laws of God . . . from [which] they all, whether they be parents, princes, magistrates, or other superiors, whatsoever they be, have all their power and authority."[21] The prerogative of these "betters" establishes and preserves peace and order in the commonwealth. Without it, the *Homilies* declare, there is chaos: "Take away kings, princes, rulers, magistrates, judges, and such estates of God's order, no man shall ride or go by the highway unrobbed; no man shall sleep in his own house or bed unkilled; no man shall keep his wife, children, and possessions in quietness; all things shall be in common; and there must needs follow all mischief and utter destruction both of souls, bodies, goods and commonwealths."[22]

The divine source of all authority rendered submission the only political posture available to the "commonalty."[23] Integral to the bifurcation of classes into high and low was an allocation in which the former reserved a monopoly on political power while the latter had none. The commons' role was summarized by Sir Thomas Smith, writing in 1565: They "have no voice nor authoritie in our common wealth, and no account is made of them but onelie to be ruled, not to rule other." Whitgift declared the religious sanction for this exclusion: "In a word, God hath appointed the multitude, how godly and learned soever they be, to obey and not to rule." The vast inequity of this political partition is measured by the fact that the ruling elite in court and country—gentlemen, county elite, and nobility—constituted only 2 percent or so of the population, while the nonelite made up about 98 percent, including, according to Smith, "day labourers, poore husbandmen . . . marchantes or retailers . . . copiholders, and all artificers, as Taylers, Shoomakers, Carpenters, Brickemakers, Bricklayers, Masons, &c."[24]

The "politics" reserved to the elite included much more than just formal authority, extending to the formulation of convictions about political matters, even to the act of reflecting on politics.[25] The exercise of "judgment," political conviction, by the "vulgar people" was typically denounced as subjecting the prince to inferiors and usurping the Crown's sovereignty (or other authority), with predictably dire consequences: "unnatural" inversion of hierarchy and the destruction of public order.[26] The queen cited this danger in suppressing John Stubbs's pamphlet, *The Gaping Gulf,* against her proposed marriage to the duc d'Alençon, "offering" as it did "to every most meanest person of judgment . . . authority to argue and determine . . . of the affairs of public estate, a thing most pernicious in any estate."[27] Judgment, the critical posture toward authority, was, in the official view, decidedly subversive. The *Homilies* asked rhetorically whether subjects should obey good princes and rebel against evil ones, answering: "God forbid. For . . . what a perilous thing were it to commit unto the subjects the judgment, which prince is wise and godly and his government good, and which is otherwise; as though the foot must judge of the head; an enterprise very heinous, and must needs breed rebellion."[28]

The prohibition against the people exercising political judgment was further justified by assertions of their innate incapacity to do so, in Whitgift's words "their disposition most unmeet to govern." Deflecting attention from the role that social structures played in limiting political participation, Whitgift spoke for the system in constructing an ideological account of disabling characteristics innate in the disenfranchised. In a sermon to the queen in 1574 he elaborated these traits as inherent in the common people ("they are so naturally inclined").[29] They are inconstant, in that they are "oftener moved with affection than reason" and "so greatly delighted with novelty" that "no man [can or should] depend upon the[ir] judgment and opinion."[30] Against those who would solicit the favor, or even the opinion, of the commons, Whitgift offered the model of Jesus, who "declareth that he nothing at all esteemed of the commendation of the people, or regarded their opinion of him." Whitgift even saw presumption in the act of interrogation by the people, affirming the church fathers who condemn "such questions as are moved to stir up strife and contention in the church of Christ" and endorsing Cyril's declaration that "silence is better than unskilful talk." This is the final imperative to which this diagnosis of "the people" leads: silence, which denies them any role at all as political agents, is what their unfitness demands.[31]

Alongside the emphasis on the differences among persons that was embedded in the structure and ideology of hierarchy, there was a recognition of its divisive impulses and an effort to blunt them. Foremost in this effort was submerging the differences the state wished at all costs to maintain in an ideal of religious uniformity—the establishment of a set of religious beliefs and experiences common to all Englishmen, regardless of degree. Elizabeth articulated this policy in a letter to her archbishop of Canterbury Matthew Parker in 1565, declaring that "no one thing" pleases God more "than unity, quietness, and concord" in both ministers and people. Indeed, unity was of the very nature of religion, God "being the God of peace and not of dissension." The means for achieving the desired unity was, according to Elizabeth, "following . . . one rule, form, and manner of order . . . and directing our people to obey humbly and live godly . . . in unity and concord, without diversities of opinions or novelties of rites and manners."[32] Official acts regulating religion were commonly carried out under these auspices, including the institution of "common prayer" itself: "And where heretofore there hath been great diversity in saying and singing in churches within this realm, some following Salisbury use, some Hereford use, some the use of Bangor, some of York, and some of Lincoln, now from henceforth all the whole realm shall have but one use."[33]

Because such homogeneity of practice could only be accomplished through conformity, the foremost political virtue among the people was "obediently to be subject," according to the *Homilies:* "Obedience is the principal virtue of all virtues, and indeed the very root of all virtues, and the cause of all felicity." Through obedience the single voice of the supreme governor would become the only voice in the realm.[34] Linked with the fundamental importance of obedience was the concomitant understanding of rebellion as "the very root of all other sins, and the first and principal cause both of all worldly and bodily miseries, sorrows, diseases, sicknesses, and deaths; and, which is infinitely worse than all these . . . the very cause of death and damnation eternal also."[35]

The concept of obedience thus became the fulcrum for what Richard Ohmann calls a "morally polarized conception of the world," a Manichaean perspective that led to the frequent equation of the Puritans and Catholics based solely on their opposition to the Crown. Both "have one

mark to shoot at," Archbishop Matthew Parker declared, "plain disobedience."[36]

"Degree and Decencie": Aesthetics and Class

By no means immune from the pervasive pressures of the ideology of
class, much Elizabethan cultural practice echoed the distinctions and ex-
clusions it embodied. To appreciate the radically innovative character of
the *Calender*'s poetics, we need to take account of just how thoroughly
class affiliations were embedded in Elizabethan aesthetic discussion. No-
where is the role class played so evident as in George Puttenham's work
The Arte of English Poesie, which, though published after the *Calender*,
represents an important cultural strain antedating it.[37] Though the social
prejudice in this work is striking, it has only recently become visible, so
carefully sealed were the categories of critical analysis previously employed to interrogate poetics. Serving as a handbook for "our courtly
maker[s]" in order "to make of a rude rimer a learned and a Courtly Poet,"
Puttenham's work establishes the court and its elite as the standard in
language use and literary practice, a valorization reflected in three topics: the hierarchy of genres, the proper language for poetry, and poetry's
audience.[38] Though important, Puttenham's views were not universal.
The diversity of perspectives among Renaissance critics is evidenced by
Sidney, whose position is similar to Puttenham's on language and genre
but diverges on the question of audience. The *Calender*, in contrast, challenges these courtly aesthetics at every point, paving the way for the
alternative poetry it puts into practice, with altogether different social
affiliations and political functions.

Through his concept of "decorum," Puttenham carefully aligned aesthetic hierarchies with political and social ones, "excellence" in both
realms converging in the queen, "the most excellent Poet."[39] Puttenham
places chief importance on "hie" matters, especially "the noble gests and
great fortunes of Princes," followed by "meane [intermediate] matters . . .
those that concerne meane men," and gives least weight to "base and
low matters . . . the doings [of men of] homely calling, degree, and bringing up." Style follows this order, "fashioned to the matters, and keep[ing]
their *decorum* and good proportion in every respect . . . . every one [is
to be set forth] in his degree and decencie." Violation of this decorum

"utterly disgrace[s]" poetry and its author, for "decencie [decorum] . . . is the chiefe praise of any writer." This decorum regulates discussion of "Princes affaires & fortunes" with particular force, because the "reverence . . . due to their estates" requires altogether different terms than those used for "meaner persons."[40]

These considerations have the most insistent bearing on tragedy, whose subject matter—princes—made it the most public and politically potent genre.[41] Puttenham stresses that historically any criticism of princes' behavior was allowed only posthumously: when alive "they were both feared and reverenced in the highest degree, [while] after their deathes . . . the posteritie stood no more in dread of them." This posthumous character muted any application to reigning princes, relegating it to "secret reprehension." Further, the "reverence . . . due" to princes demanded a "higher and more loftie" style than comedy.[42] Reserving the high style for royal and noble persons ensured that, whatever conduct might be criticized, the superior status of these figures was safely beyond question, insulated by the "due" deference that style embodied.[43]

The reservation of certain linguistic forms to the elite was also reflected in Puttenham's dicta on the language of poetry. In order to maintain its prestige as an exclusively elite activity, poetic composition had to be protected from contamination by the multitude, an imperative that extended especially to the language poetry employed, which must avoid plebeian usage—"disguising it no litle from the ordinary and accustomed." Echoing the political exclusion described earlier, Puttenham declared that excellence could be attained only by removing poetry "from the common course of ordinary speach and capacitie of the vulgar judgement." He specified at length the language to avoid, that of "the marches and frontiers, or in port townes . . . or . . . in any uplandish village or corner of a Realme, where is no resort but of poore rusticall or uncivill people: neither shall [the Poet] follow the speach of a craftes man or carter, or other of the inferiour sort, though he be inhabitant or bred in the best towne and Citie in this Realme, for such persons doe abuse good speaches by strange accents or ill shapen soundes and false ortographie." He enjoined the poet instead to "follow generally the better brought up sort . . . men civill and graciously behavoured and bred." He was able to locate them quite precisely, counseling poets to "take the usuall speach of the Court, and that of London and the shires lying about London within lx. myles, and not much above." Of particular importance in establishing this "standard" English was the earlier "company of courtly makers" who "greatly pollished our rude & homely maner of vulgar Poesie from that it had bene before" and who have passed the baton of refinement to "an other crew of Courtly makers, Noble men and Gentlemen of her Majesties own servauntes." The linguistic elitism Puttenham worked to confer on the court, centralizing value in the Crown and marginalizing those who spoke other versions of the language (relegated to the status of "dialects"), was the cultural equivalent of the political centralization of Elizabeth's regime. It served to legitimate the silencing, through the imposition of an official language of church and state, of all opposition from classes or regions whose utterance marked them as "different."[44]

Puttenham was representative of a larger group, diverse in perspectives but united in the aim of establishing normative language use and the prestige of high culture by insulating them from the common people. Many, for instance, opposed the vernacular not just because they felt it was inferior to the classical languages and inadequate as a mode of expression but also because of its association with the "vulgar."[45] The "barbarousness" attributed to the commons was seen as infecting its speech as well. Access to the vernacular by commoners sullied its usefulness as a mark of superior understanding and status, so that Roger Ascham, for example, attributed the poor quality of the language to the fact that "the least learned for the moste parte, have ben always moost redye to wryte. And they whiche had leaste hope in latin, have bene moste boulde in englyshe."[46]

Others accepted the vernacular only because they considered it redeemed—Puttenham's "pollished"—from its earlier crudeness, "purge[d] . . . from the barbarisme of the former times." In his 1577 edition of the *Chronicles* Holinshed celebrates contemporary English because it has supplanted primitive Saxon, "an hard and rough kinde of speach god wotte, when our nation was brought first into acquaintance withall, but now chaunged with us into a farre more fine and easie kind of utteraunce, and so polished and helped with new and milder wordes."[47] Many believed with Puttenham that this progress had been achieved and could only be maintained by "men civill and graciously . . . bred," who should be commissioned as custodians of the mother tongue.[48]

Echoing Whitgift's derogatory account of the people, Puttenham justified the cultural marginalization of the nonelite by their inferiority. The "naturall ignoraunce" of the common people made them "as well satis-

fied with that which is grosse, as with any other finer and more delicate."
His courtly maker therefore had to know the decisive difference between
"the rude and popular" and "the learned," so that he would "not give
such musicke to the rude and barbarous, as he would to the learned and
delicate eare."[49] Culture was to be the exclusive prerogative of the elite.

"Most Used of Country Folke": The Valorization of the Nonelite in the *Calender*

The division between the qualified and the unqualified—the cultural
version of elite and commons—disenfranchised the people as percipient
readers, producing a bifurcated audience reinforced by authors' frequent
disclaimers of any appeal to the nonelite.[50] Many writers, whether or not
formally affiliated with court, were used to bolstering the prestige of
their work by opposing it to ballads or other products of popular culture,
rendering the two as mutually exclusive.[51] As Thomas Nashe put it, if
one "love good Poets he must not countenance Ballad-makers."[52]

Superior rank and the "high" culture "true Poetry" represented were
mutually reinforcing, in large part because of the way aristocratic identity was fashioned, setting up the commons and their culture as the
"other" against which an elite image was constructed. References to
popular culture became progressively more patronizing during Elizabeth's reign as the cult of Castiglione's courtier took hold.[53] The in-
sistence on social difference embedded in cultural forms reinforced the
image of a society "stratifi[ed] by title, power, wealth, talent, and culture," consolidating the privilege of the "gentle" by rendering mobility
"unthinkable."[54] At the same time, the status of poetry as a special kind
of discourse was enhanced by association with the prestige of the percipient (and powerful) few, as opposed to the ignorant multitude. The
result was a cultural hierarchy to match the social and political one,
a development reflected in the frequent use in aesthetic discussion of
words with palpable social connotations like *base, rude, rusticall, low,*
and *barbarous* to describe popular culture.

Sidney offered an important exception to the view that poetry was intended for the perceptive few alone, removed from the ignorant mass,
because his position as a courtier makes particularly unexpected his inclusion of the people in the audience for poetry (albeit condescendingly at

times). For him poetry is "the companion of camps" and flourishes "even among the most barbarous and simple" where other "learning goeth very bare." However sublime the resources on which it draws, it is "food for the tenderest stomachs." "The poet" Sidney states, "is indeed the right popular philosopher." Just how broad he considered the audience for poetry to be is underscored by his conspicuously parallel treatment of Nathan's parable addressed to King David alone and Menenius Agrippa's fable of the belly told to "the whole people."[55] Though he once mentions the "many mysteries contained in poetry, which of purpose were written darkly, lest by profane wits it should be abused," it is clear that Sidney believed the popular audience had sufficient understanding to apprehend "that goodness whereunto they are moved."[56] However patronizing his tone is on occasion, by shifting the essential character of poetry from knowledge to motive force—to "the end of well-doing and not of well-knowing only"—Sidney substantially erodes the barrier of difficulty (the "mysteries") that reserved it to the elite.[57]

The *Calender* goes much further, challenging the alignment of linguistic practice with social position and political power that Puttenham and others espoused by affirming the status and vitality of the culture of the nonelite, starting, as E.K. does in the preface, with their language. Contradicting Puttenham's injunction not to "follow *Piers plowman* nor *Gower* nor *Lydgate* nor yet *Chaucer*, for their language is now out of use with us," E.K. emphasizes "the straungeness" of the *Calender*'s words, "the which of many thinges which in [the author] be straunge, I know will seeme the straungest" (416).[58] He acknowledges that the language of the *Calender* is "of most men unused" but sanctions it by marking the work's indebtedness to the same vernacular literary tradition Puttenham rejects: the words "them selves . . . so aunicent" echo "the sound of those auncient Poetes" (416). E.K. reverses the linguistic progress implied by the rough-polished dichotomy by installing *earlier* usage as the lost paradigm and sanctioning the project of the *Calender*'s author to reclaim it: "He hath laboured to restore, as to theyr rightfull heritage such good and naturall English words, as have ben long time out of use and almost cleane disherited" (417).

The authority for this project is the authenticity (the "rightfull heritage") of the language to be "restored." Invoking a linguistic primitivism that, not coincidentally, parallels the Edenic primitivism and the religious project of renewal discussed in chapter 4, the work aligns itself with a prior order superior to the present one and aims at repairing the break with the past ("almost cleane disherited") that has separated current language use from its true foundation.

The corruption over time has been so severe that many of the poet's contemporaries are "in their own mother tonge straungers to be counted and alienes," especially those who, disparaging English, "patched up [its] holes with peces and rags of other languages . . . [and so] made our English tongue, a gallimaufray or hodgepodge of al other speches" (417). Such borrowings by the learned would, of course, perpetuate their advantage, blunting the effect of expanded literacy in the vernacular. The "alienes" also include those who, like Puttenham, demote the "barbaric" past in favor of the "polished" present: "If they happen to here an olde word albeit very naturall and significant, [they] crye out streight way, that we speak no English, but gibbrish" (417). Their hostility to the project of restoration is captured by Mulcaster's denunciation of such "backward looking": "If this opinion had bene allwaie maintained, we had allwaie worn old *Adams* pelts, we must still have eaten, the poets akecorns, & never have sought corn, we must cleve to the eldest and not to the best."[59]

The penchant so evident in Puttenham for crediting the elite with linguistic progress is turned on its head in the *Calender*, whose challenge to the diachronic dichotomy of "rude" past and "civil" present is closely affiliated with the similar challenge to the synchronic dichotomy of "rude" low and "civil" high. Repudiating linguistic elitism, E.K. identifies the "straunge" language of the text with subordinate classes, especially in the countryside: it is "fittest for such rusticall rudenesse . . . such olde and obsolete wordes are most used of country folke" (416–17). Far from acquiescing in the marginalization of "country folke"—Puttenham's "poore rusticall or uncivill people"—he establishes them, rather than a courtly coterie, as custodians of standard English: their language "bring[s] great grace and . . . auctoritie to the verse" (417). The practice of this text does not simply diverge from the structures of power in society: it defies them by locating linguistic authority where political and social power are absent.

The text makes good on E.K.'s announcements. Not only does the *Calender* borrow John Skelton's Collyn Clout for its central poetic figure, rendered, like its author, as a rustic rhymer, "unkiste" because "uncouthe" (416), but the shepherds of the moral eclogues—Thenot, Piers, Thomalin, and Diggon—all speak from a humble social position that suffuses their diction. Robert Kinsman's comment about Skelton's Colin

applies as readily to them: "From his lips comes a flow of popular utterance—plain speech in a roughened verse marked by popular alliteration
and seasoned with proverbs." Contrary to the views of recent scholarship, these shepherd figures are neither a pose, idealized to serve as
useful disguises for the courtier, nor merely various incarnations of the
poet, but discernible representatives of certain social groups.[60] As such,
their diction—more prominent and pervasive in the moral eclogues than
elsewhere—is an important vehicle for their representation of social dynamics.[61] E.K. punctuates this usage at pivotal points: he calls attention
to Piers's use of dialect—"Northernely spoken" (440)—in introducing
the fable in May, and he emphasizes this feature of the entire September
eclogue, beginning his glosses, "The Dialecte and phrase of speache in
this Dialogue, seemeth somewhat to differ from the comen" (455).[62] As
David Richardson points out, the text lives up to this billing, for, "no-
where [is the effect of 'rusticall rudenesse'] more blatantly" created than
in the first ten lines of this eclogue. The reverberation of dialect throughout the eclogue most closely identified with the voice of the people is
striking.[63]

The functions dialect serves are amplified by the central role other
popular cultural forms play in the text. Most prominent is the fable,
brought to our attention in E.K.'s preface and a climactic element in four
of the five moral eclogues.[64] The fable was well established in medieval
society as a device for covert political comment—as it is in Sidney's
stories of Nathan and Menenius—its allegorical character "at once hid-
ing and revealing" the complaint of the author who used it.[65] Its point
was often partisan, inveighing against exploitation of the weak by the
powerful. For John Lydgate such complaint was central to the fable's art:

Of mony strange uncouth simylitude,
    Poetis of old / fablis have contryvid,
Of sheepe, of hors, / of Gees, of bestis rude,
    Bi which ther wittis / secretly apprevid,
Undir covert / tyrauntis eeke reprevid,
    Ther oppressiouns & malis to chastise
Bi exanplis / of resoun to be mevid [moved],
    For no prerogatiff / poore folk to despise.[66]

The best-known collection of fables, by Aesop, frequently represented
the exploitative dynamics of unequal power relations, its putative author
considered the spokesperson for subordinated classes—Lydgate's "poore

folk." The story of his life, which accompanied most sixteenth-century editions of his fables, emphasized his position as a slave, a status his rise to influence never completely effaced.[67]

Fables were also considered peculiarly appealing to the less educated. Sidney somewhat disdainfully comments on "Aesop's tales . . . whose pretty allegories, stealing under the formal tales of beasts, make many, more beastly than beasts, begin to hear the sound of virtue from these dumb speakers." Thomas Wilson notes how beast fables not only "delite the rude and ignorant, but also . . . helpe much for perswasion. . . . I would thinke it not amisse to speake much, according to the nature and phansie of the ignorant, that the rather they might be won through Fables, to learne more weightie and grave matters."[68]

Wilson's touting of the fables as instructional tools reflects their widespread role as standard teaching aids in the school curriculum, used "for memorizing and translating into English and Latin."[69] According to Annabel Patterson, this pedagogic use effected a "dichotomy in the cultural history of the fable, a split between a tradition of moral application that was eminently suitable for pedagogy and a tradition of political functionalism that was not."[70] Spenser's strategy in the *Calender* was, as I shall show in later chapters, to exploit this dichotomy, encouraging his readers to look for the old story of unequal power relations, even as E.K.'s commentary leads them toward a moral and banal solution. Thus, in February E.K.'s reading of the fable as an allegory of youth and age ("altogether a certaine Icon or Hypotyposis of disdainfull younkers" [426]) is so palpably at odds with the tale's rhetoric and the specifically religious description of the oak that the reader must wonder what historically specific problem is not being addressed by this commentary.

Similar to fables in their functions and social associations were proverbs. The two were generically related, the fable often dramatizing proverbial wisdom with proverbs frequently representing the aphoristic residue of the fable.[71] These "old sayd sawes" were thought of as crystallizing the wisdom of the people, "belong[ing]," as Michael Mullett says, "peculiarly to the peasants." That wisdom was often skeptical and mistrustful of claims of authority, but the anonymity of proverbs provided protection for the expression of such disbelief "in assertions which no member of the folk would dare utter as his own." The collective wisdom they represented also conferred on them a certain authority, encapsulated in the Latin proverb *Vox populi vox Dei est*. The *Calender* assumes the prestige of this lowly wisdom, mobilizing it as part of its critique of the social structure. The amount of proverbial material in the eclogues is in direct proportion to their controversial character: as with fables, the February, May, July, and September eclogues contain noticeably more than the others.[72]

When, for example, in September, Diggon reports the people's complaint that "other the fat from their beards doen lick" (123), the proverb graphically summarizes the conditions of oppression.[73] In July, Thomalin, the shepherd of "the lowly playne," even calls attention to his use of proverbs in challenging hierarchical authority:

> *This reede is ryfe,* that oftentime
>   great clymbers fall unsoft.
>
>   . . . .
>
> To Kerke the narre, from God more farre,
>   has bene *an old sayd sawe.*
>   (11–12, 97–98; my emphasis)

By invoking these "sawes," he associates himself with "the voice of the people," insistently skeptical and unimpressed by its own supposed unimportance.

Besides using dialect, fable, and proverb, the work associated itself with the culture of the nonelite in other important ways. Its very title was, as E.K. tells us, the result of "applying an olde name to a new worke" (418), borrowing from *The Kalender of Shepherdes,* a popular religious and practical manual that went through many sixteenth-century editions.[74] The earlier text had presented itself as a work by and for common people. Its shepherd speaker, who "was no clerke ne had no understandinge of the letterall sence nor of no maner of scripture nor wrytynge but of his naturall wytte & understandinge," addressed an audience of the same character: "This boke was made for them that be no Clerkes to brynge them to great understandynge."[75] Spenser's poem followed the *Kalender's* format, recalling that of almanacs as well, among the most popular works of the period. Even the decision to use the January calendar, which E.K. dwells on in "The Generall Argument," served to mark the *Calender* as popular (January 1 was popularly known as New Year's Day), while the official calendar, beginning March 25, was endorsed, as E.K. pointedly tells us, by the learned who "stoutely mainteyned with stronge reasons . . . that the yeare beginneth in March" (419).[76] Against this latter tradition, E.K. first grounds the author's choice in a religious project that echoes primitivism's impulse to reform a world fallen into corruption: "For the incarnation of our mighty Saviour and eternall redeemer the L. Christ, who as then renewing the state of the decayed world, and returning the compasse of expired yeres to theyr former date and first commencement, left to us his heires a memoriall of his birth in the ende of the last yeere and beginning of the next" (420).

There is additional, secular reason for the January format, resting "uppon good proofe of special judgement" (420). E.K. conscientiously surveys scholarly authorities on both sides of the issue, but the poet strikingly rejects both learned positions, adhering to an altogether different authority: "Our Authour respecting nether the subtiltie of thone parte, nor the antiquitie of thother, thinketh it fittest according to the simplicitie of commen understanding, to begin with Januarie" (420). The convergence of religious authority with "commen understanding" lends the latter moral weight that is later enlisted in the *Calender*'s political commentary, while the preference for "commen understanding" over "the termes of the learned" (420) recognizes the capacity of the people—whatever their "simplicitie"—to determine fundamental issues, no matter what the "experts" say.

The identity of the *Calender* as "popular" extends to its physical resemblance to the media of popular culture, highlighted by the use of woodcuts. Their prominence in the *Calender* is, according to Ruth Samson Luborsky, "unique among its kind."[77] Her research shows that "none of the poets writing during Spenser's time nor the earlier Tudor poets published works that were illustrated in this way." These illustrations were by no means ancillary to the written text but "an essential part of an eclogue unit." Their prime position at the head of the eclogue made them the first sign of the text's meaning, prior to any of E.K.'s apparatus. They thus provide an influential interpretive guide to sorting out the multiple facets and possible referents of the text, more important than their often cursory treatment by literary critics would suggest.[78]

Though rare in literary works, woodcuts were an important element in popular publications, prominently displayed at the head of broadsides.[79] According to Bernard Capp, such woodcuts were one of the few kinds of representational art the poor would see. They were found in other printed material of the period intended for wide distribution: *The Kalender of Shepherdes*, other almanacs, editions of Aesop, Foxe's *Actes and Monu-*

ments (1563), editions of the Bible, Thynne's edition of Chaucer, and the popular annotated emblem book.[80] Caxton's *Aesop*, in which every fable was accompanied by a woodcut, bears out Friedland's statement that these fables were "peculiarly suited to the purposes of emblem and woodcut."[81] Like fables, the illustrations were thought of as aids for the unlearned, because " 'commen people' . . . remember 'better that they see then that they heare' (or read)."[82]

Previous publications had exploited this educational function.[83] Sebastian Brant's 1502 edition of Virgil's works "embodied," according to Annabel Patterson, "an anti-elitist ethics of production," in which woodcuts were integral to the "explicit appeal to the intellectually underprivileged." In addition, they created an archaic aura, which was sometimes criticized, as Patterson notes, as anachronistic and aesthetically inferior to "realism." This aura is very much a part of the *Calender*'s woodcuts as well, where their "retrospective" effect reinforced the poem's project of reshaping the present by restoring the practices of an earlier time.[84]

But it is not only that the humble are represented in the text; the incorporation of their culture also includes them in the audience for it, making good on the injunction the epilogue announces:

> Goe lyttle Calender, thou hast a free passeporte,
> Goe but a lowly gate emongste the meaner sorte.
> (467)

E.K. addresses this point in discussing the language of the work: "Now for the knitting of sentences . . . and for al the compasse of the speach, it is round without roughnesse, and learned wythout hardnes, such indeede as may be perceived of the leaste, understoode of the moste, but judged onely of the learned" (417). The language would be most familiar to the "country folke" who used it, allowing the text to be "perceived of the leaste." But would the accessibility of the work to the "folke" tarnish it for the cultural elite? Was the bifurcated audience a reality that would force the *Calender*'s author to choose between mutually exclusive groups of readers? E.K. tries to maintain the cultural prestige of a work whose audience included "the leaste" by carefully allocating distinct roles ("perceived . . . understoode . . . judged") to different readers ("the leaste . . . the moste . . . the learned"). He registers the pressures of the cultural hierarchy in his tacit division into the qualified and the unqualified, reserving to "the learned" the exercise of critical (in both senses) "judgment." E.K.'s effort might reassure those who saw cultural inclusiveness as a threat, indirectly echoing a familiar response to that threat: namely allocating access on a class basis, as Henry VIII tried to do when he barred commoners from reading the Bible. Using less overtly coercive means to achieve similar ends, Spenser's own teacher Richard Mulcaster wanted to employ education to maintain social stratification and reinforce political authority by dispensing it selectively to those who already had economic or political power. Educating this elite would promote "the respect of the peple, which will obeie best, where theie be over topt most."[85]

Efforts like these to sequester the reading public, however, confronted the power of the vernacular in disseminating cultural resources. It could, Foxe recognized, empower "the simple and vulgar sort" to the extent that "they may themselves perceive the matter, and be their own judges."[86] Religious values and educational practice had by this point in Elizabeth's reign made such exclusion untenable, as shown by the spread of literacy. Once the educational barriers to participation in the reading audience were breached, as E.K. acknowledges they have been by his very inclusion of "the leaste," it is impossible for a commentator, or an author, to regulate response as E.K. tries to, both here in the preface and in his glosses.

Even more important, the poetic text repeatedly undermines the separation of "the leaste" from "judgment" enjoined by hierarchical systems like Puttenham's. The pastoral genre itself, in allowing, in Puttenham's words, "homely persons and . . . rude speeches" to deal with "greater matters" (albeit with a "glaunce"), contains the potential for challenging the politico-cultural boundaries of class.[87] The continual exercise of critical faculties in "higher matters" by representatives of "the leaste" in the shepherds' debates, in language that conspicuously incorporates the speech and culture of the "folke," makes this trespass all the more emphatic.

"Goe Little Booke": The Literate Audience

The material means whereby poetry could be made popular were available to Elizabethan writers in the printing press and the emerging publishing industry. Spenser's work appeared at a time when the circulation of writing was undergoing decisive change, poised between the patronage relationship, which was, to borrow Raymond Williams's terms, "residual" in the sense that its former dominance was on the wane, and the "emergent" commercial printing industry, which was not yet an adequate base of support for writers. The two forms were by no means mutually exclusive: print could broadcast an appeal for patronage, and patronage could generate works whose horizon extended beyond the confines of its more or less personal relationships.[88] Still, the patronage model was more conducive to the kind of flattering ingratiation Puttenham represents, while the publishing market created pressure to address subjects with a broader appeal.

Powerful cultural forces promoted the extension of literacy, especially during the mid–sixteenth century. An important factor was the increasingly complex economy, which demanded this skill, making it "a prerequisite for entry into many guilds." But Protestantism proved pivotal in establishing literacy's importance: its emphasis on individual Bible study made reading a "virtual precondition to salvation." Foxe castigated the Catholic church for keeping its members in unlettered ignorance, praising "the divine and miraculous invention of printing": he wrote that "hereby tongues are known, knowledge groweth, judgment increaseth, books are dispersed, the Scripture is seen, the doctors be read, stories be opened, times compared, truth discerned, falsehood detected. . . . through the light of printing the world beginneth now to have eyes to see, and heads to judge."[89]

The promotion of literacy went hand in hand with an expansion in educational opportunity, especially during the first two decades of Elizabeth's reign. Harrison celebrated the "great number of grammar schools throughout the realm . . . so that there are not many corporate towns now under the Queen's dominion that hath not one grammar school at the least." University education experienced a virtual explosion between the 1550s and the 1580s, with enrollments increasing threefold to a peak around 1583. This increase, in part the product of increased grammar school enrollments, in turn enlarged the pool of grammar school teachers. Despite the concerns expressed by Mulcaster and others lest educational opportunities be too widely extended, there was some significant mingling of social classes. Spenser's own career attests to the accessibility both of grammar schools—"very liberally endued," according to Harrison, "for the better relief of poor scholars"—and universities. In the latter, as a result of increased charitable bequests and expanded opportunities for sizars to work their way through school providing services to wealthier students, over half the students in the 1570s were plebeians. While those below gentle status were obviously not represented according to their share of the population, their educational opportunity was far broader than their political participation.[90]

By spreading literacy, the educational revolution had a direct impact on the size and composition of the potential reading audience. While we do not know precise literacy rates at specific times, the most detailed study to date indicates rates in 1570 for dioceses outside London of almost 90 percent for gentlemen, 30–70 percent for yeomen, 5–25 percent for husbandmen, and 25–55 percent for tradesmen. These figures must be regarded as minimal, because they are based both on less urban areas than London (where literacy rates were likely higher) and on the ability to write, which was taught independently of and after reading.[91]

In quantitative terms, printing both spurred and exploited this growing literacy—suggested by the tripling of the number of London printers between 1557–58 and 1576–77—but the qualitative questions remained for the writer: exploited for what purposes? adapted to what functions? In 1579 the publication of a volume of lyric poetry would have had a particular significance because of this genre's usual association with the court, with patronage and manuscript circulation.[92] Because court poetry, as a strategy of preferment, could reach its intended audience perfectly well through the circulation of manuscripts and because publication smacked of labor, which contradicted the ethos of *sprezzatura*, a "stigma" was attached to print production that, while it may have been exaggerated for other genres, may well have been significant for lyric poetry. Almost without exception the works of poetry before the *Calender* were published by someone other than the authors (and, in the case of *Tottel's Miscellany*, long after the composition of the works) or by those whose nonaristocratic positions gave them more of an interest in an audience like themselves.[93]

It may be that the *Calender* invoked Sidney as its dedicatee not just because he was a prominent dissenter at court but also to exploit his social status, for, as J. W. Saunders points out, a printer in general "wanted the best catchpenny display of nobility on his title-pages. . . . both poet and printer were agreed on the need to emphasize gentility." But the *Calender* contravenes the common practice of claiming gentle status for a writer, instead defining its own anonymous author as one "furre . . . from . . . vaunted titles and glorious shewes." He is presented in altogether different terms, under the name of a rustic "shepheards swayne"—Colin Cloute—whose "basenesse" is emphasized (418).[94] The *Calender* is distinctive in associating its creator with markedly inferior social orders.

In exploiting a medium, lyric poetry, that had hitherto expressed gentility, Spenser made a bold move, attempting to reclaim the most sensitive and subjective (in the strong sense of expressing a subject position) of the genres for an expanded audience and an expansive discussion of public issues.

"Baser Brests": Class Consciousness in the *Calender*

The foregoing demonstrates the intensity of this text's concern with class dynamics. The interpretation of those dynamics in the text, however, turns in large measure on how they are seen in society. Were there distinctive classes in Elizabethan society, and if so, was there a distinctive class consciousness? Despite the pervasive and formidable presence of hierarchy described above, modern social historians have tended to minimize class distinctions as localized, temporary, or confined to status differences alone, unaligned with the allocation of wealth and political power. Peter Laslett, for instance, has even asserted that Elizabeth's England was a "one-class society." Yet this view may only be a fashion, associated with British revisionism, and it has recently been challenged by Michael Mullett, who argues that the convergence of status with economic differences did create distinct classes, recognized as such at the time.[95]

Literary critics have incorporated the revisionist view into their work, describing culture against a background of social and political consensus, orchestrated by the monarchy, which is viewed as commanding the scene. According to Vernon Hall, for example, the Crown "had established itself as the representation of a national spirit so strong that it completely dominated the thinking of all classes." Its power in his view made the aristocratic culture of the minority elite "truly national." The corollary to this thesis of aristocratic hegemony, espoused by Robert Weimann, is that the nonelite, caught up in a spirit of "national pride and unity," had no distinctive identity: "Right up to the end of the six-

teenth century and well into the first decade of the seventeenth . . .
the conditions for the rise of a specifically plebeian ideology simply did
not exist."[96] Although scholarship like Hall's and Weimann's and that
of the new historicists concentrates on the social dimension of literature, it suffers from the same idealizing tendencies as formalist criticism
and earlier historical criticism like E. M. W. Tillyard's in conceiving of
society as an undifferentiated, harmonious unit, finally indistinguishable from its elite, rather than as an amalgamation of contending groups,
particularly socioeconomic classes, each with distinctive character. The
effect of this scholarship is to reproduce on the modern scene Sir Thomas
Smith's claim that "no account need be made" of the nonelite.

An alternative view with some currency—popular culture as carnivalesque—does give an account of nonelite culture, but its description
is problematic. Mikhail Bakhtin, from whom this account derives, and
his interpreters tend to overemphasize carnivalesque's "second world . . .
outside officialdom" in "its completely different, nonofficial, extraeccle-
siastical and extrapolitical aspect." Concentrating on the alternative
character of the carnivalesque, putting it outside the political world,
ignores the ways in which popular culture engaged dominant authorities on their own ground, competing for power in the system, often by
reappropriating the same cultural authorities used to buttress it, and
claiming in support of change precisely those moral sanctions used to
obviate it.[97]

Seen in this light, popular culture articulated a distinctive political
attitude. While there was no "class consciousness" exactly like that Marx
describes for the working class in industrialized society, there was an
articulable perspective, grounded in what E. P. Thompson describes as
class, which is what "happens when some men, as a result of common experiences (inherited or shared), feel and articulate the identity
of their interests as between themselves, and against other men whose
interests are different from (and usually opposed to) theirs. . . . Class-
consciousness is the way in which these experiences are handled in
cultural terms: embodied in traditions, value-systems, ideas, and institutional forms." Though it grows out of shared interests and experience,
class thus becomes "a cultural as much as an economic formation." An
integral element of the shared experience underlying the crystallization
of class ("not a thing," in Thompson's words, but "a happening") is the
differences among groups: "Class is not this or that part of the machine,

but *the way the machine works* once it is set in motion—not this interest and that interest, but the *friction* of interests—the movement itself, the heat, the thundering noise. Class is a social and cultural formation . . . which cannot be defined abstractly, or in isolation, but only in terms of relationship with other classes."[98]

The pivotal role of hierarchy in institutionalizing differences between persons—fixing their relative status, power, and wealth—went a long way toward creating classes in Thompson's sense. Those differences were, as we have seen, both public—pervasive benchmarks infusing formal institutions and everyday conventions—and subjective—integral to the identity of the privileged and the experience of the subordinate. In particular, the political exclusion of the latter was constitutive of their shared identity. While economic exploitation was more dramatic for small farmers and agricultural laborers than for others, the disenfranchisement of all the lower classes was a unifying factor among them, theoretically capable of overriding the different and often competing interests of rural and urban workers, apprentices and artisans.

More important for our purposes, the theory of rational consensus is itself shot through with contradiction, since its claim depends on our being able to hear the agreement of precisely those groups that governmental policy worked to render voiceless. When, in fact, the popular voice is articulated, however, when a record of it happens to survive, it frequently expresses, not consensus, but the critical impulse of this class perspective.[99] The people certainly flocked to welcome Elizabeth (when and where is that not the case with visiting heads of state, even today?), but they also read and circulated documents of protest, sometimes as petitions, sometimes as ballads of a more inflammatory nature.[100] It is typical of the culture I have been defining that many of the records of such ballads are in fact records of their suppression: the censorship of a 1561 broadside with facing portraits of Elizabeth and the king of Sweden, proposing marriage between them; the execution of the author of a ballad that the authorities construed as inciting the people of the north to rebellion during the Pilgrimage of Grace; the imprisonment of a printer for distributing, without license, a ballad epitaph praising Mary; the Privy Council's censorship of a ballad by William Elderton discrediting England's allies; and governmental retaliation against Thomas Deloney for his ballad "Complaint of great Want and Scarcity of Corn in the realm," portraying the queen in dialogue with the people, because, according to Victor Neuberg, "it was felt by authority that the ballad might cause discontent among the poor."[101]

The Tudor Crown did not treat such instances as isolated aberrations but, recognizing the particular critical potential of certain of the media of popular culture, took steps to regulate or suppress them, directly or through press monopolies. It imposed increasingly strict regulation on almanacs because of wariness over their subversive political potential. It tried to suppress astrological prognostications and false prophecies, the latter effort culminating in the Elizabethan ban against those constructed "upon or by thoccasion of any" heraldic signs. And it tried to regulate ballads by targeting them in censorship statutes from Henry's reign to Elizabeth's and to marginalize those who disseminated them. "Both sellers and singers," according to A. L. Beier, "were considered criminals, their performances cloaks for larceny."[102]

The specific instances of the regime's suppression betray the recognition of popular culture's potency—its ability to shape opinion and to kindle passion among the disenfranchised. The Crown's conduct reflected in particular the anxiety it shared with Puttenham over the threat of the topicality that was an important constituent of popular culture. Broadside ballads manifest this quality most clearly, reporting and commenting on current political events, often protesting the abuses to which commoners were subjected.[103] There was even a "ballad debate" over the 1569 rebellion, with a number of songs treating the rebels sympathetically, some as "folk heroes."[104] Their influence was not simply retrospective, however. Before the Pilgrimage of Grace, ballads and prophecies circulating in the north "acclimatised the commons," according to Anthony Fletcher, "to the possibilities of drastic action."[105]

The persistence of these productions in the face of government suppression demonstrated the inadequacy of censorship against these forms, because they were either allegorically indirect, like prognostications, and thus not readily identifiable as subversive, or ephemeral, like ballads— quickly printed and distributed, usually anonymous, and capable of oral transmission even if the printed versions were confiscated.[106] Denied, in James Scott's words, the "luxury of open, organized, political activity," the creators of the alternative culture persistently engaged in a "struggle over the appropriation of symbols."[107] Popular culture continued to be identified as a set of cultural forms to be reckoned with by the regime, something of which Spenser would certainly have been aware and to which he could point in the *Calender*.

It is important to recognize, also, that popular celebration of the queen herself was by no means incompatible with class consciousness and social protest (evidenced by the uprisings in 1381 and 1549, when the rebels, asserting their loyalty to the Crown, exempted the young kings from their protests). The reflexive loyalty to her, accentuated by her well-calculated development of an iconic religious aura to replace forbidden icons of the old regime, did not reflect a similar allegiance to the policies of her regime. Nor were the subordinate classes incapable of seeing through the strategies devised by the government to keep them subordinated. "The penetration of official platitudes by any subordinate class," according to Scott, "is to be expected both because those platitudes are unlikely to be as cohesive or uniform as is often imagined *and* because they are subject to different interpretations depending on the social position of the actors." He continues, "Deviant interpretations—ideological heterodoxy—are hardly astonishing when they arise among subordinate classes, which, by definition, have the least stake in the official description of reality." It is from the perspective of these classes—through what Roberto Unger calls the "undeceived eyes of the outcast"—that authority can be seen differently. The social order is most effectively reexamined by those to whom it refuses privilege.[108]

Ideological conflict necessarily involves a cultural dimension—Scott's "struggle over the appropriation of symbols"—including, as we saw earlier, the appropriation of the queen herself as icon, to articulate its critique of established social and political authority. That critique was not the only issue or the *Calender*'s final word, however. The text does not merely reverse the terms, pitting lower class against elite in an unending and irreparable social antagonism. Its dynamics are more complex and nuanced as it develops a powerful argument for popular culture's value to the culture as a whole, thus challenging the mutually reinforcing linguistic stratification and audience partition. The vernacular was not so neatly layered as the cultural elite would have had it and, given the promotion of literacy, could not be petrified into a form that precluded class "mixing." Whatever his "reservations," E.K. himself boasts of the capacity of the *Calender* to reach across social lines: it will neither put off those who look for polished language ("round without roughnesse") nor impede those for whom difficulty would prove a barrier ("learned wythout hardnes").[109] The audience for the work does not adhere to the stratification Puttenham desires.

Unlike most contemporary poetry, which put that stratification into effect by addressing an exclusively courtly audience, this text worked to include both high and low by utilizing features that would appeal to a broad readership. Roger Chartier's comments about the audience for the almanac in early modern France apply with equal force to the *Calender*: "By its very nature the almanac was open to a plural readership, for it provided a written text for those who knew how to read and signs or images to be deciphered for those who did not. . . . It seems the quintessential book for a society still unequally used to the written word and in which many different relationships with print undoubtedly existed, ranging all the way from fluent reading to halting decipherment."[110]

While certain features of the text would have particular appeal to specific segments of the audience—woodcuts, fables, and proverbs for the "low" and scholarly allusions, erudite glosses, and references to literary traditions both vernacular and Continental for the "high"—text and audience were not so neatly matched. Unlike high culture in its relation to the elite, popular culture was not the exclusive possession of the commons. While the indicia of popular culture I have discussed were distinctly associated with the nonelite, they circulated throughout the society: fables were a part of most education, proverbs were a subject of learned attention as well (e.g., in Erasmus's *Adages*), and woodcuts appeared in books read by all classes.

Even though the *Calender* is resolutely identified with the commons against the exclusiveness and exploitation of privilege and though it anticipates rejection by some of the elite, it utilizes the specific and general appeal of the various elements discussed here to seek, and to constitute, a more truly national audience. By making visible and thus negotiable the pressures for splitting courtly and popular audiences—the impulse toward hardening class lines—it casts culture as an instrument for integration, though in a different form than synthesis or consensus. It envisions culture's potential both as the forum for that negotiation—the debates central to the text—and as the model for the reformed society those debates called for, one whose resources—both political, material, and cultural—were more widely distributed. The *Calender*'s audience anticipated and prefigured that society, constituted, finally, as a more inclusive social order.

But while the *Calender* seeks to tap this potential in an expanded audience, its project is problematic: it does not yet have a fully articulated alternative to court poetics or, with the emergent printing industry still embryonic, a well-grounded social place. It attempts to invent (in both Renaissance senses of "find" and "make") a new place for poetry in both its function and its readers. Achieving some distance from the norms and functions of a poetry implicated in court dynamics, the text envisions an enlarged, public role for poetry, which would reciprocally reconstitute its audience as a "public," the foundation of a politically more inclusive commonwealth. To some extent Spenser must have succeeded, if we are to judge by the fact that the *Calender* was four times republished in his lifetime (in 1581, 1586, 1591, and 1597), and a case could even be made that its republication coincided with moments of unusual stress in the Elizabethan church and state, suggesting it had acquired a certain status as social catalyst. Yet despite this work's challenges to the social role assigned to it as "poetry," the question persists of how far it remained captive to that role, a question to which I will return in chapter 6.

3   "Labouring to Conceale It"

The Hermeneutics
of Protection

Arte made tung-tied by authoritie.
—Shakespeare, Sonnet 66

In his sermon on Ash Wednesday, 1565, Alexander Nowell, dean of St. Paul's, condemned the use of religious images. The queen, who was in the audience, responded vehemently, shouting, "Leave that alone. . . . To your text, Mr. Dean. . . . To your text! Leave that."[1] The queen's response contains in miniature the two modes of the Crown's governance of speech: prescribed speech ("To your text") and prohibited speech ("Leave that alone"). Through these two modes the regime pursued a policy of controlling public speech that built on the expansion of state power undertaken in Mary's reign to deal with religious nonconformity and opposition to the foreign marriage but that surpassed that of its predecessors in comprehensiveness and intensity. The Crown under Elizabeth extended the effort to govern speech to all the major institutions and media of society: the church, the press, the universities, Parliament, and court. In each instance there was no reluctance to "draw out" Whitgift's "sword of discipline" against those who violated government restrictions.[2]

The result of this policy was an ominous shrinkage of the space for discussion of important public issues, even while public concern persisted over social and political questions, expressed in all the arenas just mentioned. The discussion continued, often as debate, but always under the threat of official retaliation, which constrained the way it was conducted (through veiled language, hidden presses, and so on). Moreover, by problematizing public speech, the official policy also affected the substantive terms of the debate itself, highlighting the questions of who could speak, by what authority one could speak, and what could legitimately be said.

The blockage of channels for public comment, complaint, and criticism created pressure for the literary media to serve these functions. This was not a novel role for literature: official restraint required strategies of evasion for which it was well suited. The *Calender* employs several of these in its veiled language, ambivalent relationship between text and commentary, and format of dialogue between shepherds, allowing it to engage matters the regime tried to quarantine, as well as the issues that policy brought to the fore concerning participation in the discussion itself.

The Crown's two modes of governing speech—prescription and proscription—were executed through several methods of control: rationing speakers, structuring occasions for public speech, and ordering its content. In the first, the Crown governed access to the forums in which public speech could be uttered by licensing preachers, requiring the oath of supremacy of all secular and ecclesiastical officers and university graduates, enlisting the presses as its agent through the printers' monopoly, and enjoining the Stationers' Company to police its 1559 injunctions against unorthodox works.[3]

The ruling elite utilized the second strategy, structuring occasions for public speech, to promote its vision of social and political relations. The most important of these occasions were religious services, whose function in England was much like that described by Montaigne: "Politike and wel ordered common-wealths endevor rather carefully to unite and assemble their Citizens together; as in serious offices of devotion. . . . Common societie and loving friendship is thereby cherished and increased." The regular services prescribed by *The Book of Common Prayer*, a work described by John Booty as "an instrument of state," were dramatic enactments of the foundations of the national community. The social harmony implied was made explicit in the requirement that any contention among members of the congregation be reconciled before the antagonists were admitted to the service.[4] A further major vehicle for promoting the regime's views was *The Book of Homilies*, which Elizabeth's administration revived, augmented, and required to be read.[5] The Crown's emphasis on prescribed speech—*The Book of Com-*

mon Prayer and the *Homilies*—relegated the communicants to passive
roles as hearers only, who should give, in the words of the *Homilies*,
"diligent ear with all reverence and silence" to the minister's words, to
which they merely "should assent, and . . . say *Amen*."[6]

Besides the regular religious services, government sponsorship of
speeches in Parliament, the public sessions of Star Chamber and ecclesiastical courts, public trials, proclamations, books and pamphlets, and
ballads provided important opportunities for fashioning public opinion.[7]
The Crown was especially adept at "tuning pulpits" on important occasions for its own purposes.[8] A special homily against disobedience was
prepared and disseminated in response to the Northern Rebellion of
1569, and the government promulgated a "state of the nation" speech to
be "read in Elizabeth's name and by her command from the pulpits of
all churches." In another instance, to counter the effect of John Stubbs's
pamphlet condemning the Alençon match, the Privy Council instructed
the bishops to inform the clergy that "the seditious suggestions [in the
book] were without foundation and that special noted preachers should
declare the same to the people."[9]

The last and most visible of the regime's strategies was its management of the content of speech through a regulatory apparatus consisting
of the treason and sedition statutes, and prohibitions directed at more
specific classes of works, defined either by content or by genre.[10] The
treason and sedition statutes were expanded throughout the Tudor period
to bring various kinds of speech, both oral and printed, more squarely
within their scope.[11] Despite the fact that Elizabeth's religious policies
overthrew those of her sister, her regime immediately renewed these
statutes of Mary's because they "hathe bene proved to bee . . . verye good
and necessarye Lawe[s]." The sedition act prohibited "any false Newes
lyes or other such lyke false thinges" of nobles or officers of the regime,
as well as "false sedicious and sclaunderous Newes Rumours Sayenges
and Tales" against the prince. Like the treason statute, this act gave particular attention to printed material—"Writinges Rimes Ballades Letters
Papers and Bookes"—extending not just to the authors of the works
(punished by having an ear cut off) but also to printers and anyone who
"procure[d]" them (subject to losing their right hands). The chilling effect
of these laws certainly discouraged political critique, especially of the
prince, "of whom," in the words of the sedition statute, "we ar forbidden
to thinck evill and muche more to speake evell."[12]

Not content with the prohibition of specific "Sayenges" against the established order or its officials, the regime attempted to bar certain subjects from public discussion altogether—an early form of executive privilege over "matters of state."[13] In one of her earliest proclamations Elizabeth instructed her censors to "permit no [plays] . . . wherein either matters of religion or of the governance of the estate of the commonweal shall be handled or treated." These subjects "were no meet matters to be written or treated upon but by men of authority, learning, and wisdom, nor to be handled before any audience but of grave and discreet persons."[14]

Claiming an exclusive "prerogative" in these areas, the Crown denied others any role in formulating policy, instead characterizing their participation as "interference."[15] In one well-known instance, the queen's treasurer justified the interrogation and detention of William Strickland, a member of the House of Commons, for introducing a bill to reform the Prayer Book, on the grounds that such legislation was "against the prerogatives of the Queene, which was not to bee tollerated."[16] The proper role, even for members of Parliament, was to be "hearers" who only gave assent, rather than active parties to the making of policy.

Because of their public prominence, the pulpits were most dramatically "tuned" by silencing obstreperous preachers. John Field, one of the authors of the 1572 *Admonition to the Parliament*, was deprived of his license from that date to 1580; the Privy Council intervened in 1566 to exile the "most obstreperous of the antivestiarian clergy" from London; and Edward Dering, long a thorn in the side of the Crown both for his bluntness and his popularity, was suppressed in 1573.[17]

The most notorious repression, however, came in August 1579, during the height of negotiations over the queen's marriage to the French duc d'Alençon, when John Stubbs published his pamphlet denouncing it, *The Gaping Gulf*. Occasioned in part by the failure of the normal institutional means of advice—the Crown had not called Parliament into session for three years, and dissenters on the council were for the most part gagged by the queen—the work identifies itself with the tradition of plain speaking. "For," as Stubbs wrote, "true, plain men are the best spies of a prince; they . . . will ring a timely alarum in your ear before the danger approach."[18] The Crown suppressed the work and campaigned to counter its effect by denouncing it, enlisting the church to discredit it with the people, and, despite his claim of loyalty, prosecuting Stubbs, his publisher, and printer. Stubbs was convicted of sedition and had his right hand cut off.

This fresh evidence of the Crown's willingness to exile, imprison, and maim even loyal supporters in order to stifle dissent made menacingly clear that to engage public issues was to trespass on the terrain the political authority claimed as exclusively its own. How, then, could one deal with such issues without compelling suppression by that authority? Spenser's project had to take a form that would provide a measure of protection from reprisal, yet the project was worthless if it was so muted as to be unrecognizable, if it was, in Annabel Patterson's words, "safe but unheard or misinterpreted." His dilemma was that of all writers under a regime of censorship: strategies that would protect him also risked rendering unintelligible the sensitive material that required protection in the first place. The poet needed to fashion his work so that it was, as Frank Whigham put it, "simultaneously visible and deniable."[19]

One facet of its visibility was the *Calender*'s conspicuous affiliation with the party of silenced speakers. Spenser was associated with Sir Philip Sidney in 1579, when Sidney was an increasingly obstreperous dissenter from both the decorum of court life and the substance of royal policy. By the fall of 1579 Sidney was known to vigorously oppose the Alençon match, so vigorously that he ran afoul of the accepted hierarchical structures of authority. He was identified with his uncle Leicester's faction, which strenuously opposed the marriage and prompted him to write a personal letter to the queen, probably in the fall of 1579, around the time John Stubbs's pamphlet against the marriage was published.[20] Although his rank and the private character of the letter must have given him some measure of protection, Sidney seems to have experienced the queen's displeasure, since he withdrew from court for almost a year. The *Calender*'s identification with him is announced frontally in a dedication that may well have been written when Sidney was in exile from court.

Another well-known dissenter is shadowed in the shepherd Algrind, a paradigmatic figure invoked several times in the moral eclogues. The name is a thinly veiled anagram for the name of Elizabeth's archbishop of Canterbury Edmund Grindal, who in 1579 was under house arrest for flatly disobeying the queen's orders to suppress prophesyings and to "abridge" the number of preachers in the church, so that most preaching would consist of merely reciting the official texts. Animated by his concern for the spiritual welfare of those deprived of effective preaching, Grindal squarely challenged the queen's prerogative in religious matters. In a letter to her in December 1576, he cast his refusal to carry out her orders as a matter of conscience, pitting religious demands against political commands: "I cannot with safe conscience, and without the offence of the majesty of God, give my assent to the suppressing of the said exercises. . . . Bear with me, I beseech you, Madam, if I choose rather to offend your earthly majesty, than to offend the heavenly majesty of God." His position was not just a matter of private scruple. He elaborated the institutional implications of his stance, questioning the allocation of religious authority between ecclesiastical and political officers. In a direct challenge to royal supremacy, he urged Elizabeth to defer to the church in "all these ecclesiastical matters which touch religion, or the doctrine and discipline of the church." Citing and quoting Ambrose, Grindal repudiated the Constantinian model of church governance by temporal authority, which, he said, "ended ill, because [the emperor] took upon him *de fide intra palatium judicare* [To judge of faith within the palace]." He forthrightly challenged Elizabeth's "peremptory" exercise of authority in religious matters, audaciously comparing it to "the anti-christian voice of the pope, *Sic volo, sic jubeo; stet pro ratione voluntas* [So I will have it; so I command: let my will stand for a reason]." The regime's response to Grindal's challenge was flatly stated in a memorandum to justify his deprivation: "A thing not sufferable that any shall set up any things in the Church without public authority: neither hath the bishop such power."[21]

Finally, the *Calender* is directly associated with Stubbs's work through Hugh Singleton, who printed them both. His printing of Stubbs's pamphlet underscores Singleton's identification, dating back to Mary's reign, with the oppositionist press.[22] The *Calender* was the very next work he printed, registered with the Stationers' Company only a month after Stubbs's mutilation. Singleton's notoriety as a printer would have encouraged expectation of further topical, controversial material from his press, associated as it now was with resistance to royal policy.

The text's internal form and dynamics confirm these external associations, evoking the contest surrounding public speech. The introductory poem "To His Booke" anticipates a hostile reception ("And if that Envie barke at thee, / As sure it will" [416]) and the danger ("jeopardee") that would accompany it. Such signs of alertness to a censorship culture are even more distinct in the eclogues, where the dialogue form dramatizes the potentially threatening reception to challenges like those just recounted.

In the February eclogue, for example, Thenot's fable is, as E.K. tells us, "cutte of by Cuddye" (427), who characterizes it as a "lewd tale" (l. 245). This phrase, accompanied by Cuddie's injunction "tel it not forth" (239), echoes the official characterization of proscribed speech. "Tales" were frequently identified, as in the sedition act, as one of the media for such material, while *lewd* was a common official designation for an outlawed work. The word's association with ignorant commoners (as in the conventional "lerned"/"lewed" antithesis) casts dissent as the presumptuous meddling of the unqualified in matters beyond their station. Stubbs's work, for example, was described as "lewd" several times in the proclamation denouncing it, and the queen used the word to brand the 1569 rebels, referring to their "lewd practices" and "lewd . . . tales."[23] The link between the term and governmental suppression reverberates ominously in Cuddie's usage.

Less subtle is the thinly veiled threat with which Morrell, in the July eclogue, responds to Thomalin's speech:

> . . . harme may come of melling.
> Thou medlest more, then shall have thanke,
> to wyten [censure] shepheards welth.
>   (208–10)

The word *meddle* was frequently used by the Crown to describe unauthorized "intrusion" into matters within its prerogative, as in the frequent royal warnings to Parliament against interference.[24] In Morrell's threat it marks Thomalin's speech as subversive, and the reality of the threat of retaliation is driven home by the fable of Algrind, which immediately follows.

But how could a poem succeed in addressing controversial public issues when notable figures like Edward Dering, Thomas Cartwright, Peter Wentworth, and even Edmund Grindal had been silenced? The September eclogue dramatizes the poet's dilemma. When Diggon utters his critique of "false shepheards" in indirect terms, Hobbinol cannot understand it:

> Diggon, I praye thee speake not so dirke.
> Such myster saying me seemeth to mirke.
>   (102–3)

When he repeats his complaints with more clarity, however, Hobbinol warns him:

Nowe Diggon, I see thou speakest to plaine:
Better it were, a little to feyne,
And cleanly cover, that cannot be cured.
(136–38)

This exchange delineates the passage the poet-critic had to negotiate to be understood by his audience without being suppressed by his antagonists.

Equivocation was fundamental to achieving this double-edged goal. As Patterson points out, quoting an anonymous seventeenth-century romance: "Ambiguity remain[ed] the key to intellectual freedom, 'disguiz'd Discourses' paradoxically 'ha[d] liberty to speak out.' "[25] While such disguise is a palpable sign of political pressure, the proliferation of meanings in the text makes it impossible to prove that critique is the *Calender's* project. It is possible to test any interpretation, including my own, though, by its plausibility—whether it makes coherent sense under the conventions we use to determine these matters—and its comprehensiveness—whether it accounts for major elements of the text.

Spenser disguised his discourse by proliferating meanings in the text, so that at every level it resists being distilled to a single interpretation. Because, as E.K. emphasizes, its words are "straunge," they cannot be readily pinned down by familiar usage. Even where not obscure, they are often multifaceted, with one of the several meanings pointedly political, as with *lewd tales* in February, *meddle* in July, and *wander* in September. The allegorical character of the inserted Aesopian fables also opens them to a variety of interpretations, as the critical history of the *Calender* demonstrates. Voices in the text itself are multiplied by the dialogue form of the eclogues. The interaction of the text and its own commentary further complicates the interpretive process. These features all contribute to an interpretive pluralism that prevents definitive attribution of any one meaning to the author. At the same time, the text usually makes available an apparently authoritative voice that would mollify and reassure those who resisted the critique the *Calender* undertakes. As we shall see, E.K. is a major source of this reassurance.

The cover that plural meanings could provide was also integral to the pastoral genre in which the *Calender* is so prominently located by its title and division into "Æglogues." This genre was chosen, E.K. tells us, by the need for indirection in a project of this kind: the author "chose rather to unfold great matter of argument covertly, then professing it, not suffice thereto accordingly. Which moved him rather in Æglogues, then other wise to write" (418). There was widespread recognition that pastoral was the appropriate vehicle for "covertly" engaging the public issues that made up "great matter of argument." George Puttenham locates the origin of the genre in just this function: "The Poet devised the *Eglogue* . . . not of purpose to counterfait or represent the rusticall manner of loves and communication, but under the vaile of homely persons and in rude speeches to insinuate and glaunce at greater matters, and such as perchance had not bene safe to have beene disclosed in any other sort."[26] Pastoral's characteristic feature—its "vaile" of indirectness—is the means of addressing sensitive matters in the face of the threat of political reprisal.

The announcement of covertness, however, would seem to blow pastoral's cover: how can a veil known to be such function to conceal? The public discussion of pastoral's cover indicates that there was cultural license to raise these issues in this mediated form, a tacit agreement "between authors and authorities."[27] Pastoral's covertness was integral to this contract, because it made the "matter" of pastoral less available— less public—thereby relieving the pressure on the authorities to repress it. Its covert nature even created a dilemma for them, because repression would necessarily draw attention to the work, certifying the presence of a subversive interpretation.

Puttenham's declaration of the need for safety itself marks pastoral as implicating those who have the means for reprisal, namely the powerful. His commentary affirms that political allegory was integral to the pastoral tradition, central to Petrarch and prominent in Renaissance readings of Virgil.[28] Sidney in his *Defence* elaborates on this function: "Is the poor pipe disdained, which sometime out of Meliboeus' mouth can show the misery of people under hard lords or ravening soldiers, and again, by Tityrus, what blessedness is derived to them that lie lowest from the goodness of them that sit highest; sometimes, under the pretty tales of wolves and sheep, can include the whole considerations of wrongdoing and patience." This extraordinary passage identifies pastoral as the very means for examining class dynamics in society, the relationship between those who "sit highest" and those who "lie lowest," whether that relationship is oppressive (as in Meliboeus's case) or beneficial (as it was to Tityrus). The genre was used for just this purpose in the *Calender*, articulating with emphasis the exploitation of the lower classes by the powerful. At least one contemporary, writing in 1586, acknowledged this dimension of the work. After giving capsule summaries of the "Morrall lessons . . . contained" in the moral eclogues, William Webbe added a discreet but incisive description: "There is also much matter uttered somewhat covertly, especially the abuses of some whom he would not be too playne withall."[29]

Pastoral's indirectness was largely achieved through its allegorical character, but this feature was not confined to this genre. Works of all kinds were read allegorically as social criticism. The style of reading required was summarized by Arthur Golding in the preface to his translation of Ovid's *Metamorphoses*:

> Now when thou readst of God or man, in stone, in beast, or
> tree
> It is a myrrour for thy self thyne owne estate to see.
> For under feyned names of Goddes it was the Poets guyse,
> The vice and faultes of all estates to taunt in covert wyse.[30]

This passage specifically marks the *critical* potential of allegory, "in feyneyng of Fables," according to Robert Crowley, "greate Vices to blame." This conception guided the interpretation of many sixteenth-century works, including, notably, tales attributed to Chaucer. Foxe, for one, saw in Chaucer a critique of the Catholic church: "What finger can point out more directly the pope with his prelates to be Antichrist, than doth the poor pelican reasoning against the greedy griffon?" He also recognized the protection this allegorical technique provided: "Under shadows covertly, as under a visor, he suborneth truth in such sort, as both privily she may profit the godly minded, and yet not be espied of the crafty adversary."[31]

The authorities were sensitive to the use of allegory for political comment and took steps to prevent it—by, for example, prohibiting "fonde and phantasticall prophesyes," which were typically rendered allegorically—and to punish it when they believed it had occurred.[32] In one notable instance in 1582 they arrested the printer William Carter for printing an edition of Gregory Martin's *A Treatise of Schism*, claiming that a passage alluding to the biblical story of Judith's murder of Holofernes was an allegory intended to incite the women at court to assassinate Queen Elizabeth. Though Carter argued it did not apply to Elizabeth and "that its meaning was strained by the lawyers," he was convicted of treason in 1584 and hanged, disemboweled, and quartered.[33]

The allegorical dimension of pastoral has important implications for modern criticism. While this technique allows for the introduction of material conditions and historical persons and events, its primary mode is not verisimilitude. It is not amenable to conventions of realism that take literary shepherds simply and solely as historical shepherds—the "purpose to counterfait or represent" that Puttenham specifically rejects. In particular, allegory does not by any means require "the tight system of equivalences" critics have often applied to the *Calender*. Paul McLane, for example, taking E.K. at face value, treats Spenser's allegory as "specifically personal," the figures standing in for what E.K. refers to as the author's "familiar freendes and best acquayntaunce[s]" (455). This assumption propels him on a hunt for a single historical person with which to equate each figure. Such identification is, at times, indicated by the poem (as in September's Roffyn or July's Algrind), but single-minded treatment of every figure in this way excludes the "broad analogy and symbolic transfer" Patterson describes, especially the social allegory— "the vice and faultes of all estates"—to which Golding refers.[34] Different interpretive methods must be used, through which literary shepherds can be seen as ministers, church hierarchs, political officials, the ruling elite, the prince, or other persons, groups, or institutions in the society. Only this perspective can uncover the work's engagement with more comprehensive cultural dynamics.

The equivocation implicit in allegory was underscored by other devices Spenser used to proliferate meanings. The classical allusions in the text, for example, often evoke a range of references. Mythological stories have multiple facets, with the concomitant difficulty of determining which ones are pertinent. The single figure of Pan—the most frequently recurring figure in the text—can evoke religious, political, or literary references, the multivalent character of "the shepeheards God" emphasized by E.K.: "So that by Pan is here meant the most famous and victorious King . . . Henry the eyght. And by that name, oftymes (as hereafter appeareth) be noted kings and mighty Potentates: And in some place Christ himselfe, who is the verye Pan and god of Shepheardes" (434).

Most important, the structure of the work dispersed authorial voice: the division of the work into apparently separate eclogues, with an array of figures engaged in debate, mitigates against the simple identification of the poet with any single voice.[35] Even though E.K. identifies Colin

Cloute as "the author self," this figure appears in only four eclogues, among the least controversial. He is not even quoted in the so-called moral eclogues, even October, which deals with poetry. Moreover, Colin's appearances themselves are often equivocal: in April his song is sung in his absence, and while he seems to be present in both January and December, another voice introduces each eclogue and concludes January. The reader cannot get very far in "fixing" the author's perspective by relying on Colin.

Perhaps the most important protective device is the misreading of the text that takes place within the work itself. This misreading is not, in one sense, surprising, for the *Calender* presents itself as a difficult work. Its commentator, E.K., emphasizes that it will seem "straunge" and "hard," in part because of its covert procedures, the author's not only withholding an account of his "intention" but also "labouring to conceale it."[36] E.K., however, presents himself as a reliable interpretive guide, able, through his "exposition" (the implication of *exposing* is important), to make intelligible passages that would "passe . . . either as unknowen, or as not marked." He asserts the privilege of one "made privie to [the author's] counsell and secret meaning" (418). His persona is thus that of the authoritative reader, who can subdue the proliferation of meaning by designation and specification. He characteristically works against that proliferation to stabilize the meaning of the text in a single, acceptable form. He attempts to do so by containing the eclogues (though not the woodcuts) he purports to explain, "coming," in Jonathan Goldberg's words, "before in his arguments, after in his glosses."[37] His air of final authority gives the author a measure of protection against other, more dangerous interpretations.

But E.K.'s role is more complex, integral to the *Calender*'s double-edged project. He only appears authoritative. For the discerning reader, he fails to establish his authority unequivocally. The result is an apparatus that is itself a devious device, an interpretation that requires interpreting.[38] Many critics have noted the redundancy of E.K.'s comments, his "prolix prolusions" and "pedantic digressions" that have been identified as "misinformation" or "mystification," but insufficient attention has been given to E.K.'s complex role in the *Calender*'s protective strategy. Too often critics, sharing with him what Leigh DeNeef calls "a particularly literary perspective," have uncritically accepted his authority.[39] The accumulated weight of his allusions to other literary works or maxims from classical authors, an important element in that perspective, goes a long way toward situating the *Calender* in a merely literary frame, encouraging the reader to make connections only to other texts rather than to society.

Other elements in his perspective that similarly divert attention from the social and political registration of the poem are the focus on style—characteristics of the language itself, rather than its reference—and situating interpretation in the realm of philosophical abstraction, in the universal character of human experience.[40] Each is exemplified in E.K.'s treatment of the February eclogue. His argument begins by vaulting interpretation into the category of a universal human condition, excluding any topical political application: "This Æglogue is rather morall and generall, then bent to any secrete or particular purpose. It specially conteyneth a discourse of old age." Coyly alluding to the alternative to his own interpretive perspective—the "secrete or particular purpose" he quickly shunts aside—he buttresses the eclogue's universality with his analogy to "the season of the moneth, the yeare now drouping, and as it were, drawing to his last age" (423). His effusive praise for the artful effect of the tale—told "so lively and so feelingly" (423)—is also a distraction away from its topical reference. He repeats these emphases in his gloss on the fable, declaring it "very excellente for pleasaunt descriptions" and analyzing it as "a certaine Icon or Hypotyposis of disdainfull younkers" (426)—a terminological flourish that deflects attention from substance to technique. He closes with a discussion of the emblems that for the most part perpetuates the philosophical terms of age and youth in which he frames the eclogue.

Throughout the eclogue E.K. confines his interpretation to the surface, to the most obvious features of the speakers: their ages. But this restriction proves progressively more inadequate as the eclogue introduces additional elements. In particular, E.K. fails to account for the royal rhetoric in February's fable or the religious references to "holy eld" (206), "Sacred ... mysteree[s]," "priestes crewe," and "halowed with holy water dewe" (208–10). These omissions render his interpretation increasingly unsatisfying, especially concerning the fable of the oak and the brier itself, encouraging the reader to reconsider the "secrete or particular purpose" he initially discounted.

When he does acknowledge an intersection with topical issues, E.K. is often careful to channel that reference into safer waters, frequently invoking an apocalyptic struggle between "true religion" and papism. He sees the fable in May, for example, as inveighing against the "doubling deceit [of] the false and faithlesse Papistes" (440), the critique of July as directed against "Popes and Cardinalles" (447), and the September eclogue as aimed at the "loose living of Popish prelates" (452). In configuring the poem's censure in this way, E.K. echoes the antipapist rhetoric of apologists for the established church and the political regime, who used such language to spur unity by invoking real or supposed threats at home and abroad. But this orientation fails to account for prominent nonreligious elements in the eclogues—the political valence of "motherly care" in May's fable, July's focus on the familiar class designations of "high" and "low", and the palpably economic complaints of September.[41]

Even in its own terms, E.K.'s effort to contain the eclogues in an exclusively religious context is problematic, as antipapal discourse was itself very fluid, having been appropriated by church reformers, including Puritans, and redirected against the politico-religious establishment.[42] The fluctuating political uses of such discourse made it impossible to confine it to a single target.

Though E.K. usually inoculates the text in this fashion against subversive interpretations, his role is not limited simply to diversion. Operating as a double or triple agent in the text, his comments on occasion even steer the allegory in the direction of the political, as in his gloss of the "great hunt" of September (l. 159) as the "Executing of lawes and justice" (455). On other occasions he calls attention to topical meaning in less direct fashion. For example, by changing the fox to an ape in the Aesopian fable he cites in his gloss on February's emblems (427), he evokes Elizabeth's well-known nickname for the duc d'Alençon's representative Simier: *le petit singe* (the little ape). Or, by glossing *orphane* in May as one who "needeth a Tutour and governour" (440), he punningly introduces Elizabeth into the fable, undermining his own apparent effort to fix it in an exclusively antipapal context. At other crucial points his professed ignorance, in the face of his vaunted access to the author's secret meaning, calls attention to interpretive cruxes and suggests a reticence accounted for by the political charge of the reference. Such, for example, are his declared ignorance of the "particular Action" of the tale of Roffyn (455) in September and his striking vagueness about the identities of that shepherd and Algrind (439, 447–48), both of whom can be readily identified as men who challenged the Crown. At other times the very inappropriateness of his gloss calls attention to other contexts of meaning. For example, he explains the word *loord* in July—meaning "lout"—by incongruously recounting the history of the phrase *Lord Danes* (447). He thus introduces lordship, especially its oppressive dimension, into the eclogue, preparing for polemic against that oppression later in the poem.

Perhaps the most notable instance of a misleading gloss that produces interpretive richness for the diligent reader is E.K.'s reference to the song contest between Pan and Phoebus in June (68–69). Contrary to his gloss (443), Midas did not *judge* their contest but was, instead, the audience and was punished by having an ass's ears affixed to his head for *disputing* the judgment.[43] When the story is reexamined in detail, in Golding's *Ovid*, several provocative elements stand out. A sharp contrast is drawn between the contestants' music, their contest originating in Pan's claim that "Apollos musick was not like to his" (*Met.* 11.174). Indeed it was not: Pan plays a "country pype of reedes" (11.181), Apollo a viol "made of precious stones and Ivorye intermixt" (11.187); Pan plays "lowd and strong," a "rude and homely song" (11.180–81), while Apollo "smites" or plays "with conning hand the tuned strings" (11.190). The differences suggest wholly different milieus and audiences for these singers— a courtly, aristocratic one for Apollo and a rustic one for Pan. This implication is underscored by the suggestions of royalty in Apollo—whose attire includes "a crowne of Bay" (11.185) and a scarlet robe that sweeps the ground (11.186)—and in the judge himself, Tmole (who is a mountain), who "from loftye toppe to seaward looketh downe" (11.168) on his extensive domain and who renders judgment from a hill (11.176). These powerful regal figures are set in sharp contrast to Pan and Midas, who became Pan's companion because he "hat[ed] riches" (11.164).

There is a compelling association between Apollo and Elisa of the April eclogue, who is also "yclad in Scarlot" (57). "Upon her head a Cremosin coronet" sat with bay leaves in it (59, 61). The Muses also bring bay leaves to her (104). They come with "their Violines" (103), instruments identified with courtly entertainment and depicted in the woodcut for April.[44] Elisa herself is expressly identified with Apollo: she is "another Sunne belowe" (77). The point is not that, by means of some sort of mechanical substitution, Elizabeth is Apollo, but that through these associations the June eclogue implicates the April eclogue (the most courtly of the *Calender*'s poems) in the preference for an Apollonian royal aesthetic over Pan's pastoral song.

What is especially striking about that preference is the way it is rendered in Ovid: no judgment is given in favor of Apollo, declaring his songs superior. What we have instead is the judge's "delyght" with their "sweetnesse," a response echoing the importance of pleasure to court aesthetics. The product is a judgment against Pan:

That Pan was willed for to put his Reedepype in his cace,
And not to fiddle nor to sing where viols were in place.
                    (*Met.* 11:192–93)

Because his music is inimical to Apollo's, Pan is penalized by being silenced in the halls of power. Moreover, the audience, Midas, who "found fault therwith and wrongfull did it call" (11.195) is punished for doing so. He is disciplined for asserting the capacity to make an independent judgment, a capacity that challenges the judge's status. His punishment is directed at "the part that did offend for want of skill" (11.201), his ears. In transforming them to an ass's ears Apollo inscribes on Midas's body his judgment that Pan's companion is not fit to judge this matter, disabling him from rendering any future evaluation, in much the same way the people's alleged unfitness barred them from either aesthetic or political determination.

What the diligent reader thus finds at the end of the trail marked, however covertly, by E.K. is the hostility of the powerful to the kind of poetic enterprise with which the *Calender* is identified, hostility expressed in the reprisal they exercise not only against the poet but against his audience as well. The reader finds, in short, the reason for the poet's laboring to conceal in the first place.

Whatever his particular function at any given point in the text, E.K. consistently spurs the reader to interpretive labor. Though his commentary is intended to channel and ultimately to satisfy that effort, his inadequate procedures sabotage this aim, leading the discerning reader to focus on just those issues he fails to resolve. His failure thus redoubles the pressure for alternative interpretations, even while giving apparent credence to safely orthodox ones. The dynamic E.K. thus sets in motion gives the reading experience itself political overtones. The pressure to understand the poem leads the reader to challenge or to set aside E.K.'s interpretations, to resist, like Midas, the authority he represents.[45] This process leads the reader out of the orthodox channels E.K. has so carefully plowed and into more dangerous territory. By challenging authority in this fashion the reader of the *Calender* reproduces the dynamics of the debates in it.

Misreading similar to that which E.K. performs on the poetic text also occurs elsewhere within it. At times the audiences inside the eclogues recognize the subversive implications of the debate or fable, responding with cautionary advice (Hobbinol in September) or a threat (Morrell in July), while at other times those implications are missed or muffled. In May, for example, Palinode reads the message of the fable as "Foxes bene . . . crafty" (312). In proposing to use it as a church homily, he either overlooks or represses the implied criticism of the regime that Piers's fable contains. His desire to do so, of course, offers reassurance that the fable is benign enough to serve this function. Similarly, in July Morrell responds to Thomalin's fable of Algrind with a blithe optimism that is at odds with its political character:

> Ah good *Algrin*, his hap was ill,
>   but shall be better in time.
>   (229–30)

He reads the tale literally, as recounting a physical injury that time will "naturally" heal. By maintaining the invisibility of the power struggle behind the fable, this bland perspective frustrates the political impulse, while Morrell's focus on accident (Algrind's "hap"), which he shares with E.K., blinds him to the fully intentional confrontation between monarch and archbishop—an interpretation permitted but not required by the fable of the eagle and the shellfish.[46] Finally, in September, Hobbinol, having warned Diggon to "cleanly cover" (138) his complaints, shortly tries to do so himself. In response to Diggon's claim that sheep "been of ravenous Wolves yrent" (148), he objects,

> Fye on thee Diggon, and all thy foule leasing,
> Well is knowne that sith the Saxon king,
> Never was Woolfe seene many nor some,
> Nor in all Kent, nor in Christendome.
>   (150–53)

He chooses to read Diggon's statement as one of historical zoology and to rebut it on that basis, thus suppressing the political overtones generated by its allegorical dimension.

Like E.K., these speakers demonstrate the penchant for easy, and safe,

readings, taking the surface meanings of the words for their deep structure and confining interpretation to that single register. Such an interpretive strategy neither demands the effort required by allegory nor allows
for its political valence.[47] Instead, the misreaders take the "vaile," the
pastoral guise, for the matter itself. While the shallow character of these
responses may have been intended to guide more conscientious readers
to look further, it serves as a self-fulfilling prophecy of the poem's possible reception among those who, then and now, prefer that literature
not disturb their complacency. In other words, Spenser himself wrote
into the *Calender* signs of the fragility of its project and its author's
vulnerability.

Sometimes the impulse to repress social and political understanding
even takes the shape of folk wisdom, providing a salutary reminder that
inhibition can arise out of inertia from below as well as imposition from
above. The proverbial "thilke . . . rule were too straight" (September
236), God giveth good for pleasure only, not duty (May 64–72), the optimism of it "shall be better in time" (July 230), and the resignation of it
"cannot be cured" (September 138) each justify mental disengagement
at the point where recognition of a social problem might demand some
practical intervention.

The complacency such responses embody is only the less dramatic
aspect of the poet's dilemma. It is not just misunderstanding by his audience that he risks, but perceptive understanding as well. For the poet
who would "teach . . . shepheards," it is precisely those whom he would
teach that he must fear. The audience that needs most to understand is
most likely to act on its understanding by retaliating. There is no sat-
isfactory resolution to this dilemma, only the reassuring expectation
that there will be a fit audience, however few. Our own efforts to understand this work anew themselves spring from the hope that we might be
among them.

4

"The Time Was Once"

The Configuration of
Authority in the Poem

However comprehensive its worldview or compelling its moral force may be, ideology is never total or exclusive. Even apparent acquiescence in the worldview that ideology promulgates may conceal extensive resistance, constrained by the weakness of the resisters, but durable and palpable, especially behind the public stage that those in power control.[1] As we have seen, popular culture, without imprimatur and circulating in unofficial channels, frequently contains signs of this resistance. Further, persons and groups with divergent interests and perspectives may share the same ideology up to a point, until changed circumstances bring their differences to the fore. The uneasy alliance between Elizabeth's regime and the Protestant reformers, many of them Marian exiles, is a case in point, dramatically exemplified by Archbishop Grindal's challenge to Elizabeth's prerogative. Or ideology may be challenged in a more comprehensive way by others using the same resources it draws on to reach very different conclusions. When Hannah Arendt refers to the reliance of an authoritarian regime on a transcendent source for its legitimacy, she notes that that same sanction also provides a standard "against which [the authorities'] power can be checked."[2]

Each form of ideological contest has an ineradicable cultural dimension, consisting of what James Scott describes as "a struggle over the appropriation of symbols, a struggle over how the past and present shall be understood and labeled, a struggle to identify causes and assess blame."[3]

The Puritans engaged in just such a confrontation during Elizabeth's reign, forcing the ruling ideology to be more sharply stated than it otherwise would have been. The *Calender's* renegotiation of religious authority, as we shall see, reverberates with the echoes of this conflict.

The poet's predicament required him to muster authority for voicing criticism, however deniably. The regime might attempt to enforce a monopoly on speech under an ideology of uniformity, but the native culture was not monolithic. It offered traditions potentially antagonistic to that ideology, traditions that could authorize critical engagement of political issues, including the prestige of "antiquity" against which any supervening institution could be evaluated; the resources of Christianity as at once a locus of egalitarian thought, a history of resistance to oppression, and a powerful source of icons and unimpeachable metaphors; and the national, vernacular literary tradition. Not only were these authorities congruent with one another in aims and sympathies, but by the sixteenth century they were inextricably woven together, reinforcing and reconfiguring one another. It is possible, however, to track each in the culture and to describe the *Calender's* particular appropriation of each to ground its critique.

Situating the poem in the pastoral tradition did more for Spenser than allow him to circumvent government suppression of criticism. It lent his project specifically literary authority that did not derive from the Crown or the ideologies of the ruling elite. In particular, the pastoral tradition evoked the authority of its founders, Theocritus and Virgil, as E.K. does in his introductory epistle. It also allowed Spenser to summon, as E.K. does, Mantuan, Petrarch, Marot, and Sannazaro, a group "whose foting this Author every where followeth" (418). Placing the text in this tradition rendered it an "image of antiquitie" (417), thus conferring on it the sanctity of time. In the Renaissance this sanction carried considerable weight, for, as David Miller observes, "priority of time [was] regularly associated with moral perfection and political authority." It is important to stress the political importance of temporal location, as Keith Thomas does: "Most political thought [was] essentially an inquiry into origins; happenings in the state of nature or some other version of the primitive past still determined men's political obligations in the present."[4]

The authority of the ancient past did not take a single shape but was invoked by antagonistic parties in political and religious debates, reflecting decisively different attitudes toward the present. On the one hand, apologists for the regime saw Elizabeth's reign as the fulfillment of the destiny heralded by the distant past. They forged a continuity between the two that surmounted the intervening periods, cast as interruptions. Foxe praised Elizabeth for having overcome "the iniquity of time" (between the Norman Conquest and her accession) to usher in "these halcyon days." E. J. Hobsbawm calls this usage "primitive legitimation": it is "a return to or rediscovery of . . . some part of the past which has been mistakenly forgotten or abandoned."[5] The interruptions in the providential movement, especially Mary's Catholic regime, served to intensify the sense of renovation, expressed by the final tableau presented to Elizabeth on her passage through London before her coronation:

> . . . O worthy Quene, . . . our hope is sure
> That into errours place, thou wilt now trueth restore.[6]

The dedication to Elizabeth in *A Theatre for Worldlings* (1569) was more explicit: "The Kingdom of Saturn and the Golden world is come again." The Act of Supremacy similarly inscribed the broad powers granted the monarchy in a narrative of restitution, "restoring to the crown [its] ancient jurisdiction." Such declarations used the past to confirm the present by *"closing* the gap" between the two.[7]

But the past was available not only for celebration of the present; it could support a critique of contemporary conditions as well. Rather than "closing the gap," critics used versions of a primordial golden age like the utopian Eden to drive a wedge between past and present, censuring officials and institutions for that disjunction. Best known is the Puritans' invocation of the primitive church as the "true" one to measure just how far short the established church had fallen. The litany of "Then . . . . [and] . . . Now" on which the *Admonition to the Parliament* is built sharply delineates this gulf.[8] The pressure the paradigmatic past can exert on the present is made explicit in an Elizabethan ballad that begins with the announcement "The golden world is now come agayne" and proceeds to describe the model behavior of princes, other political and religious officials, the commons, and family members in this renovated world. The actual conduct of these groups, though, was so clearly at odds with these models that explicit commentary was unnecessary. The refrain, however, drove their force home: "Other [either] thus it is, or thus it shoulde bee."[9]

Such moralized primitivism could support a powerful attack on existing conditions by denying them the sanction of antiquity. When seen as the heirs of a lineage whose genesis lay beyond memory, present institutions were invested with a necessity that put them outside human intention and action. Changing them became both literally unimaginable and morally suspect. But when their originary character was described as altogether different from their present one, their alteration became not just a possibility, but an imperative: to restore them to their primary condition. In these circumstances only change could be faithful to the past.

This disjunction between past and present constitutes an important thread running through the *Calender*. It may be implied, as in Cuddie's plaint in the October eclogue—"all the worthies liggen wrapt in leade, / That matter made for Poets on to play" (63–64)—with its unavoidable conclusion that any praise of present dignitaries amounts to unwarranted flattery. Or the critique may be more explicit, as in Piers's depiction of a golden age in the May eclogue (103–31), introduced by the affirmation "The time was once, and may againe retorne" (103). The disjunction between that earlier time and the present represents a fall from the paradigmatic original, an alienation from true morality that occurs through "tract of time" (117). At the same time, the past exerts pressure on the contemporary situation because it reveals a possibility latent therein, a condition that could be actualized in society: "For ought may happen, that hath bene beforne" (104).[10]

The close association between the golden age and social pessimism in Spenser can be seen in the chiding his friend Gabriel Harvey gave him in a 1580 letter: "You suppose the first age was the goulde age. It is nothinge soe. Bodin defendith the goulde age to flourishe nowe, and owr first grandfathers to have rubbid thorowghe in the iron and brasen age at the beginninge when all thinges were rude and unperfitt in comparison of the exquisite finesse and delicacye, that we ar growen unto at these dayes."[11] Harvey's equation of the present with the golden age precludes using the past to exert any leverage for reform.

The golden age motif is, of course, associated with a classical education, but Scripture provided its own equivalent in an Edenic primitivism more readily accessible to the less educated. This primitivism was an integral part of an important alternative tradition deriving from the fourteenth century, which enlisted religion in the call for a society both much more equal in social status and much more inclusive in the political participation of its citizens. The Puritan challenge to the established church in the 1570s, though in some ways less radical than the older tradition, echoed it by invoking religious authority in support of its protests. It was clearly antihierarchical in its theory of how the church should be governed and occasionally extended its spiritual egalitarianism into secular matters.

This alternative tradition challenged hierarchy by emphasizing the common status of all persons before God, bringing to the fore the "contradiction between the secular claims of aristocratic prerogative and the religious claims of common origins, shared fallenness, and spiritual equality among men, gentle and base alike."[12] These elements, together with Protestantism's emphasis on direct access to God, unmediated by priest or church, gave all persons a significant religious dignity, regardless of social position. In 1540 Archbishop Thomas Cranmer, arguing against excluding the lower classes from education, had relied on their status as creatures of God, who is no respecter of social position: "Utterly to exclude the ploughman's son and the poor man's son from the benefit of learning, as though they were unworthy to have the gifts of the Holy Ghost bestowed upon them, as well as upon others, is as much to say, as that Almighty God should not be at liberty to bestow his great gifts of grace upon any person . . . . [He] giveth his gifts both of learning, and other perfections in all sciences, unto all kinds and states of people indifferently."[13]

The Puritans drew on this tradition in their critique of hierarchy, which they repudiated as fundamentally inimical to the Word of God, "forbidden by Christ," and a "tyrannous Lordshippe [that] can not stande wyth Christes kingdome . . . . It is the speciall mischiefe of oure Englishe churche, and the cheefe cause of backwardenesse and of all breache and dissention."[14] The animus toward hierarchical distinctions went hand in hand with an emphasis, like Cranmer's, on the dignity of the people in the church. Cartwright retorted to Whitgift, "How vile account soever you will make of them, they are the people of God." The political structure that most accorded with this religious affirmation was popular election, in which, according to Cartwright, "some must be governed by all, and not all by some."[15] Though ambivalent about the qualities of the lower classes, the Puritans provided a religious rationale for a more inclusive polity, a model whose sanction for popular participation in governance could not be wholly removed from the political realm.

That, however, is precisely what the establishmentarians tried to do. Whitgift accused Cartwright of "seek[ing] so great an equality" as well as "mak[ing] the ignorant subject lofty and arrogant, [and] tak[ing] from princes their due authority in ecclesiastical matters." Significantly, however, he was compelled to acknowledge that, as far as salvation was concerned, "God . . . hath neither respect to nobility, learning, riches, or any such thing." This concession forced him to quarantine equality "to the spiritual realm," wholly isolated from society: "In the spiritual kingdom of Christ, and regiment of his church, there is no respect of persons, but all be equal: in the external regiment and government there is and must be degrees of persons."[16] The need Whitgift felt to segregate religious parity from political hierarchy reveals with particular clarity the tension implicit in using religious resources to legitimate that hierarchy.

At the heart of the religious challenge to hierarchy lay a narrative contesting the assertion that social status was primordial and derived from God. This account argued that unfallen society in Eden was classless and that rank and property were later corruptions of a divine intention. A popular couplet exemplified these notions:

When Adam delved and Eve span,
Who was then the gentleman?

This proverbial verse was deeply ingrained in the popular tradition "for centuries," according to Ruth Kelso, and was in the sixteenth century "still the taunt and challenge of the common people to a system which bade them labor contentedly for their betters." The most famous instance of its invocation was as the text for John Ball's celebrated sermon at Blackheath during the Peasants' Revolt of 1381.[17] Ball made the couplet's challenge to hierarchy explicit: "By what right are they whom men call lords greater folk than we? If all come from the same father and mother, Adam and Eve, how can they say or prove that they are better than we?"[18] Attacking the institution of serfdom, Ball eloquently exploited the authority of a primitive vision to sanction fundamental social change, arguing, according to a contemporary historian, that "from the beginning all men were created equal by nature, and that servitude had been introduced by the unjust and evil oppression of men, against the will of God, who, if it had pleased Him to create serfs, surely in the beginning of the world would have appointed who should be a serf and who a lord."[19]

The *Calender* echoes the Edenic egalitarianism of Ball's text in Thomalin's rendition of "the first shepheard" in July:

> As meeke he was, as meeke mought be,
>   simple, as simple sheepe,
> Humble, and like in eche degree
>   the flocke, which he did keepe.
>   (129–32)

The prestige of the primitive is here set squarely against the social differentiation of hierarchy. Far from celebrating the present, this version of the primitive judges it. Thomalin makes that judgment explicit by pointing to the reversal that has occurred:

> But now (thanked be God therefore)
>   the world is well amend
>   (169–70)

His irony accentuates the corruption time has brought with it, for shepherds now

> reigne and rulen over all,
> and lord it, as they list.
>   (175–77)

The *Calender* further incorporated Christianity into a unique melding of literary with religious pastoral, a convergence that provided the work with potent cultural authority. The overdetermined nature of the presiding deity, Pan, either a religious, literary, or political figure, and sometimes something of each, exemplifies this effect. The most important merger of the two traditions, however, was through the figure of the shepherd, whose New Testament associations had long since been blended with those of classical pastoral. By Spenser's time this already composite figure had taken on two different functions, representing either the model leader—with legal power and the accompanying responsibility for the care of the flock—or the collective voice of the common people who were subjected to the abuses of that power.[20]

Religious apologists drew on the figure of Christ as the Good Shepherd—familiar and well established in Elizabethan worship—to fuse the religious and political dimensions of secular leadership, rendering Elizabeth as "chief shepherd" commissioned "to govern [Christ's] Flock committed to her charge."[21] Such constructions enhanced the monarchy's prestige and shaped its policies by investing it with a specifically religious mission. But as an emblem for the moral responsibility of those in power, the shepherd metaphor also facilitated criticism of the prince and others in authority. This criticism was integral to the religious tradition, as ancient as the prophets of the Old Testament. Ezekiel had protested: "Thus saith the Lord God unto the shepherdes, Wo *be* unto the shepherdes of Israel, that fede them selves: shulde not the shepherdes feed the flockes? Ye eat the fat, and ye clothe you with the woll: ye kil them that are fed, but ye fede not the shepe. The weake have ye not strengthened: the sick have ye not healed, neither have ye bounde up the broken, nor broght againe that which was driven away, neither have ye soght that which was lost, but with cruelty, & with rigour have ye ruled them."[22] The Geneva Bible removed any doubt that his indictment encompassed political leadership: "By the shepherds he meaneth the King, the magistrates, Priests, & Prophetes."[23]

Robert Crowley demonstrated the continuing vitality of this tradition when he too invoked the shepherd's responsibility for the poor, faulting him for not being "a diligent watchman." Had he been, he "wold have steppeth betwene [the poor man] and [his] enemi" and "enstructed" him, so that he "shoulde not have [been] deceived." But the shepherd "hathe bene negligent as (alas the while) all shepeherdes be at this daie. . . . He espied not the wolfe . . . or happlye he knewe him not frome a shepe."[24] The shepherd's dereliction is dramatically imaged by his absence, which provided the opportunity for predation, a common figure for socioeconomic exploitation, as in the comment by the Norfolk peasant who was a part of Kett's Rebellion in 1549: "As sheep or lambs are a prey to the wolf or lion, so are the poor men to the rich men."[25]

The *Calender* fully exploits the simultaneously religious and political character of this metaphor. Its complaint is typically directed against shepherds, for social dereliction that is indistinguishable from religious malfeasance. Bad shepherds "leaving [their] Lords taske" (May 53) will be subject to religious judgment when "great *Pan* [glossed here as Christ] account of shepeherdes shall aske" (May 54). The affirmative obligations that religion imposes on the powerful subjects them to criticism not just for actively exploiting their flock—"get[ting] all the gayne, paying but a peece" (May 50), and "lord[ing] it, as they list" (July 176)—but also, as in Crowley's complaint, for neglecting it—leaving it "unfedde" (May 44),

in the charge of hirelings (May 47–48 and July 195–96), or "wander[ing]
at wil, and stray[ing] at pleasure" (September 144).[26] Most important, the
fable in the May eclogue of the goat who leaves her kid alone pointedly
interrogates the responsibility of those in power who, despite professions
of concern, leave their charges vulnerable to oppression.

In his other cultural function, the shepherd stands for the people's
voice, articulating their complaints, a tradition that goes back at least as
far as the mystery plays.[27] *The Second Shepherds' Play* (still performed
in the mid–sixteenth century) opens with a shepherd recounting the
condition of the poor and identifying its cause in economic exploitation:

> No wonder, as it standys,   if we be poore,
> For the tylthe of oure landys   lyys falow as the floore,
> As ye ken.
> We are so hamyd [hamstrung]
> For-taxed [overtaxed] and ramyd [oppressed],
> We are mayde hand tamyd [tamed]
> With thys gentlery men [gentry].[28]

The shepherd does more than report this oppression. He challenges the
justifications offered for it: "That men say is for the best, we fynde it
contrary."[29]

Sixteenth-century critics continued the tradition of the shepherd as the
blunt spokesman for the lower classes, "along with the ploughman . . . a
favourite persona of mid-century writers," according to David Norbrook,
"who like[d] to present themselves as speaking simple truths in the voice
of the people."[30] An important example is the poem *Vox populi vox Dei*
(c. 1547–48), in which the speaker describes himself:

> for I a sheparde ame,
> A sory powre man[31]

He reports what the people have already written with their labor:

> for the comenes of this Lande
> hat sone [sowen] this in there sande,
> plowghyng it with ther hande.
> I fonde it where I stonnde,
> And I ame but the hayne [wretch]
> that wrythe new agayne
> The copy, for to see.

What they have written is what

> . . . god him-Self he knothe,
> and as all men understandes,
> bothe lordeshipes and landes
> are now in few mens handes.

The result of this condition is that "the fermer and the powre" are

> redy for to steale
> for very pure neede.

In the *Calender* the "seely shepherds swayne[s]" (July 30) who articulate complaints against the powerful echo this tradition. In September the theme of popular spokesmanship is foregrounded in Diggon, whose sharpest critique is composed of the complaints of "the people" (104–35). He gives voice to what "they sayne" (108). Thomalin, in July, enlists religious authority in support of that voice, invoking Christ as the Good Shepherd

> that bought his flocke so deare,
> And them did save with bloudy sweat
> from Wolves, that would them teare.
>   (54–56)

Mobilizing religious pastoral with its long-standing concern for the weak, these lines strongly imply that Christ's original sacrifice remains effective against oppression, or at least that it continues to justify those who speak out against it.

It is important to realize that by invoking the moral authority of religious pastoral in this way Spenser was opposing himself (if only prophetically) to the mainstream of Elizabethan pastoral. As Louis Montrose has argued, the subversive aspects of religious pastoral "had to be expunged or transformed if pastoral metaphors were to function effectively as benign images of the stable and rigorously hierarchical social order which Tudor governments sought to establish and preserve."[32] He contends that this potential was transformed in Elizabethan literary pastoral to serve the interests of that order, but at the least, the *Calender* stands as a dramatic exception to this claim.

There are other signs of the continuing vitality of the tradition yoking religious authority with the perspective of the lower classes, crystallized in the proverb *Vox populi vox Dei est*. These signs are particularly evident in the repeated efforts to sever the two. In George Gascoigne's poem *Dulce bellum inexpertis*, to take one example, the speaker castigates "the common voice" for its skeptical attitude toward war—"That Princes pryde is cause of warre alway"—but then feels it necessary to discredit that voice altogether for its indictment of exploitation by the powerful:

> And though it have bene thought as true as steele,
> Which people prate, and preach above the rest,
> Yet could I never any reason feele,
> To think *Vox populi vox Dei est,*
> As for my skill, I compt him but a beast,
> Which trusteth truth to dwell in common speeche,
> Where every lourden will become a leech.[33]

Whether or not these lines represent Gascoigne's own view, their defensiveness underscores the prestige religion continued to bestow on the voice of the people.

The same pattern can be seen in Spenser's use of the vernacular literary tradition, especially the genre of complaint with which it was heavily identified. The *Calender* is distinctive in paying homage to this tradition, in contrast to the work of others, who conspicuously subordinated it to classical and Continental precedents. Sidney, for example, rebuked Spenser in the *Defence* for not adhering to those precedents, omitting William Langland and John Skelton altogether from his account of English literature and equivocating about Geoffrey Chaucer, who "had . . . great wants," though "fit to be forgiven." Puttenham is blunter, charging Langland with being "a malcontent" and Skelton "a rude rayling rimer & all his doings ridiculous" and dismissing the language of all the earlier vernacular poets as obsolete. For him, Thomas Wyatt and the earl of Surrey, influenced by the "Italian Poesie . . . of *Dante, Arioste,* and *Petrarch,*" provide the poetic models. His assessments of Langland and Skelton betray hostility to the strain of social criticism in their work (their "rayling"), which is dominated by the genre of complaint. According to John Peter, this genre was the primary mode of literary protest until late in the sixteenth century, when it was replaced by neoclassical satire.[34] Though in distinguishing complaint from satire Peter overstates the morally generalized character of the former at the expense of its social specificity, he does show how the genre became more particular and concrete in the sixteenth century.

The *Calender* calls on this vernacular tradition most clearly through its appropriation of John Skelton's persona Collyn Clout, highlighted in E.K.'s very first gloss (422).[35] In Skelton, Collyn is one of the common people:

> . . . wandrynge as I walke
> I here the people talke.

He reports what they say—"Thus the people telles"—which provides him with his "maner of cause to moane,"

> Of hygh and lowe degre
> Of the spirytualte,
> Or of the temporalte.

His complaint is directed primarily against the politico-religious establishment represented by Cardinal Wolsey, not so much for its theological shortcomings as for its social policies. Prelates, for example, are criticized for their material exploitation of the people:

> Howe they take no hede
> Theyr sely shepe to fede,
> But plucke away and pull
> Theyr fleces of wull.

Such complaint responds to the biblical epigram to Skelton's poem: "Who will rise up for me against the evil doers? or who will stand up for me against the workers of iniquity? No man, Lord!" The poet speaks against oppression when no one else will.[36]

The prominent references to Chaucer in the *Calender*, especially to what was thought to be his *Plowman's Tale*, also place the text in the tradition of complaint, as Chaucer in the Renaissance was widely considered a reformist writer on social and religious questions.[37] The epilogue celebrates Chaucer's work, even while disclaiming equal status with it, as the model for the kind of poetry the *Calender* represents:

> Dare not to match thy pype with Tityrus hys style,[38]
> Nor with the Pilgrim that the Ploughman playde a whyle:
> But followe them farre off, and their high steppes
> adore.
> (467)

The Piers figures in the May and October eclogues must be read in the light of this unequivocal designation of the poem's lineage.[39]

Drawing on Chaucer's substantial cultural authority reinforced the *Calender*'s effort to license its social and political critique. His work had established a precedent for exemption from government censorship, explicitly excepted as it was from "the prohibicion" of Henry VIII's "Acte for thadvauncement of true Religion," which instituted an index of proscribed works.[40] Reformers took advantage of this exemption by including "The Complaint of the Plowman," a fifteenth-century poem, in the 1542 (and later) editions of Chaucer's works, under the title *The Plowman's Tale*, to which the epilogue refers.[41]

The *Calender*'s multiple references to this tale of "Chaucer's" would have accentuated its identification with the vernacular tradition of reform.[42] While the tale concerns mainly church abuses, the plowman figure, like the shepherd, is represented as speaking for the lower classes in society.[43] He is depicted in the General Prologue to *The Canterbury Tales* as a common laborer who, out of religious motivation, works on behalf of the poor:

> A trewe swynkere, and a good was he,
> Lyvynge in pees, and parfit charitee.
> God loved he best with al his hoole herte
> At alle tymes, thogh him gamed or smerte,
> And thanne his neighebor right as hymselve.
> He wolde thresshe, and therto dyke and delve,
> For Cristes sake, for every povre wight,
> Withouten hire, if it lay in his myght.[44]

Though the bulk of his complaints are directed against church officials, he repeatedly indicts them for their exploitation of "the pore" and "the people."[45] He is more concerned with social justice than with theological correctness.

The plowman figures in Chaucer and Spenser derive from and evoke the tradition of social and religious commentary instituted by Langland's *Piers Plowman*. The prestige of Langland's work lent cultural authority to the plowman figure as spokesman for the common people, the voice of complaint against oppression by those in power.[46] After Langland there were various incarnations of this figure, but in virtually every instance he decried abuses against the poor and called for reform, often weaving political with religious critique.[47] The importance of religious values in this tradition is evidenced by Hugh Latimer's "Sermon on the Plowers" (1548), in which he equated the plowman with the preacher. Adopting the persona of the plowman himself, he proceeded to castigate the "rich citizens of London," whom he compared unfavorably with the residents of the city of Nebo denounced by Jeremiah: "London is never so ill as it is now. In times past men were full of pity and compassion, but now there is no pity. For in London their brother shall die in the streets for cold; he shall lie sick at their door . . . and perish there for hunger."[48]

The plowman tradition also included more straightforward social and political commentary. In *Newes from the North, Otherwise Called the Conference Between Simon Certain, and Pierce Plowman* (1579), Pierce, like the *Calender*, combines populism with a literate culture. A "woorthy Clown," he is "a Countrie man . . . bringing under his arme a fardel of Bookes." This combination produces a skeptical view of power. He will have none of Simon's celebration of the character and godly motivation of public officials, contending instead that their power corrupts them. He cites "the old Proverbe, Honors chaunge maners. . . . many are wurse disposed, and much more ungodly in high and honorable calling: then while they were in meane estate and degree." Against Simon's efforts to identify the government officials with God, he counters sarcastically "that many of them buy their offices, and pay very deerely therfore. . . . now did I never read that ever God received Money for an office, howe be it I refer my self heerein to my Maisters that are learned." His critique rubs off on the author, "T.F., a student," who denounces the double standards applied to different classes: "Prerogatives [of the rich] are great and many, but chiefly these that in the rich: vices get credit and estimation due to vertue . . . robbery and extortion is purchase, and lechery is solace, and so of the rest as it pleaseth their flatterers to magnify them in their folyes, and contrarywise in the pore: vertues are slaundered, simplicitie and playne dealing are holden foolishnes because they do not advaunce."[49]

Writers who placed their works in the plowman tradition did not limit them to exposing moral abuses but included economic analysis of social ills and specific proposals for reform, best exemplified by *Pyers plowmans exhortation unto the lordes knightes and burgoysses of the Parlyamenthouse* (c. 1550). The author adopts the voice of the plowman to trace the effect of the closing of the abbeys on rural employment. He is especially critical of the concentration of landholding among fewer and fewer owners, because this disparity in wealth violates fundamental religious principles: "It is not agreable with the gospel that a fewe parsons shall lyve in so great abondaunce of wealth and suffer so many their christen brothers to lyve in extreme povretie." He views poverty not as a moral defect in the individual but as a structural problem in the society, not remediable by voluntary charity. Instead, Parliament must enact measures to provide more work. Without such steps the whole realm will be exposed to judgment for "this cruell oppression of the poor." He asks, "What can folowe but the just vengeance of God?"[50]

Tracing the plowman tradition is particularly instructive in demonstrating the two-way influences that pertain between social fact and textual record, response, or representation. It is widely recognized, for instance, that *Piers Plowman* informed the thought and language of the peasant leader John Ball, quite against Langland's intentions.[51] The historian Rodney Hilton describes this influence: "If, as has been argued, there was a long-term apocalyptic vision in *Piers the Ploughman*, in Ball it was to be of immediate effect." Ball himself said he "biddeth Peres Ploughman go to his werk."[52] One chronicle from the period even listed "per plouman" as a conspirator in the revolt.[53] This episode exemplifies the process by which literature informs the social imagination, issuing not only in more literature but in political expression and action as well.

The exchange between literary text—*Piers Plowman*—and political action—the Peasants' Revolt, which was in turn incorporated into literature, especially the drama—warn us that one can never securely disentangle "traditions" like "literature" and "political action" in the complex circuitry of cultural exchange.[54] It should also warn us against any simple assumption that because we have assimilated the *Calender* into our categories of the "literary," in it Spenser must have been seeking what modern culture has believed to be a valuable condition—artistic autonomy—removed from the contentious and sometimes dangerous realm of sociopolitical conversation. Unlike Langland, Spenser, utilizing the forms of the culturally articulate but politically mute, seems to have conspicuously located his work in and courted appropriation by an oppositional culture. The precise shape that opposition took in this work is revealed in a detailed examination of the heart of the *Calender*, the moral eclogues.

5

"I Dare Undersaye"

The Social Commentary of
the Moral Eclogues

Privilege in Elizabethan society was em-
bodied in a variety of ideological and institutional forms. The *Calender*'s
critique of privilege is focused in what E.K. called the moral eclogues,
whose subjects include patronage and its centralization in the Crown
at the expense of the church (February); the stated benevolence of the
regime toward the people, which did not square with its actual neglect of
their welfare (May); the ideology of hierarchy, with its religious under-
pinnings (July); and the exploitative relations of the rural economy (September). In each instance, through a network of allusions to social and
political dynamics that infuse the eclogue's debate or fable, or both,
the social form is subjected to critical examination in a manner that
is at once blunt and indirect. Detailed examination of these eclogues
demonstrates how thoroughly this work, skillfully drawing on the resources of culture, addresses the major issues confronting the Elizabethan social order.

**"Ranckorous Rigour": The February Eclogue and the
Royal Captivity of the Church**

The officially moderate tone and philosophical tidiness of the rationales
for the Crown's supremacy over the church should not blind us to the
blunt exercise of power it entailed, the flavor of which is expressed by the

queen's words to the bishop of Ely: "PROUD PRELATE, You know what you were before I made you what you are now. If you do not immediately comply with my request, I will unfrock you, by God."[1] The dominion over the church was inextricably bound up with patronage, an institution integral to the Crown's power because it centralized the distribution of wealth and status in the court, thereby fostering a competitive ethos among courtiers for the material and symbolic benefits the Crown could confer. To maintain the power patronage provided, however, the Crown had to replenish the system with new wealth, a major source of which was the church.

The February eclogue offers a critique of these dynamics of patronage. As is often the case in the *Calender*, the key to that critique is the fable of the "Ambitious" and "spitefull" brier, who induces the husbandman, a palpably royal figure, to cut down the "auncient," "Sacred" oak. While the competitive ethos of patronage and the rhetorical strategies through which it was played out are woven into the fable, it is the court's exploitation of the church to provide fuel for the system of royal rewards that is its focus.

Patronage has played an important role in recent criticism, often serving as an explanatory paradigm in the interpretation of Renaissance literature. In that role, however, patronage has generally been described as individual relationships between artists and princes, rather than as a set of institutional dynamics central to political power. Further, while contemporary literary critics acknowledge that writers bridled from time to time at the constraints of the patronage system, there has not been adequate recognition of the capacity of the early modern artist to analyze its destructive character. The February eclogue sheds light on the structural dimensions of patronage, while demonstrating how even those institutions in which the artist is implicated can be subject to his scrutiny. It is particularly valuable in reminding us that patronage in Elizabethan England was not merely a practice affecting courtiers and what we would now call the civil service, but it had decisive effects on the institutional church as well. It is part of the story I mean to tell here that, thanks to Elizabeth's policies of church governance, the state's political patronage and the church's social mission had become inextricably intertwined.

The intelligence of Thenot's fable in this eclogue lies in just that link, which he recognizes, between patronage at court and the exploitation of the church. The interpretive crux of the fable is found in the lines about the oak that have been discounted by many critics:[2]

For it had bene an auncient tree,
Sacred with many a mysteree,
And often crost with the priestes crewe,
And often halowed with holy water dewe.
But sike fancies weren foolerie,
And broughten this Oake to this miserye.
                                                            (207–12)

These lines associate the oak with the Catholic church, or what "had bene" the Catholic church, picking up on a common metaphor, for "the fall of Catholicism in England was often compared to the fall of a great tree, or reformers were urged to cut down the tree of Catholicism."[3] While these lines link the oak's destruction to its superstitious practices, the fable refuses to condemn it on that ground, instead affirming the value of the "goodly Oake" (103).

How do we reconcile this favorable treatment with the "foolerie" of "papist" practices? The repudiation of ritual invites us to look to other institutional functions of the old religion as the explanation for the respect accorded it. The fable's tragic tone grows out of the waste resulting from the oak's destruction, pointing to social benefits once provided by it but now cut off. Moreover, that destruction is unjust: the brier's complaint, we are told, is "causlesse" (148), and the ax that is the instrument of its destruction is reluctant "to wrong" the tree (206). But if injustice has been done, who is responsible? The fable's answer to that question is both comprehensive and nuanced, and in it lies the kernel of this eclogue's critique.

As we saw above, Thenot, through his choice of words, locates the tale he tells in the court. The forest is described as "trees of state" (146), and the brier employs the rhetoric of lordship ("my soveraigne, Lord of creatures all" [163], "my liege Lord" [150]). Thenot's reference to "your Coronall" (178) casts the husbandman as a royal figure. The brier's flowers— "Lilly white, and Cremsin redde" (130)—which anticipate Elizabeth's in April, and his praise for them as "Colours meete to clothe a mayden Queene" (132) go a long way toward including the reigning monarch in their scope. Underscoring this association is the pun on *husband*, which evokes the spousal metaphor commonly applied to and used by Elizabeth to describe her relationship to the kingdom. Capitalizing on the queen's unmarried status, Anthony Munday, for instance, referred to Elizabeth as "the husband of the common weale, maried to the Realme." The queen herself frequently invoked the image of marriage, declaring in 1561: "I was once married to this realm at my coronation, in token whereof I wear this ring."[4]

The royal character of the husbandman is emphasized by his coming "of custome for to servewe his grownd" (145), for it was through the survey that the Crown determined the extent and value of its holdings. In particular, the survey served as an integral element in the Crown's program of acquiring church property, going back to Henry VIII's reign. The 1535 survey, known as the *Valor Ecclesiasticus*, inventoried and valued the property to be turned over to the Crown on the dissolution of church institutions. In the legislation authorizing that appropriation, the word *survey* was used to describe the Crown's jurisdiction over this property: "All hereditaments appertaining or belonging . . . to any [of] the said monasteries . . . shal be in [its] order, survey and governance." Elizabeth also employed surveys of property she acquired from the bishops, with the same term appearing in her legislation: "thorder survey rule and governance."[5]

The supervision of property implied by *survey* underscores the ostensible setting of Thenot's fable in husbandry, the prudent management of resources. Such management provided an important rationale for the expropriation of church property. The Crown's early actions were justified by the claim that the religious inhabitants would, if left in possession, "spoil, destroy, consume and utterly waste" their property.[6] According to Joyce Youings, "government propaganda never allowed the point to be lost sight of that the whole process of the Dissolution was directed towards the transfer of monastic property into the hands of those better fitted to make use of it."[7] The image persisted, invoked during Elizabeth's reign by Protestants, like Foxe, sponsoring royal supremacy. Foxe describes the dissolution in language implying that the bad husbandry of the monastic orders had transformed them into noxious plants, which the good husband in charge of the Protestant church and state had extracted from the national soil: "All friars, monks, canons, nuns, and other sects of religion were then so rooted out of this realm from the very

The woodcut from the February eclogue
(Huntington Library).

foundation, that there seemeth, by God's grace, no possibility hereafter left, for the generation of those strange weeds to grow here any more. . . . [Quoting Jesus] 'Every plantation, being not planted of my Father, shall be plucked up by the roots.' "[8]

The brier in the fable echoes this Protestant polemic, complaining that the tree "hinder[s] with his shade my lovely light" (173), so that "untimely my flowres [are] forced to fall" (177), and that with worms and leaves from the oak "my fresh flowretts bene defast" (182). Yet in fact, as Spenser put it later in *Mother Hubberds Tale,* what is represented as "care of thrift, and husbandry" (l. 1170) was actually the "cloke" of simple acquisitiveness. The graphic description of the oak's decay (111–14) seems to rationalize its destruction as a pruning of dead growth, but the implication of decadence is undermined by the difficulty the husbandman has in bringing the tree down. The *Calender*'s woodcut also questions his action as an instance of prudent husbandry: as Ruth Samson Luborsky points out, the oak is depicted "in leaf, contrary to other February illustrations" in the calendrical tradition.[9] It is a living tree that is cut down.

The associations of the oak with the church and the brier and husbandman with court and monarchy thus evoke the history of the Crown's exploitation of the church. But in order to understand the poem's tone and textual details more deeply, we will need to broaden our account of that history. The most dramatic period, the dissolution of the monasteries and other religious institutions under Henry VIII from 1536 to 1544, transferred enormous wealth to the Crown, some nine hundred thousand pounds before it was complete.[10] The animus against superstitious practices like those the eclogue describes played its part in prompting this confiscation, but the overriding motivations, according to Geoffrey Elton, were that "the government wanted the wealth of the monasteries, and the gentry hoped to obtain it from the Crown after confiscation." In fact, that was exactly what happened. Though much of the land may have been sold at something close to its value, acquiring it represented a tremendous opportunity for the Crown's lay clients, an opportunity they took advantage of, often initiating the transfers themselves.[11]

The appropriation of church property continued through Edward's reign and into Elizabeth's. She extended her predecessors' policy by issuing commissions to search for property that should have been transferred to the Crown in earlier confiscations but that was "concealed." Just as important were her own extractions, which took a number of different forms. Pursuant to a statute in her first Parliament, any estates still held by the church institutions and those restored during Mary's reign were appropriated, while the Crown was also authorized to take church land in exchange for the right to collect tithes.[12] Since the former was often undervalued and the latter was of dubious validity, such exchanges enriched the Crown at the church's expense. According to Claire Cross, this act "set the precedent for the royal treatment of ecclesiastical revenues for the whole of the reign." Parliament also restricted the bishops' leases of church land, funneling any arrangements between church and courtier through the Crown, which made such full use of this power that favorable leases of church lands became "the cheapest and most popular way for [it] to reward a courtier or a civil servant."[13] The Crown also left sees vacant so that it could collect the income from their property, shuffled bishops to take advantage of the "first fruits" that went to the Crown, and assessed disproportionately high taxes against the church.[14] Though the queen was, as Cross put it, "nominally the guardian of the church, she felt no compunction in plundering its estates and permitting

favoured lay subjects to follow her example." So they did: "The conviction," according to Felicity Heal, "that there was still an easy profit to be
made from the church . . . remained alive and well under Elizabeth."[15]

The Crown's plunder of the church had several important effects. First,
it decisively impaired the system of social services, especially in the
countryside. Education, the care of the sick, and hospitality for travelers
were all sharply diminished. At the same time, there arose widespread
unemployment among former employees of the monasteries and some
abuse of tenants by their new landlords.[16] Most important, however, was
the damage to the system of poor relief, since it was the church and not
the state that played the predominant role in caring for the poor during
this period. The exact impact of the dissolution on this role is uncertain,
but it was considerable. According to Joyce Youings, "When, in the mid
sixteenth century, the Church was relieved of a substantial part of [its]
wealth, the poor were almost forgotten in the scramble of the laity at
large, including the Crown, to repossess the resources bestowed on the
clergy by their ancestors."[17]

This diversion of the church's resources to patronage did not go unchal-
lenged. Contemporary complaint, even by Protestant reformers, decried
the reduction in care for the poor prior to Elizabeth's reign. In 1542 Henry
Brinklow ridiculed the aim of "amending that was amysse" in the abbeys:
"The monkes gave to lytle almesse. . . . But now, where .xx. pownd was
geven yearly to the poore, in moo than an .C. places in Ingland, is not one
meales meat geven. This is a fayre amendment." He unsuccessfully urged
on Parliament the example of "Christen Germanys . . . [w]hich dyvyded
not such goodys and landys among the pryncys, lordes, and rych men,
that had no neede theroff; but thei put it to the use of the comon welth,
and unto the provysyon for the pore, acordyng to the doctryne of the
Scrypture." And in Robert Crowley's poem "Of Almes Houses" (1550),
a merchant returns from abroad, finding "a lordely house . . . where the
hospitall should be."[18] A beggar he meets tells him:

> we are all turned oute,
> And lye and dye in corners,
>   here and there aboute.
> Men of greate riches
>   have bought our dwellinge place,

And when we crave of them,
they turne awaye their face.

The merchant is shocked, declaring that even in Turkey,

emonge those heathen
none such crueltie have I sene.

The impact of the dissolution on the lower classes in rural society
was dramatically demonstrated by the Pilgrimage of Grace in 1536–37.
Though this uprising was a response to Henry VIII's initial expropriation
of church property, the rebels were animated by more than religious motives. According to Anthony Fletcher, "They simply identified the threat
to the Church with the threat to the poor." The first of their articles to
the king asserted that by reason of the suppression "the service of our
God is not wel [maintained] but also the [commons] of yor realme be
unrelevyed, the which as we think is a gret hurt to the common welthe."
Elaborating on this "gret hurt," their leader, Robert Aske, declared that
"in the north parts much of the relief of the commons was by succour of
abbeys." He emphasized the importance of these indigenous institutions
to the local economy: "The profites of thies abbeys yerley goith out of
the contrey to the Kinges highnes, so that in short space little money . . .
should be left in the said countrey. . . . when the . . . abbeys stud, the . . .
peuple not only had worldly refreshing in their bodies but also sperituall
refuge both by gostly liffing of them and also by spiritual informacion,
and preching; and many ther tenountes wer ther feed servaundes to them,
and serving men, wel socored by abbeys."[19]
    Thenot's fable evokes this economic impact of the Crown's policy by
locating the oak's value not in theology or the ritual of religion but in
the material benefit rendered to the nonelite in rural society, for "with
his nuts [the oak] larded many swine" (110). In accordance with the proverb, this line affirms that this tree is known by and valued for its fruit.
Given the importance of swine in the countryside—pigs were especially
suited to the small farmer, often raised for domestic needs, "one of the
peasant's standbys"—the line casts the oak as an integral part of the
rural economy. The proverbial association between acorns and primitive
society also underscores the allusion to the uncultured rustics in that
economy.[20] There, among the unlearned and the poor, the church provided an institutional network of important services, both material and

educational. Echoing the complaint of the commons in the Pilgrimage of Grace, the *Calender* implies that by providing these benefits to the rural poor the church strengthened the national government as well: the oak "mochell mast to the husband did yielde" (109).

Thus, the detriment to the poor from the dissolutions was profit to the upper classes, whose financial gain affected their attitude toward Protestantism, ensuring their commitment, according to Reinhard Bendix, to the Reformation: "Whatever the religious sentiment involved, landowning families had a manifest interest in the validity of titles to former monastic estates which they had purchased from the Crown." Even when the winds of religious policy shifted, as they did in Mary's reign, there was no political support for restoring property to the church. This attitude persisted in Elizabeth's reign, expressed in the hostility of the landowning classes to any ecclesiastical reform that might reduce their control over church assets.[21] The great proportion of the benefices for supporting the parish clergy was now in the hands of laymen, who, having received their lands as royal patronage, became patrons in their turn. Hence lay patronage of the clergy increased.[22] Arrangements such as pluralism and the sale of benefices, which treated the material resources of the church as so many economic commodities with little or no regard for the church's ministry, led to a poor and ill-prepared clergy. Archbishop Grindal complained to Elizabeth in 1576 of the erosion of preaching, tracing the diversion of resources that were to be used for that purpose: they "were first annexed to abbeys; and after came to the crown; and now are dispersed to private men's possessions, without hope to reduce the same to the [church]."[23]

At the same time that that diversion created a large lay faction opposed to institutional reform of the church, it solidified their alliance with the Crown by committing them to its supremacy in all matters "temporal and ecclesiastical" (the language of the Act of Supremacy). This policy, which was central to Elizabeth's government and its vision of national identity, created a symbiotic bond between Elizabeth and the landed elite: she "was seeking the revival of the royal supremacy over the Church, and [they] knew that the supremacy would assure their continued possession of the alienated Church property."[24]

Spenser's fable in the February eclogue draws attention to this question of supremacy. The oak "whilome had bene the King of the field" (108). Though it has been supplanted, the savvy brier recognizes that the most effective way to inflame the husbandman is to invoke the oak's power (its "felonous force" [156], its "cruell constraint" [152] and "might" [185]), accusing it of aspiring to "tyrannie" (172). In response, the husbandman demonstrates his supremacy over the rival institution by the graphic image of felling it.

While creating support for supremacy, the exploitation of the church also enhanced the Crown's role as the dispenser of patronage, for, as Grindal noted, the church's assets were funneled through it. Church property provided a significant proportion of "the raw materials of the political system, the bricks out of which loyal service, and consequently a reliable administration, were constructed." On the individual level, the reciprocity expected of the beneficiary was succinctly stated by Elizabeth's grandfather to one of his courtiers: "Study to serve me and I will study to enrich you." Institutionally, centralizing patronage augmented the Crown's power "at the expense of the system of aristocratic patronage, making the Court more than ever the focus for men's hopes and ambitions," so that, as Cecil advised the queen in 1579, "you shall have all men of value in the realme to depend only upon yourselfe."[25] At the church's expense, the Crown's position as the creator of hierarchy—the "placer of plants both humble and tall" (l. 164 in the February eclogue)— was solidified.

The courtiers' dependence on the Crown for status and material benefit is figured in the brier's references to himself as the husbandman's "Suppliant" (151) and "poore Vassall" (153) who is "like for desperate doole to dye" (155) without intercession. Such dependence intensified the competition the queen fostered at court, reflected in the rivalry of the brier and oak, which "stir[red] up sterne strife" (149).[26] A contemporary and one of Elizabeth's earliest historians commented that "the principall note of her Reign will be, that she ruled much by faction and parties, which she her self both made, upheld, and weakened, as her own great judgment advised."[27] It is just such factionalism that the fable implies is the seedbed for the destruction of the oak, for the parties to the conflict, in the words of *Mother Hubberds Tale*,

... would be Lords alone:
For Love and Lordship bide no paragone.
(ll. 1025–26)

The same phrase is used in the eclogue to describe the brier's short-lived triumph: "Now stands the Brere like a Lord alone" (222). While the dynamics of competition rendered "alone" as success, the brier's ultimate demise shows how costly that success could be.

The changes in the fable from its sources emphasize these court dynamics as the cause of the oak's destruction. As E.K.'s statement that it is "like to Æsopes fables" (426) hints, the kinship with Aesop's fables of the tree and the reed and the bush and the aubier tree is unmistakable, while the differences are striking.[28] In both of Aesop's fables the tree is destroyed for its pride, while the smaller plant is advanced or preserved for its humility or low status. In Thenot's rendering, however, it is the smaller plant who, "puffed up with pryde and vaine pleasaunce" (223), initiates the oak's downfall. This reversal, together with the husbandman's prominent role, shifts attention away from moral qualities to political dynamics, from the oak to those who conspire against it.

In similar fashion, Thenot's fable alludes to but reverses roles in a contemporary political dispute about the literal felling of trees. It is true that chopping wood, depicted in the eclogue's woodcut, was "a traditional labor" for the month of February. The activity commonly appeared in almanac illustrations, including those of *The Kalender of Shepherdes*. Yet the image of felled trees also recalled a more specific and topical issue. In the face of depletion by the Crown and courtiers, timber became for the bishops a particularly important asset, its harvesting "a common expedient with churchmen to make both ends meet." In 1579, concerned by reports that church prelates were "wasting . . . revenues" by cutting down trees, the bishops were ordered not to take any more great trees and to report on those already felled.[29] Thenot's use of the same image to render the church as victim rather than agent graphically shifts responsibility for that waste.

The Crown's dominance of the church made it impossible for the latter, as an institution, to serve as an independent voice in the commonwealth. The haughty attitude displayed by the queen in her letter to the bishop of Ely captures the personal flavor of that dominance. Although one might not wish to put it as strongly as F. O. White, whose research on the Elizabethan bishops led him to see the queen as "a cruel despot tyrannising over a helpless set of men whom she regarded as being peculiarly her own creatures," Elizabeth was certainly more "absolutist" in policy and more of a bully in temperament than some historians and many literary critics have been willing to admit. With her economic power and legal sanction, the queen could use both carrot and stick to keep her churchmen in line. As a result, "the temptations to prefer the easy course of *adulator* were," according to Collinson, "as numerous and strong as in Old Testament days of false prophecy. It would be naïve to suppose that many, and perhaps most, ecclesiastical careerists did not succumb." The product was a church "governed as another department of the State," whose voice so often represented royal ventriloquism, an institution disabled as a potential critic of the Crown.[30]

Yet occasional stubborn figures like Dering or Grindal refused the role of flatterer and spoke the truth, to their own disadvantage. In Spenser's fable, also, the oak does not participate in the language of compliment the brier employs. As his inept responses to the brier show (140–42, 189–90), he lacks the rhetorical skills so necessary to the courtier's advancement. In fact, he interferes with the courtly rhetoric of flattery: the brier claims he damaged the *flowers* (176, 182) of which the husband-man's "Coronall" was to be composed. In such a context, the oak's lack of rhetorical skill is a virtue on the order of Cordelia's.

It scarcely needs saying that the symbolic force of each of the eclogues in the *Calender* is enhanced (though seldom clearly explained) by the final emblems, which usually require an explanation of their own. In this case, the two emblems appear to be directed to the youth-age contest but evidently also involve the location of religious authority. Playing off the identification of the oak, the "aged Tree" (102) and "holy eld" (206), with ancientness, Thenot's emblem, *Iddio perche è vecchio, / Fa suoi al suo essempio* (426), associates it with "God, who is old, [and who] will bring others to himself by his example." Cuddie's emblem, on the other hand, *Niuno vecchio, / Spaventa Iddio* (426), "spoken," according to E.K., "in contempt of old age" (427), drives a wedge between God and age by asserting that "none who are old fear God."[31] The effect is to set against each other two incomparable claims about the old religion, which is either close to God or alienated from him. Hence the rival emblems leave unresolved the issue supposed to have been settled by the Reformation and the dissolution of the monasteries, or rather, they reopen the question, not in theological terms, but from the vantage of the institutional dynamics central to the fable.

Earlier readings of the fable overlooked those dynamics in their emphasis on factionalism sparked by the "Ambitious" brier. These readings cannot take account of what is at first glance the curious religious affiliation of the oak. In order for Paul McLane, for example, to identify this figure with Leicester, the leader of the hard-line Protestant faction (at least in foreign affairs), he must discount its association with "the priestes crewe."[32] The institutional dimension of the fable points beyond the damage inflicted on one or another of the factions competing at court to the destructiveness to the whole commonwealth from the institution itself: the patronage system dominated by the Crown, which looted the church for the benefit of its clients and its own power.

"Motherly Care" in May: The Political Dimension of the Parental Metaphor

The narrowest account of the May eclogue is that offered by E.K. in a gloss to its enclosed fable of the fox and the kid: that it represents anti-Catholic satire.[33] A somewhat broader interpretation can be found in the work of certain modern literary critics, who have read the entire eclogue as religious satire, aimed at the papist tendencies of the Anglican clergy.[34] But this would be an accurate account of only a part of the eclogue, Piers's critique of the prelates (81–131). It does not satisfactorily describe the other, apparently disparate, elements of the eclogue or the relationship among them: Palinode's description of May Day festivities (1–36); the debates between Piers and Palinode over the conduct of shepherds who participate in them (37–72) and over the propriety of Piers's criticism itself (132–71); and, most important, Piers's extended rewriting of a familiar Aesopian fable (174–305) and Palinode's reaction to it (306–13). These sections are held together in large measure by the eclogue's concern with social responsibility, signified by the word *care*.[35] This concern is most sharply focused on parental care, an image with important ramifications in Elizabethan political culture because it was central to the Crown's self-representation, an encapsulation of the queen's relationship with her subjects. Overlooking the importance of this metaphor, modern criticism has failed to recognize the implication of the Crown in the abuses to which Piers alludes. The fable's importance to this eclogue is hinted at early, in the woodcut. Unlike the *Calender*'s other fables, this one is depicted in three places, "ringing the [May Day] festival" in

The woodcut from the May eclogue
(Huntington Library).

the center.[36] Its interrogatation of the Crown's claim of "motherly care"
toward the English church and people brings together the other elements
of the eclogue.

The eclogue opens with Palinode's envious descriptions of typical May
Day celebrations (1–16 and 19–36), whose participants Piers denounces:

> Those faytours little regarden their charge,
> While they letting their sheepe runne at large,
> Passen their time, that should be sparely spent,
> In lustihede and wanton meryment.
> Thilke same bene shepeheards for the Devils stedde,
> That playen, while their flockes be unfedde.
>
> (39–44)

To fully appreciate the nuanced character of this critique, it is necessary
to look at May Day celebrations and Puritan criticism of them. While
the May Day festival was very popular in the countryside, it was not confined to rural England or to the common people but cut across regional
and class boundaries. It is true that as a popular event these festivals
carried with them a subversive potential, actualized in the Suffolk May
play in 1557 concerning "a king, how he should rule his realm," in which
one character "played husbandry, and said many things against gentle-

men, more than was in the book of the play." But what Robert Weimann says of other popular rituals is particularly true of these activities: they were "based on . . . heterogeneous social foundations . . . [and] simply cannot be reduced to any single sociological formula." John Stow notes that Londoners "of all estates" participated in May Day festivities and that the games were "made by the governors and Maisters of this citie." Elizabeth's court, as well as those of her father and grandfather, also participated.[37]

There were unmistakable sexual overtones to May Day celebrations, which Palinode hints at with his emphasis on the pleasures of the event, especially the dancing "eche one with his mayd" (24), and the pun in his expressed desire "to helpen the Ladyes their Maybush beare" (34). This aspect of the celebrations called forth denunciations by Puritans such as Phillip Stubbes, who lamented the "credible reports" that told "that of forty, threescore, or a hundred maides going to the wood over night, there have scarcely the third part of them returned home undefiled. These be the frutes which these cursed pastimes bring foorth."[38]

Though Palinode's leering invites Piers to voice similar complaints, his criticism of the festival takes a quite different tack. While acknowledging the promiscuity of the celebration—its "lustihede and wanton meryment"—he chastises the participants not for sexual license, but for the irresponsibility the celebration entails: they "playen, while their flockes be unfedde." The participation by all estates in these festivities gives these lines multiple registration. They reflect first a nuanced attitude toward popular culture, critical without wholesale condemnation. Avoiding the Puritans' typical censures, Piers escapes the "disabling ambivalence toward the queen's subjects—'the people'" that the reformers often betrayed.[39] Instead, he subjects these festivals to the *Calender*'s characteristic imperative of social responsibility, while making clear that, for the elite who participate in these festivals, the temporary delinquency of pastime is emblematic of their systematic neglect: they "little regarden their charge" (39).

In Piers's critique, proper care has been sacrificed for "hire," economic transactions substituted for personal relationships between the powerful and their charges:

Well is it seene, theyr sheepe bene not their owne,
That letten them runne at randon alone.

But they bene hyred for little pay
Of other, that caren as little as they,
What fallen the flocke, so they han the fleece,
And get all the gayne, paying but a peece.
                                                (45–50)

Piers's reproach is religiously grounded, the neglect of responsibility en-
visioned as courting divine judgment:

I muse, what account both these will make,
The one for the hire, which he doth take,
And thother for leaving his Lords taske,
When great *Pan* account of shepeherdes shall aske.
                                                (51–54)

The first and most obvious register of meaning in Piers's analysis is
that of ecclesiastical government. His language closely tracks complaints
made by both reformers and some church officials about the decayed
state of the church as a result of lay patronage and pluralism. As we have
seen, upon the dissolution of the monasteries a great deal of ecclesiastical property was converted to lay control.[40] Much of that property, originally intended for the livings of local ministers, was accompanied by the
right to present a minister for a specific parish. Piers's complaint about
economic motives echoes the *Admonition to the Parliament* (1572) in its
denunciation of the "unlawful sute & buying," the marketplace that the
appointment of clergy had become: "Now, by the letters commendatorie
of some one man, noble or other, tag and rag, learned and unlearned,
of the basest sorte of the people . . . are freely receaved. . . . now every
one picketh out for himself some notable good benefice [the minister's
living], he obtaineth the next advouson, by money or by favour, and so
thinketh hymself to be sufficiently chosen." In 1584 even Whitgift acknowledged that patrons "get all the gayne, paying but a peece": he wrote
that they "nowadays search not the universities for a most fit pastor, but
they post up and down the country for a most gainful chapman [trader].
He that hath the biggest purse to pay largely, not he that hath the best
gift to preach learnedly, is presented."[41]

The exploitation of livings by patrons fueled the trend toward pluralism (the holding of two or more livings by one person) in two ways:
offering an additional source of revenue for the patron or providing the

holder of a living with adequate support in the face of the patron's extraction.[42] In each case the funds intended for the church's mission were diverted to the wealthy. As Archbishop Parker complained about one diocese in 1567, "The best of the county, not under the degree of knights, were infected with this sore, so far that some one knight had four or five, some seven or eight benefices clouted together, fleecing them all." Not only lay patrons profited from pluralism. It was also an important source of episcopal income, employed to replace revenue lost to the Crown and laity. The Crown benefited, too, because royal dispensations were necessary for most clergy to hold more than one benefice. The economic benefits of pluralism increased the value and thus the price of these dispensations. All these parties were enriched at the expense of the local parish and its parishioners. Despite widespread acknowledgment of the damage pluralism inflicted, the alliance of these powerful groups successfully resisted repeated efforts at reform.[43]

For the reformers, the worst consequence of pluralism was "the dissociation of benefices from pastoral duties." The *Admonition* complained that in the primitive church "every pastor had his flocke, and every flocke his shepheard, or els shepheards: Now they doe not onely run fyskyng [moving briskly about] from place to place . . . but covetously joine living to living, making shipwracke of their owne consciences, and being but one shepherd (nay, wold to God they were shepheards and not wolves) have many flockes." Cartwright argued (in language echoed by Piers's complaint) that the responsibility of the minister could only be fulfilled by personal involvement with those to whom that responsibility was owed, requiring that "every man ha[ve] a certain possession committed unto him, *which he should care for* and take charge of. . . . And so the Lord . . . ordained that the church should be divided in divers parts, and that *everyone should have a piece to care for* and to give account for."[44]

The personal character of the responsibility central to these complaints was figured by the trope of presence. The debate over pastoral residence revolved around whether, as Phillip Stubbes put it, ministers "may not as well be absent, or present." The nonresidence inherent in pluralism eroded the pastor's responsibility, making the shepherd's "absence from his flocke a dangerous and perilous thing," which delegation to deputies "shall not excuse . . . at the day of judgment."[45] Piers defines neglect in the same terms, as the replacement of personal with impersonal relationships—"theyr sheepe bene not their owne"—and as physical withdrawal—"leaving his Lords taske."

Piers develops his analysis of these abuses by focusing on misplaced care: the excessive concern the prelates showed for their families, their "care for their heire" (77). As Joyce Youings describes it, that concern often took the form of using church resources to promote the family's wealth and status: "Having for the most part come from humble backgrounds, once in possession of what, by contemporary standards, was great wealth, the higher clergy felt more obliged than their lesser brethren to find patrimonies and dowries sufficient to ensure all their children a standard of life such as they had enjoyed in the palace." However natural the sentiment, providing for families opened the prelacy up to charges of abuse, not just from the Puritans but also from the queen, who was opposed to clerical marriage in the first place. The bishops' "greed on behalf of their children and kin . . . became [a] common theme . . . in the repertoire of royal anger."[46] While Elizabeth typically invoked that greed to get the bishops to turn over property to the Crown or its clients and the Puritans focused on the diversion of resources from the church's preaching ministry, however, Piers emphasizes the self-defeating quality of accumulating wealth to pass on:

> For if he mislive in leudnes and lust,
> Little bootes all the welth and the trust,
> That his father left by inheritaunce:
> All will be soone wasted with misgovernaunce.
> But through this, and other their miscreaunce,
> They maken many a wrong chevisaunce,
> Heaping up waves of welth and woe,
> The floddes whereof shall them overflowe.
>   (87–94)

Piers expands his critique of misdirected parental care with a vision of a primordial utopia (103–31). Against the active accumulation of wealth by contemporary shepherds he sets the simplicity of primitive ones whose material needs were met without such "heaping up": "little them served for their mayntenaunce . . . of nought they were unprovided" (112, 114). The conveyance of wealth to the next generation is, in Piers's vision, supplanted by the transmission of moral values represented by religion, "for *Pan* himselfe was their inheritaunce" (111).[47] His vision posits a nonexploitative relationship with the flock that provides the minimal necessary material support. The fall from this utopia comes when, against Piers's imperative "not [to] live ylike, as men of the laye" (76), religious shepherds aspired to a life like that of the powerful, marked by the appetite for wealth, social status, and political power.[48] That is when shepherds began to "leave to live hard, and learne to ligge soft" (125), "gan to gape for greedie governaunce" (121), and became "Lovers of Lordship and troublers of states" (123).

This passage also echoes contemporary complaints by church reformers. Though the resources of the higher clergy were exploited by the Crown and patrons, the bishops (often through pluralism) remained wealthy landowners heading large households, officials who "need[ed] to maintain their station and fulfil the expectations of secular society." The reformers complained of this status, contrasting it with the simplicity of the primitive church: "Then it was paineful: now gaineful. Then poore and ignominious: now rich and glorious." They should be "abridged of their huge livings," which should be returned to the local ministry. As Piers's complaint suggests, an important mark of the bishops' status was their title as "lords." In the Puritans' view this title signified the contamination of the hierarchy with extraneous temporal concerns that detracted from the pastoral mission of the church. To the reformers the title was inimical to the religious tradition, "for the name bishop is not the name of a Lord." It is "against the word of God" and "drawne out of the Popes shop." They need to "lay aside this Lording," to be "unlorded." The degradation of the church by temporal ambitions stood in the way of "the restitution of true religion and reformation of Gods church."[49]

In May the fable of the mother goat, her kid, and the fox recombines important elements of this complaint, namely the figure of personal presence as an emblem of social responsibility and the concept of parental care. Together they accent the questionable character of the goat's departure from home, leaving her child alone. Piers's tale is a substantial revision of Aesop's of "the wulf and of the kydde."[50] E.K. draws our attention to the different outcome (in Aesop the kid successfully resists the intruder), but there are other significant differences as well. In particular, though framed with references to the kid's shortcomings, Piers's fable gives a great deal of attention to the mother's words and actions— not only her departure but also the instruction she gives the kid as she leaves. The narrative, for instance, is not sequential but opens with that departure, leaving the kid alone:

For on a tyme in Sommer season,
The Gate her dame, that had good reason,
Yode forth abroade unto the greene wood,
To brouze, or play, or what shee thought good.
                                        (176–79)

Her "good reason" is qualified by the catalog of possible motives, especially the subjective "what shee thought good," rendering that motive
far less definitive or compelling than the "honger" that in Aesop's fable
"toke her . . . to the feldes for to ete some grasse."[51] Furthermore, unlike
Aesop, who does not describe the goat's exit, Piers dwells on it:

Tho went the pensife Damme out of dore,
And chaunst to stomble at the threshold flore:
Her stombling steppe some what her amazed,
(For such, as signes of ill luck bene dispraised)
Yet forth shee yode thereat halfe aghast.
                                        (229–33)

The warnings she perceives further problematize her withdrawal.[52] But
her departure is most severely compromised by its association with the
May Day revelers described earlier in the eclogue. Her action of going
"forth abroade" mirrors theirs (marked by the repetition of *yode* from
line 22 in lines 178 and 233), and she is headed for the same destination,
"the greene Wood" (27 and 178). The possibility that she is going to the
woods to "play," like the revelers, brings her within the ambit of Piers's
critique of them.

Juxtaposed to her "doubtfull" absence is the concern the dame pro-
fesses for her "youngling": "But for she had a motherly care" (180).[53] She
repeats the word *care* in introducing her "warning" to him,

Kiddie (quoth shee) thou kenst the great care,
I have of thy health and thy welfare.
                                        (215–16)

The word's prominence in the fable recalls its earlier uses in the eclogue,
in Piers's critique of both the "outgoing" shepherds (48) and clerical
parents (77 and 96).[54]

In addition, the centrality of *care* in the fable, as well as its distinctively
maternal context, suggest a secular register for the analysis of social ir-

responsibility. Elizabeth frequently invoked the term *care* to describe the Crown's benevolent attitude toward the people—personalizing the political relationship—particularly when its action might be unpopular, viewed as antagonistic to their interests. In rejecting Parliament's 1567 petition that she marry, for example, Elizabeth assured the members that she was not "unmyndfull of your suretie by successyon, wherein is all my care. . . . although perhappe you may have after me on bettere learned or wiser, yet I assure you non more carefull over you."[55] She denounced John Stubbs's *Gaping Gulf* because it called her concern into question: "The crooked nature of the seditious libeler will not imagine any . . . princely care in her majesty." She considered her solicitude beyond dispute, self-evident and acknowledged by her subjects: "Her majesty needeth not by words to express her princely care in all her public actions, for that the effects hereof do plentifully give testimony, and so she daily findeth her good subjects thankful to her for the same."[56]

The Crown's invocation of "motherly care" articulated the central Elizabethan metaphor of prince as parent. We have already seen how the parental metaphor was employed to provide political power with a footing in the Fifth Commandment, giving civic obedience religious sanction.[57] The regime's adaptation of this trope became what was perhaps the most important self-representation of the queen, as mother of her people.[58] The Crown promoted the image in public and private (though published) prayers, and in Elizabeth's public speech.[59] According to Alison Heisch, "Throughout her reign, in a metaphor her sex made plausible, [Elizabeth] picture[d] and present[ed] herself as a loving and yet virginal mother." Like *care*, the image was often invoked defensively by the queen to reassure those whom she rebuffed. "Though after my death you may have many stepdames," she told the Commons as she rejected their 1563 petition that she marry, "yet shall yow never have any a more naturall mother then I meane to be unto you all."[60]

This image effectively combined, to borrow Louis Montrose's phrase, "intimacy and benignity with authoritarianism," presenting coercive rule in the guise of affection and kinship while still affirming its prerogatives.[61] According to John Hayward, Elizabeth was mistress of this strategy: "If ever any persone had eyther the gift or the stile to winne the hearts of the people, it was this Queene . . . in coupling mildnesse with majesty . . . and in stately stouping to the meanest sort."[62]

The image of "motherly care" also fashioned a role for the people as grateful children who celebrated Elizabeth for her solicitous concern. Mulcaster based the subject's obligation on the image, declaring that the queen "clameth a prerogative in dewtie, both for the excellencie of hir place . . . and for the greatnesse of hir care, wherewith she is charged, as our parent."[63] Casting the subjects as children figuratively disempowered them, allowing the queen to "correct" them while retaining their loyalty as "loving subjects."[64] She chastised the Commons through the Speaker in 1585, for example, for its efforts to legislate ecclesiastical reform: "Her majestie is greatlye greved that she hathe occasyon to cause this thus to be delyvered unto you whom she dothe know and affyrmethe to be as loving subjectes as any prynce in the world hathe. And therfore of her great and tender favor she could not choose but as a mother over her children eftsones to warne you to forbeare any further procedinges in this course."[65]

As in Piers's fable, there was no inconsistency here between "motherly care" and command. The subjects' role as children, in fact, demanded more than obedience from them. "For by the name of parents," Nowell's *Catechism* declared, "we are charged not only to yield and obey to magistrates, but also to honour and love them."[66] The maternal image dictated a filial response that would satisfy Elizabeth's desire to "have the obedience of all our subjects of all sorts, both high and low, by love and not by compulsion, by their own yielding and not by our exacting."[67]

The parental metaphor was so central to the Crown's rhetorical self-fashioning that the phrase *motherly care* by itself would implicate it in the dynamics of the fable. But E.K. reinforces its involvement by his punning gloss on *orphane* as one who "needeth a Tutour and governour" (440).[68] There are other hints at the monarchy's implication as well, each slight on its own, but cumulatively suggestive. The word *dame* (177) that Piers uses, which is not in Aesop, not only referred to a mother or the mistress of a household but was also a title of rank, used for a female ruler, as in the speech welcoming the queen on progress to Norwich in 1578, praising her as "so great a Dame."[69] Further, during the 1570s Elizabeth often retired to a "green" place in spring or summer: Greenwich. That site, Elizabeth's birthplace and a "favourite residence," may well be evoked by the emphasis Palinode and E.K. put on the "pleasaunce" of the season, for, according to William Harrison, the royal residence there was called Pleasance.[70]

This eclogue is also linked in subtle ways with the preceding April eclogue, so closely identified with Elizabeth. Their woodcuts share distinctive features, and Palinode's description of May Day, which continues April's festive tone, is marked by references to features found in the previous eclogue as well: "girlonds of roses and Sopps in wine" (14; see April 62, 68, 138), the dance (24–26; April 111–13), the nymphs (33; April 37), and April's "meriment" (112) that has, for Piers, become "wanton" (42).[71] These combined elements—the festive air Palinode evokes, the music and dance, the destination in the green wood, and the entourage of nymphs and shepherds under the genial rule of a queen—suggest a royal progress in the countryside. Harrison's description of that activity—"when it pleaseth [the queen] in the summer season to recreate herself abroad"—aligns strikingly with the importance of "pleasure" in the celebration of May Day, the "Sommer season" (176) of the fable, and its emphasis on the dame's going "abroade" (178 and 223). The royal progress—referred to by one historian as a "public-relations exercise"—may well stand as the exemplar of the irresponsibility the eclogue castigates.[72]

The conduct of the dame in the fable scrutinizes the parental metaphor and the profession of care that accompanies it. Although she knows the fox's superior craft (she calls him the "maister of collusion" [219]) and is aware of the kid's "tender state" (218), she leaves the young goat alone (just as the derelict shepherds of Piers's complaint left their flock "alone" [46]), protected only by her "school[ing]" (227) of him. There is also more than a suggestion of a causal relationship between her departure and the fox's assault:

It was not long, after shee was gone,
But the false Foxe came to the dore anone.
(235–36)

Not only the dame's absence bears on the question of her responsibility, however; there is also her advice to the kid, which, though well intentioned, is singularly unhelpful. It closely resembles the goat's advice in Aesop: "Yf the wulf come hyder to ete the . . . opene not the dore to hym." But the change from Aesop's wolf to a fox, a more furtively cunning predator, puts an added premium on the ability to detect the "fraude" (224) the dame mentions. The problem is that the fox comes "not as a Foxe, for then he had be kend" (237), for the dame has not instructed her kid on the shape his "collusion" might take.[73] As a result he is unable to see through the fox's disguise to recognize the predator. Her advice is virtually worthless because it presumes what it is intended to achieve, namely the ability to discern the fox. It is especially difficult to perceive the threat of the fox because it is cloaked in the claim of solidarity: he presents himself as "very sybbe to" his victim (269). Only instruction like the fable itself, echoing the Puritan critique of the people's attraction to papist "tryfles" (239) of the kind with which the fox lures the kid, can supply the deficiency in the dame's conduct by delineating the nature of the threat to the church. Because it offers what she failed to provide, the fox will now be more recognizable.

Instead of instruction, the dame relies on her authority as parent. She wants that authority to substitute for the vigilance implied by presence, to let it serve in her absence. Her injunction to "be ruld by mee" (221) reflects one of the abuses of which the reformers complained, "the excessive concern with rule and jurisdiction to the neglect of instruction." Taking the metaphor of prince-as-parent seriously, the fable charges the monarchy with responsibility for the inculcation and transmission of true religious values in society. That responsibility cannot be fulfilled by simply commanding the populace, in the words of the *Homilies*, "obediently to be subject."[74] In the terms of the eclogue, the reliance on rule, in place of proper instruction, also anticipates the cultural backlash of the 1580s, especially the replacement of Grindal's pastoral perspective with Whitgift's disciplinary policies. But the outcome of the fable, where the dame's unquestioned authority proves inadequate, challenges the assertion that its "catastrophe" could be averted by imposing more discipline. The eclogue contains additional warning against just such a policy, in the fable of the mother ape:

> Sike mens follie I cannot compare
> Better, then to the Apes folish care,
> That is so enamoured of her young one,
> (And yet God wote, such cause hath she none)
> That with her hard hold, and straight embracing,
> She stoppeth the breath of her youngling.
> (95–100)

The two fables are linked by the word *youngling* (100 and 182), which focuses on the model of parental care they present.[75] Each embodies an instance of "folish care," one dramatizing neglect through absence, the other abuse (albeit inadvertent) through suffocation. The ape's "hard hold, and straight embracing" is the analogue to the policy whose goal was, to use Elizabeth's words, to "stop the mouths" of dissenters.[76] The claim of benign motive integral to the Crown's "motherly care" does not save that policy. The ape's good faith is assumed but nullified by the consequences of her action:

So often times, when as good is meant,
Evil ensueth of wrong entent.
(101–2)

By repeatedly tracing such consequences, the eclogue raises the broader question of cultural transmission from those in authority—the religious and political leadership—to their charges. This transmission, which takes place both across time, as "inheritaunce" (105 and 111), and synchronically, from the leadership to the people (the ape's "hard hold" and the dame's "school[ing]"), evokes a more comprehensive dimension of "care": the nurture of the charge's own moral and political capacities, needed to serve them where passive obedience cannot. In the terms the eclogue proposes, this task of nurture can be inhibited by neglect, wealth, or the misuse of political authority.

As Palinode's response to the fable indicates, however, its lessons (and those of the eclogue as a whole) may be least understood by those who need most to hear them. Though critics usually explain Palinode's name, which means "a recantation," in a religious context, it also evokes one who rewrites to please the powerful.[77] Palinode first tries to defuse the fable by impugning its teller: "Thou art beside thy wit" (306). Then he denies its relevance: it is "furthest fro the mark" (307). But his reference to a minister named Sir John (309) confirms all that he would deny, evoking not only Catholic priests but unlearned clergy in general, especially those installed by the patronage system.[78] Sir John's ignorance identifies him as just "such an one who will be content to share, and on Sunday to say nothing."[79] His good intent ("well he meanes" [311]) is undone by the institutional dynamics that have set this misfit in a shepherd's position. His muteness ("little can [he] say" [311]) is the institutional product of the irresponsibility of the powerful—the bishops and the Crown—whose "misgovernaunce" has replaced careful attention to their flock.

The interpretation of the May eclogue I am offering here, combining ecclesiastical and secular analysis, helps to explain the special quality

The woodcut from the July eclogue
(Huntington Library).

of Spenser's Protestantism. It integrated the best elements of religious reformers with a vision of the Crown's responsible governance. Though accepting the basic constitution of the Elizabethan social order, he calls to account its foremost institutions—Crown and church—in the name of their responsibility for the moral integrity and social welfare of that order. He did so precisely by unfolding and rewriting the tropes used to buttress the authority that had been abused.

"High" and "Low" in July: The Contest over Hierarchy

Visually depicting the vertical imagery of *high* and *low*, terms commonly applied to social status in Elizabethan England, July's woodcut draws the reader's attention to the class dynamics that are at the heart of this eclogue.[80] Morrell's elevation, his "sitting hye" (103), while Thomalin stands on the "lowly playne" (7), announces the respective class positions of the two, within the church or elsewhere. This contrast is a striking departure from Mantuan's eighth eclogue, from which July borrows, in which the shepherds have equal status.[81] The emphasis on their status affects the way we read their debate, rendering their competing claims as rationales for the social positions they represent, rather than as philosophical arguments over the virtues of different mental attitudes. The social structure at issue in the shepherds' debate is hierarchy, both ecclesiastical and secular. Though a number of critics treat the eclogue as directed solely at the abuses of the Anglican church, important elements cannot be accounted for by confining it to church polity.[82] The emphasis on physical labor, the important nonreligious contexts of "lordship," and the fable of the shepherd Algrind all attest to the eclogue's broader import. Even the attention given to religious authority in the debate reverberates with the ideology of a divinely justified secular hierarchy, whose omnipresence in Elizabethan culture I have already described.

The eclogue is distinctive in how specifically the debating shepherds, Morrell and Thomalin, respond to one another's assertions. Each rebuts the other by either rewriting the particular authority that has just been invoked or presenting a matching counterstory to nullify its effect. The specific point-counterpoint procedure draws attention to the verbal practices the shepherds use, making the eclogue a virtual anatomy of the processes by which social institutions are legitimated, a dramatization of how authority is mobilized to either support or critique social structures.

The woodcut also draws attention to the differences in the shepherds' flocks, which Luborsky finds "contrasted more clearly here than in any other cut. Morrell's are unruly and unattended, while Thomalin's are grouped together obediently."[83] This contrast alerts us that hierarchy will here be examined in its relationship to social responsibility (the major topic of May), and in fact, Thomalin's initial speech does just that, linking Morrell's elevated status as "a goteheard prowde, / that sittes on yonder bancke" (1–2) with the abandoned, wandering condition of his flock:[84]

Whose straying heard them selfe doth shrowde
   emong the bushes rancke?
      (3–4)

Morrell hastens to rebut the implied charge of irresponsibility with his claim that high status is both personally more rewarding and socially more beneficial:[85]

Better is, then the lowly playne,
als for thy flocke, and thee.
(7–8)

Thomalin at this point rejects Morrell's invitation to tacitly affirm hierarchy—"come up thc hyll to me" (6)—on prudential grounds:

great clymbers fall unsoft.
In humble dales is footing fast.
(12–13)

But he goes beyond these proverbial moralisms in a cryptic narrative of the passage of the "Sonne":

The rampant Lyon hunts he fast,
   with Dogge of noysome breath,
Whose balefull barking brings in hast
   pyne, plagues, and dreery death.
Agaynst his cruell scortching heate
   where hast thou coverture?
The wastefull hylls unto his threate
   is a playne overture.
(21–28)

It is altogether possible that these lines have the neutral astrological meaning given to them by E.K., "that in July the sonne is in Leo. At which tyme the Dogge starre . . . reigneth, with immoderate heate causing Pestilence, drougth, and many diseases" (447). But several elements of the passage encourage the reader to seek more controversial material embedded here. First, in his response Morrell seems unduly defensive about what is merely an astrological digression. In disparaging Thomalin's "fond termes" he suggests they import another level of meaning. Further, as we will see in a moment, besides the constellation Leo, "the rampant Lyon" could also refer to the technical term for this animal's customary posture on Elizabethan coats of arms.[86] Such an allusion becomes far less improbable when we recall that well-known heraldic symbols were often employed in "prophecies" for disguised political commentary, a practice so troubling to the authorities that it was outlawed during Elizabeth's reign. It was, in fact, discredited with the same word Morrell uses: *fond*.[87] Thomalin may be employing precisely this kind of allegorization here and, just as in November's imagining of the queen's death, engaging in criminal conduct by doing so.

Finally, the astrological reading of the lines is disturbed by their subtle but palpable religious aura. It derives not only from the common Elizabethan pun of son/sun suggested by the Sonne of line 17 (and by E.K.'s gloss, which includes both spellings) but also from the more substantive fact that in this society the naturalistic account of catastrophes, like E.K.'s, rarely stood alone. It was usually folded into a religious doctrine of divine judgment: "It was . . . customary," Keith Thomas explains, "for natural disasters to be regarded as God's response to the sins of the people."[88] There is even literary precedent for using this very story to suggest the moral status of meteorological events in Barnaby Googe's poetry:

> Now ragethe Titan fyerce above
>   his Beames on earth do beate.
> Whose hote reflection makes us feale
>   an over fervent heate:
> Wyth fyery Dog, he forward flames
>   hote Agues up he dryves:
> And sends them downe, with boylyng blud
>   to shorten Mysers lyves.[89]

If there is political commentary here, to what might the hunt's target—"the rampant Lyon"—refer? The lion was the most common animal figure in the crests of English nobility, and this symbolism was absorbed into the collective consciousness through constant physical display, literature (especially emblem books), and the political prophecies.[90] The lion was also closely associated with the Crown, prominently displayed in the rampant posture on the royal coat of arms, a tradition dating back to "the time that [the kings of England] first possessed any true armorial insignia."[91] The royal status of the lion was also a commonplace in popular literature like Aesop and the Reynard the Fox cycle of fables and was incorporated into Spenser's own Mother Hubberds Tale.[92]

These associations allow us to read Thomalin's narrative as a religiously sanctioned judgment upon the elite of Elizabethan society, those who were "highest" on the sociopolitical spectrum, providing ample reason for Morrell, who shared that status, to be antagonistic. Indeed, Thomalin brings Morrell personally within the scope of his indictment,

Elizabeth I's Arms, St. Margaret's Church,
Tivetshall, Norfolk (photograph by H. Felton).

with the *thou* of line 26 and the charge that the position the "wastefull hylls" represent is an invitation to judgment (27–28). Returning to the topographical metaphor completes Thomalin's elaboration of the hills' treacherous "footing" into a morally questionable slippery slope that calls for justification (the other meaning of *coverture*). By invoking religious sanction, Thomalin's narrative drives a wedge between the secular privilege embodied in hierarchy and the religious authority so often used to validate it. He thus polemically poses at the outset of the eclogue the question of the alignment between that privilege and that authority, a major issue in the shepherds' debate to follow.

In the balance of the eclogue Morrell attempts to rehabilitate "the hills" with religious authority, but he begins his response by discrediting his accuser as precisely what he himself is not—hardworking.

Syker, thous but a laesie loord,
and rekes much of thy swinck.
(33–34)

While E.K.'s paraphrase of this line (as "counts much of thy paynes" [447]) has Morrell chastising Thomalin for pride over his verbal handiwork (often a clue, as we have seen, to a line's allegorical character), the pivotal word *reke* also meant "reek," making Morrell's comment a punning insult to Thomalin for body odor resulting from physical work. In any case, Morrell's introduction of "swinck" in this debate over hierarchy is significant, for labor was the definitive mark dividing gentry from commons. It was the single characteristic joining the disparate groups—ranging from "day labourers" to "marchantes or retailers and artificers"—that constituted the "low" in Sir Thomas Smith's definition, serving to disqualify these citizens from gentle status. According to Lawrence Stone, "An essential prerequisite for membership of the *élite* was financial independence, the capacity to live idly without the necessity of undertaking manual, mechanic, or even professional tasks. . . . Active personal occupation in a trade or profession was generally thought to be humiliating."[93] The *Calender*'s Morrell, in stigmatizing "swinck," reveals his affiliations with an elite who in fact deserve the opprobrious ephithet *laesie*. But Thomalin quickly rebuts this insult by revealing the sacred original of useful sweat, invoking Christ as the

> . . . shepheard great,
> that bought his flocke so deare,
> And them did save with bloudy sweat
> from Wolves, that would them teare.
>   (53–56)

The heart of Christianity is thus placed squarely on the side of the working poor, against their oppression by the powerful.

Thomalin later focuses on this exploitation when he castigates shepherds who "leade" their lives "as Lordes" (185–86):

> Theyr sheepe han crustes, and they the bread:
> the chippes [parings of crust], and they the chere [ample fare]:
> They han the fleece, and eke the flesh,
> (O seely sheepe the while)
> The corne is theyrs, let other thresh,
> their hands they may not file.
>   (187–92)

The association between idleness and high status ("their hands they may not file") is also graphically depicted by Morrell's posture in the woodcut—sitting with his back to the farm workers. Though in Thomalin's passage those who work have only "crustes" and "chippes," while the idle powerful take the "bread" and "chere," the "fleece" and "flesh," some saw no injustice in the lower classes doing all the work, representing it as a natural division of functions. "Men of lower degrees," Bishop Edwin Sandys declared in a sermon before the queen, "are set as inferior parts in the body, painfully to travail for the necessary sustenation both of themselves and others."[94]

From the earliest days of popular protest in England, however, the charge was made that an unequal society exploited the laboring classes. The *Calender*'s complaint about lords' privileges echoes that of John Ball in 1381: "They are clothed in velvet, and are warm in their furs and ermines, while we are covered in rags. They have wine and spices and fair bread, and we oatcake and straw, and water to drink. They have leisure and fine houses; we have pain and labour, the wind and rain in the fields. And yet it is of us and our toil that these men hold their state."[95] Thomalin, speaking on behalf of others, submerges Ball's powerful "they . . . we" formula in what is grammatically a less polarized indictment, yet his promise that this exploitative economy will "heapen hylles of wrath" (202) marks the resentment such disproportionate wealth engenders.

Morrell responds to Thomalin's effort "to wyten [blame] shepheards welth" (210) by trying to recuperate their affluence as a sign of social well-being:

> When folke bene fat, and riches rancke,
>   it is a signe of helth.
>   (211–12)[96]

He echoes the tendency of some of Spenser's contemporaries to see prosperity in the context of divine providence, as a sign of God's favor. "It was impossible to reiterate the view that sin was the most probable cause of misfortune," according to Keith Thomas, "without conveying the implication that godliness was somehow linked with prosperity." Such a rationale, diverting attention from the means by which wealth was acquired, foreclosed any structural analysis of economic matters, relegating them instead to the private sphere of personal morality. Anointing the wealthy with moral authority and blaming the poor for their own situation, this perspective reinforced the early version of the "trickle-down" theory, namely that poverty did not require governmental intervention on behalf of the poor, just personal charity.[97]

Thomalin's use of the word *lord* in complaining about exploitation

(186) returns us to Morrell's attack on Thomalin as a "laesie loord" (33). E.K.'s gloss, while purporting to explain *loord* as meaning "lout" (derived from the French *lourd*, or "heavy"), actually focuses attention on the homophonic *lord*, for "master" (from the Old English for "the keeper of the bread"). That title, the common rendering of the Latin *dominus*, was an important sign of status in Elizabethan England, used by noblemen of various degrees, as well as by important secular and church officials.[98] The regime defended the title as integral to hierarchical authority, "teaching us," according to Whitgift, "to acknowledge our duty towards our superiors, and their authority over us. . . . it is antichristian, that is, proud, presumptuous, disdainful, arrogant, and contemptuous, to refuse to give to every one that name and title that by law, civility, and duty of us is required, and expresseth our reverence, duty, and obedience." For their part, the Puritans unequivocally repudiated "tyrannous Lordshippe" in the church as inimical to Christianity: it "can not stande wyth Christes kingdome."[99]

E.K. elaborates on the meaning of *lord* by calmly announcing that "the old Britons" used *loord* "to signifie a Lorde," attributing this usage to the "Tyrannie" of the Danes over the Britons, conduct for which they came to be called "Lurdanes" or "Lord Danes." He then dramatizes this oppression with the story of the Briton who, meeting a Dane on a bridge, had to give way or suffer death. This incongruous migration of the gloss from *loord* to *lord* has the effect of removing the insult from Thomalin and attaching it instead to Morrell. More important, by associating lordship with hated foreigners, the gloss encourages the English audience to identify with the native victims of oppression ("the old Britons") against "the insolencie and pryde" of "Lurdanes," foreign or domestic (447).[100]

The negative overtones of *lord* are also evoked by Thomalin in criticizing another important sign of hierarchical status: dress. He ironically compares contemporary customs with the primitive models of Moses and Aaron, who

. . . never stroven to be chiefe,
    and simple was theyr weede.
But now (thanked be God therefore)
    the world is well amend,
Their weedes bene not so nighly [sparingly] wore,
    such simplesse mought them shend [disgrace]:

They bene yclad in purple and pall,
  so hath theyr god them blist,
They reigne and rulen over all,
  and lord it, as they list:
Ygyrt with belts of glitterand gold,
  (mought they good sheepeheards bene).
                    (167–78)

Thomalin's references to "pall," fine cloth, and "gold" echo the attention given by sumptuary regulation to such materials as velvet, satin, and silk and to the use of gold. The difference in the contemporary dress of the elite—"purple and pall" and "belts of glitterand gold"—from that of Moses and Aaron measures their moral distance from these paradigmatic figures. Thomalin's sarcastic parenthesis—"now (thanked be God therefore) / the world is well amend"—mocks the claim that sartorial decoration is a sign of real value, either divine approval ("so hath theyr god them blist") or moral quality ("mought they good sheepeheards bene").

In an effort to rehabilitate the religious defense of hierarchy, Morrell tries to transform Thomalin's "wastefull hylls" into "holy hylles" (38) by recalling their association (through names alone) with saints' legends:

For sacred unto saints they stond,
  and of them han theyr name.
S. Michels mount who does not know,
  that wardes the Westerne coste?
And of S. Brigets bowre I trow,
  all Kent can rightly boaste.
                    (39–44)

These lines reveal Morrell's nominalist strategy, the way social and political power taps the reservoir of authority in other discourses. The name (of the saint) comes to stand for the status of the institution (the hill), so that the latter is taken to embody suprahuman quality. In the examples he gives, Morrell adds to the religious element the sanction of national pride, the association with well-known landmarks like the actual hills mentioned (and the Thames and Medway rivers [79–84]) rendering the figurative hills as integral to national identity. Through their locations, encompassing the country from coast to coast, and the suggestions of protection they provide ("ward[ing] the Westerne coste") and popular pride they engender ("all Kent can rightly boast"), he depicts hierarchy as a source of security and esteem for the entire land.

Thomalin counters Morrell's strategy by making it visible:

> The hylls, where dwelled holy saints,
>   I reverence and adore:
> Not for themselfe, but for the sayncts,
>   Which han be dead of yore.
>   (113–16)

These lines echo in striking fashion the Protestant critique of idolatry. The "Homily Against the Peril of Idolatry," for example, does not reject saints, "who were the true servants of God, and did give all honour to him, taking none unto themselves, and are blessed souls with God," but, denouncing pilgrimages to the sites of saints' images, inveighs "against such as had any superstition in the holiness of the place, as though they should be heard for the place sake." It specifically attacks the tactic Morrell uses in citing the protection of St. Michaels Mount because it "attribute[s to saints] the defence of certain countries, spoiling God of his due honour herein."[101] Applying this orthodox critique in unorthodox fashion to Morrell's sanctioning of hierarchy, Thomalin accuses him of idolatrous logic: of misdirecting religious power by first investing a human institution with divine credentials, and then revering it as something more than human. In diverting religious value from its authentic locus, this investment spoils God of his due honor.

Morrell's next example of a "holy hylle" is Christ on the Mount of Olives:

> And wonned not the great God *Pan,*
>   upon mount *Olivet:*
> Feeding the blessed flocke of *Dan,*
>   which dyd himselfe beget?
>   (49–52)

But Thomalin, in the move I have already described, responds by alluding to the story of Christ's "bloudy sweat" in the garden the night of his arrest, selecting Luke's account (22:39–44) as the only one in which the place is described as "the mount of olives" and where Christ's agony is perceived in "his sweate . . . like droppes of blood, trickling downe to the grounde."[102] Once again, Thomalin's rejoinder deflects attention from the topography of the site to the material content of Christ's sacrifice. Morrell next presents hills as part of a primordial paradise:

> Whilome there used shepheards all
>   to feede theyr flocks at will,
> Till by his foly one did fall,
>   that all the rest did spill.
> And sithens shepheardes bene foresayd
>   from places of delight:
> For thy I weene thou be affrayd,
>   to clime this hilles height.
>   (65–72)

In the prelapsarian world of this story all were "high." Lowness originated with Adam's Fall and thus becomes a sign of culpability. With this narrative Morrell counters popular culture's claim that equality was the Edenic condition, offering instead what Louis Montrose has described as "a *differential* subjection to the penalty of fallen Adam, a selective dispensation from the original injunction [to labor]."[103]

In turn, Thomalin counters Morrell's story with a quite different narrative of origins:

> Such one he was, (as I have heard
>   old Algrind often sayne)
> That whilome was the first shepheard,
>   and lived with little gayne:
> As meeke he was, as meeke mought be,
>   simple, as simple sheepe,
> Humble, and like in eche degree
>   the flocke, which he did keepe.
>   (125–32)

In Thomalin's story the Fall did not institute social differentiation, for in his model, a postlapsarian shepherd (whom E.K. identifies as Abel), is "like in eche degree" those in his charge.[104] And following Abel came Moses and Aaron, here presented as equally humble and honorable even after the Fall:

Whilome all these were lowe, and lief,
and loved their flocks to feede,
They never stroven to be chiefe.
(165–67)

Thomalin chooses to ignore the fact that Aaron, as E.K. remembers, "committed Idolatry" (447), whereas Moses' superiority to Aaron was cited by religious apologists to justify civil supremacy over the church.[105] The parity that Thomalin asserts existed between these figures therefore encapsulates an altogether different view of the church's relationship to political power. It is much to Spenser's point that here Algrind (Grindal), retelling the stories of these shepherds, is a source of instruction about how humility and equality in the church's leaders survived the Fall. Algrind will later reappear (albeit heavily disguised) as a victim of the ironic consequence of accepting hierarchy in the church, namely the supremacy of the monarch at the apex of the entire system.

Morrell's last and best hope for a "holy hylle" is Sinai: "Of Synah can I tell thee more" (73). E.K. underscores the religious association, identifying Sinai as a hill "where God appeared" (447). Moses went up there to meet God, there God gave him the law, and from there Moses carried it down to the people.[106] But Thomalin counters even this allusion with a story conspicuously free of vertical metaphors, in which Moses

. . . sawe hys makers face,
His face more cleare, then Christall glasse,
and spake to him in place.
(158–60)

He refers to the only biblical instance in which Moses does not go up to meet God on Sinai but meets him on the plain beside it, "in place." There "the Lord spake unto Moses, face to face, as a man speaketh unto his friend" (Exodus 33:11). God does not appear on mountains only, and even divine authority does not preclude conversation. If conversation of the intimate kind Thomalin describes took place between two ontologically different figures, a fortiori it can take place between human persons, whatever their status.[107]

Finally, the shepherds contest the composition of the flock that is the beneficiary of Christ's sacrifice. Morrell singles out "the blessed flocke of *Dan"* (51), apparently referring to the Israelite tribe.[108] But "Dan" was also an honorific title, equivalent to "Master" or "Sir," for those promi- nent in the nobility, in the church, and in learning. Through this pun Morrell privileges the elite as religiously "chosen." Social distinction becomes religious distinction: the high are "thc blessed."[109] E.K. tries to mute this privilege by his gloss: "One trybe is put for the whole nation per Synecdochen" (447). Far more than a linguistic convenience, how- ever, the trope stands as an emblem of Morrell's strategy: identifying this single group with the character and welfare of the entire nation.

Thomalin highlights Morrell's device by countering his story with that of "the brethren . . . that came from *Canaan"* (141–42):

> The brethren twelve, that kept yfere [together]
> the flockes of mighty *Pan*.
> (143–44)

In contrast to Morrell's effort to privilege one group, Thomalin empha- sizes the collaborative character of community under God, both in the "brethren" (the word is repeated in lines 141 and 143) who keep the flocks and in the flocks themselves, "kept yfere."[110]

Morrell concludes his defense of hierarchy by asserting that such high status is a sign of divine favor:

> Hereto, the hills bene nigher heven,
> and thence the passage ethe [easy].
> As well can prove the piercing levin [lightning],
> that seeldome falls bynethe.
> (89–92)

The support religious authority gives social and political status is here imaged by a proximity ("nigher heven") that embodies the metaphorical logic of hierarchy. The *Homilies*, for example, repeatedly associate "high powers" with God, the "Most Highest," who "set [those powers] in au- thority."[111] Morrell hopes to capitalize on the coincidence of the vertical metaphors for social and divine status to sanction the former.

E.K., however, points out the faulty literalism of the logic, which he attributes to "the shepheards simpleness" (447). Thomalin flatly rejects the logic, claiming an equality of access that violates Morrell's vertical decorum:

Alsoone may shepheard clymbe to skye,
    that leades in lowly dales,
As Goteherd prowd that sitting hye,
    upon the Mountaine sayles.
        (101–4)

Moreover, Morrell undermines his own claim by citing lightning as evidence of divine favor, for it was widely regarded as an instrument of
divine judgment.[112] When St. Paul's was struck by lightning in 1561, for
example, "upon one thing only was everybody agreed, that the storm
and lightning and consequent fire were acts of God."[113] The false note
struck here by treating a sign of judgment as evidence of favor implies
an arrogant obliviousness to divine action.

The arrogance becomes more pronounced in the self-validating quality
of Morrell's arguments. The comment he makes about the authorities
he has marshaled reveals that hills need not, finally, be validated by
externals:

But little needes to strow [display] my store,
    suffice this hill of our.
        (75–76)

He tacitly acknowledges that his efforts are, after all, but embellish-
ments to a prestige that is at its heart self-authenticating. More precisely,
that prestige turns on a power that has little, if anything, to do with
the sanctions offered for it. Given the fact that any authority Morrell
invokes—especially, as we have seen, religious authority—can be mobilized against hierarchy, the continued status of this institution would
rest in large measure on the power to control the distribution of stories
that sanction or critique it. Morrell invokes this power in his final response to Thomalin's criticism:

Here is a great deale of good matter,
    lost for lacke of telling,
Now sicker I see, thou doest but clatter:
    harme may come of melling.
Thou medlest more, then shall have thanke.
        (205–9)

Again claiming there is much more to be said, he shuts off the debate
with a threat of force. As we saw earlier, the word *meddle* was often
used, as here, to regulate public discussion, marking the intrusion by
a speaker into matters for which the political authority deemed him
unfit.[114] Speaking for the nonelite in this eclogue, Thomalin has done
just that, asserting an authority for that voice capable of challenging
established institutions. Especially dramatic in this regard is his rejection of Morrell's assertion that hills are "nigher heven," citing an "old
sayd sawe":

> How be I am but rude and borrell,
>   yet nearer wayes I knowe.
> To Kerke the narre, from God more farre.
> (95–97)

The provocative assertion Thomalin makes here is that the knowledge
of the "meanest" is nearer the truth and the wisdom of the people, crystallized here in the proverb, has sufficient force to contest the orthodoxy
produced and patrolled by established institutions. Thomalin's presumption in even engaging Morrell, who voices that orthodoxy, in debate is
audacious enough. Matching him point for point challenges the pur-
ported inability of the "rude and borrell" classes to participate as competent political agents.

The fable of Algrind evokes in dramatic fashion the question of conversation, bringing together the issues of the people's participation and
the relationship between religion and political power. Told as the story
of the eagle and the shellfish, however, it is not immediately clear how
the fable relates to the rest of the eclogue:

> He is a shepheard great in gree,
>   but hath bene long ypent.
> One daye he sat upon a hyll,
>   (as now thou wouldest me:
> But I am taught by *Algrins* ill,
>   to love the lowe degree.)
> For sitting so with bared scalpe,
>   an Eagle sored hye,
> That weening hys whyte head was chalke,
>   a shell fish downe let flye:

She weend the shell fishe to have broake,
   but therewith bruzd his brayne,
So now astonied with the stroke,
   he lyes in lingring payne.
     (215–28)

Despite E.K.'s reticence about the identity of Algrind, the name, an anagram for the name of Elizabeth's archbishop Edmund Grindal, provides
the key to the fable's meaning. In late 1576 Grindal challenged orders
of the queen concerning the prophesyings, for which he was "seques-
tered"—stripped of his powers and effectively kept under house arrest
until his death in 1583 ("the lingring payne" of the fable).

The confrontation between prelate and prince brought to the fore in
particularly dramatic fashion two issues that had an important bearing
on the Crown's control: the participation of the people and the autonomy
of the church. The queen saw the prophesyings as "meddling" because
they involved the people in matters for which they were not fit. She was
not mollified by the fact that these conferences were carefully controlled
so that, according to Grindal, "no controversy of this present time and
state shall be moved or dealt withal" and "none is suffered to glance
openly or covertly at persons public or private," indeed "no layman be
suffered to speak at any time." Despite these constraints, the queen objected to the exercises precisely because the people were involved: the
conferences "procur[ed] unlawful assemblies of a great number of our
people out of their ordinary parishes and from place far distant." More
important, they aired "disputations, and new devised opinions, upon
points of divinity, far and unmeet of unlearned people," and threatened
disruption in the economic order: "Great numbers of our people, especially the vulgar sort, meet to be otherwise occupied with honest labour
for their living, are brought to idleness and seduced."[115] Just how important a factor the government's fearful resistance to popular participation
was is evidenced by the compromise Leicester and Cecil proposed to
Grindal: that the exercises continue, but without the presence of the
people. Grindal rejected the proposal, saying: "I see no reason why the
people should be excluded . . . especially for the benefit that groweth
thereby to the hearers."[116]

This strain of the Grindal episode, participation by the nonelite, and
that discussed earlier, religious dissent among the elite, converge prob-

lematically in the figure of Algrind. On the one hand, as the source for the story of the lowly shepherd who shared the humble status of his flock, he is a fitting champion for Thomalin, the "shepheards swayne" (5). On the other hand, Algrind is not himself one of the low, but "a shepheard great in gree," implicated in the entanglements of power, a fact from which Thomalin draws a simple lesson: he is

> . . . taught by *Algrins* ill,
> to love the lowe degree.
> (219–20)

Despite this disclaimer, it is not so easy to segregate moral authority from social status. Grindal's own prominence did not derive from exemplary virtue alone, but from temporal power as well, power of the kind the *Calender* so thoroughly interrogates. It was his position as chief executive officer of the national church that enabled him to confront the queen and required her to deal with him. Had he not been "great in gree," his challenge would have gone unnoticed. There would have been no fable for Thomalin to tell. Grindal's own status questions any simple opposition between political power and social responsibility.

At least equally problematic, however, is the facile identification of high status with humility as suggested by Whitgift: "Christ, in suppressing ambition, pride, and arrogance, and exhorting to humility, doth not condemn superiority . . . but requireth humbleness of spirit, and lowliness of mind in all degrees of persons, especially in superiors, whom this virtue doth more adorn; the mightiest and noblest prince in the world may come nearer this admonition of Christ than the poorest slave."[117] Carefully channeling humility into personality allowed Whitgift to ignore the pressures that social and political institutions put on "lowliness of mind." The qualities that identify Algrind with the "meek shepherd" and make him less interested in "great freendes" (194) than religious principle are precisely those that led Grindal to promote the popular participation in the prophesyings so actively opposed by the Crown. His fate sharply dramatizes the question of whether high status that takes its social responsibility seriously can survive in such a hierarchical political order.

The conflicting emblems and E.K.'s discussion of them echo these issues without providing any definitive resolution. E.K. underscores the contradiction running through the eclogue in his final sentence, citing two "doctours" who espouse opposing paradigms: *Suorum Christus humillimus* versus *Suorum deus altissimus*. Reiterating the eclogue's debate, the phrases embody antagonistic views of the relationship of divinity to humanity. In the first—"Christ, the humblest of his own people"—recalling "the first shepheard," who was "like in eche degree / the flocke," the affirmation of religion's affiliation with the socially inferior could hardly be stronger. The contrary model of the second—"God, the highest of his people"—proposed by "a gentle man," echoes Morrell's vertical metaphors working to secure the status of the elite. The antagonism of these paradigms, each supported by the prestige of learning, elicits a comment by E.K. that summarizes the contest in the eclogue: one authority is "beate backe again with lyke saying of another," each side "taking [the other] at the rebownd" (448).[118]

The emblems are also part of that conflict. Morrell's, *In summo fœlicitas*, which E.K. reads in relation to "supremacie" (448), would repel Grindal's challenge by reasserting the dominion of political power over religion. The logic of supremacy that E.K. articulates, none "higher or better," opposes not only the right of conscience claimed by the archbishop but also the franchise implied by Thomalin's emblem. At first glance it is surprising that Thomalin should have as his emblem *In medio virtus*, since *medio* is commonly taken to refer to "middle." E.K. seems to use it this way in reporting "the saying of olde Philosophers, that vertue dwelleth in the middest" (448). But he also sees in the emblem "prayse [for] the meane and lowly state" Thomalin represents, referring to the other meaning of *in medio* as "in public" or "available to all," which evokes an inclusiveness at odds with the segregationist premises of hierarchy.[119] Equally suggestive are E.K.'s references to *medio* as "mediocrity," the term used to describe the *via media* of the established church, and his use of the word *sequestred*, the term describing Grindal's punishment, which bring within the scope of the emblem the issues of church and state the archbishop's challenge so forcefully posed.[120] Though the emblem remains at the symbolic level, by yoking the non-elite to these fundamental questions of Elizabethan polity it suggests that no authentic resolution of the latter can be made that ignores the fate of the former, thus acknowledging that some account of the lower classes must be made in constructing the commonwealth.

"Such Il As Is Forced": Economic Justice and the Problem of Order in September

Unlike the other moral eclogues, and most unlike July with its tightly structured repartee, September is less a debate than an exposition by one of the shepherds, Diggon Davie, who has just returned from extended travels. The narrative of that experience structures the eclogue, holding together its three segments: the report of his visit to "a farre countrye" (as E.K. refers to it), a set of complaints linked with the conditions in that country, and a story about the shepherd Roffyn. Most critics, following E.K.'s lead, treat the eclogue solely as ecclesiastical satire, aimed only at what he calls the "loose living of Popish prelates" (452).[121] This description, however, becomes less and less persuasive as the eclogue progresses, unable to account either for the complaints Diggon reports or for the tale of Roffyn, his dog, and the wolf. These elements reveal with particular clarity the questions of economic justice and the problem of order that are at the heart of the eclogue's concern. Through them Diggon articulates a critique of the rapidly changing agrarian relations in Elizabethan England, in the process engaging such controversial issues as vagrancy, poverty, class exploitation, and internal security.

His travels mark Diggon himself, by Elizabethan legal definition, as a vagrant. The phenomenon of vagrancy was the focus of a debate in the society over fundamental questions: how to account for the poverty it represented? did it pose a threat to the social order? if so, what was the nature of that threat, and how best to deal with it? In order to trace how the eclogue engages these issues it is necessary to review the economic and cultural status of vagrancy in some detail.

September was a fitting month for evoking the phenomenon of vagrancy, as vagrants were especially visible then. Traveling in search of harvest work, they were most mobile during late summer, particularly prominent at local fairs, where they gathered in groups. Because of their visibility, efforts to suppress them were usually mounted during this period. September also brought to mind the strains in agrarian relations. As the month in which rents were payable (generally on Michaelmas in late September) and tenancies renewed, it was the point at which tenants' tenure was most vulnerable, resting on both the landlord's plans for the land and the adequacy of the harvest to meet obligations to him.[122]

The month thus brought together the explosive issues that, if we are sensitive to them, suddenly become prominent in this eclogue.

Spenser highlighted Diggon's role as wanderer by changing the relative importance of the two shepherds from that in Mantuan's ninth eclogue, his model, shifting the role of the principal expositor from the shepherd who stays at home to the one who travels, "that in hope of more gayne, drove his sheepe into a farre countrye" (E.K.'s argument, p. 452). Hobbinol underscores Diggon's perambulation early in the eclogue:

> . . . thou hast measured much grownd,
> And wandred I wene about the world rounde.
>   (21–22)

The word *wander* fixes Diggon as a vagrant. It was a salient part of official terminology, used in statutory definitions of vagrancy in 1547 and 1572.[123] In 1562 the Privy Council wrote the sheriffs of a number of counties "to have spetiall reguarde to the . . . keping in order of such as wander in those counties without certaine habitacions." The moral investment against wandering is demonstrated by the *Homilies'* denunciation of "wilful wandering," coupled with praise for "the sharp and severe laws" against vagabonds. The word was also used by the popular press to censure vagabonds. Harrison refers to them as continuing "to stray and wander about," and William Harman, in his pamphlet *A Caveat or Warening for Commen Cursetors Vulgarely Called Vagabondes*, repeatedly uses the word to characterize vagrants as those who are "wyly wanderars."[124] The attention given to vagrancy in Elizabethan society in part reflects the magnitude of the phenomenon. The vagrant poor were a substantial minority, "the enormous class of casual laborers and masterless men, demobbed soldiers, orphans, paupers, prostitutes and thieves." A. L. Beier finds vagrancy "one of the most pressing social problems of the age." It may be true, as Frank Aydelotte claims, that the number of vagabonds in the sixteenth century was a larger proportion of the population than ever before or since. There were certainly significant increases in vagrancy in Elizabethan London, evidenced by the threefold jump in the number of vagrants dealt with by the Court of Governors between 1560 and 1578–79.[125]

But it was not just the numbers of vagrants that concerned the authorities. It was what they represented: they were indeed "masterless men," outside the hierarchical arrangements thought to be fundamental to the social order. Integral to hierarchy was the allocation to every person of a fixed "place," ordained by God. The projection of this conception of order onto the landscape made the vagabond a lightning rod for anxieties about the security of that social structure. Wandering became the geographic analogue to forbidden mobility across social categories. Its prohibition was an effort to stabilize those categories, as a means of securing order.[126]

The anxiety associated with the vagabond was intense. "Those in authority," according to Joyce Youings, commonly "viewed all people on the move with . . . fear and suspicion as potential disturbers of the peace." The threat they were believed to pose was not limited to criminal activity such as theft but also included sedition. The Privy Council wrote in 1571: "For there ys no greater disorder nor no greater root of theftes murders pickinge stealinge debate and sedicion then ys in these Vagabonds and that riseth of them." "Into what country and place soever they come," the Geneva Bible flatly declared, "they cause sedition and tumults." This association of vagrancy with sedition crystallized around the Northern Rebellion of 1569. According to Paul Slack, "Although there was no justification for the view that vagabonds caused rebellion, the myth was a potent force in the years immediately after 1569, as it had been after 1549." Beier reports that another "insurrection reportedly planned in Suffolk in 1569 was suppressed, it was claimed, by a round-up of 13,000 masterless men." While the strategy of searching out vagrants had begun earlier, the 1569 revolt gave that strategy new impetus, resulting in a whipping campaign that lasted for years: "As late as 1572 [the earl of] Huntingdon was still flogging vagabonds in order 'to stay the spreading of false and seditious rumours and the sending of messages from the late rebels.'" The Speaker of the 1572 Parliament identified the "punishment of vagabonds" as a principal reason for calling that session, a motive reflected in the penalties for vagrancy in the 1572 act: whipping and boring the right ear, with death for a repeated offense.[127]

Because vagrants were poor, the phenomenon of vagrancy was inextricable from the question of economic distribution, an association made explicit in the title of the 1572 act itself: "An acte for the punishment of vacabondes, and for the relief of the poore and impotent." The official view tried to negotiate this association by distinguishing the "deserving" poor who were "impotent" from vagabonds, who were able-bodied, "sturdy" beggars.[128] For the latter it was assumed that, as the *Homilies* succinctly put it, "poverty followeth idleness," a willful failing, subject to severe punishment.[129]

In locating the cause of poverty in the individual's moral condition, the distinction between the deserving and undeserving poor overlooked two important social dynamics that contributed to poverty in this period: inflation, especially in food prices, and population growth. Prices more than doubled from 1540 to 1560, rising an additional 79 percent from 1559 to 1602. This inflation hurt the poor far more than the rich, as Penry Williams explains: "There can be no reasonable doubt that the real incomes of artisans and farm-labourers fell during the inflation of the sixteenth century. The glamour and brilliance of the Tudor court and the Elizabethan theatre shine against a backdrop of dark suffering for the majority of the population."[130]

The rise in food prices had a particularly dire impact on the landless laboring classes. This rise itself reflected the pressure that population growth put on the land, resulting in increased rent costs and changes in agrarian landholding patterns. Though some historians believe rents failed to keep pace with rising prices in the sixteenth century, there were ample grounds for the contemporary complaints of burdensome rents. Harrison reports what were common grievances regarding increases in rent, fines, and fees for renewing leases. Like inflation, these increases hit the lower classes the hardest, often forcing even those tenants with the most secure estates to vacate the land and become landless, transient laborers.[131]

Vagrancy was not the product of these general economic trends alone, however. There were specific causes, particularly enclosures, the appropriation of the commons for pasture or for a single landowner's use. The visibility and impact of this practice made it a focal point for complaint over the upheavals taking place in the countryside. While there may not have been a significant increase in their number during this period, the continuing enlargement of arable fields at the expense of common pasture frequently reached the point where the pasture could no longer support the stock on which the small farmer depended. Harrison identified this process as a cause of vagrancy, indicting the greedy, "such I mean as have the cast [trick] daily to make beggars enough whereby to pester the land, espying a further commodity in their commons, holds, and tenures, [and who] doth find such means as thereby to wipe many out of their occupyings and turn the same unto his private gains."[132]

Because enclosures "deprived the community of common rights," many "viewed the enclosure of their commons as symbolic of the loss of a sense of community" and responded with frequent and persistent protest, sometimes violent, throughout the sixteenth century. There were "hundreds of riots protesting enclosures of commons and wastes" from 1530 to 1640, "numerous and widely dispersed" during Elizabeth's reign, and many reports of destruction of enclosures and pending enclosure disputes throughout the 1570s.[133] The government was well aware of the potential for such local disputes to turn violent and escalate.[134] Kett's Rebellion in 1549, for example, had begun with the destruction of the hedges of a local landlord who had enclosed part of the commons, and one of the demands of the rebels was "that from hensforth noman shall enclose any more" and "that no lord of no mannor shall comon uppon the Comons."[135]

Despite the threat to order represented by enclosures, the government only selectively opposed them, focusing (as in the 1563 Act for Maintaining Tillage and the 1569 proclamation for enforcing the same) on those that converted arable land to pasture. While it gave lip service to encroachment on the commons, it was far less concerned with enclosures that maintained or "improved" arable land, perhaps because it considered dearth a more serious threat than the depopulation that accompanied those enclosures. Above all, it wanted to ensure, as the queen wrote the Council of the North in 1574, "that the common people do not violently redress themselves, but wait the redress of law."[136]

That redress, however, was in most cases illusory. Although a series of statutes as far back as the Statute of Merton (1235) and as recent as the 1563 Act for Maintaining Tillage limited the power to enclose, the impotence of the law to protect peasant farmers was a recurring grievance. This situation had important implications for public order, as dramatically illustrated by the following sequence: a statute against enclosure was enacted in 1563, only to be followed in 1566 by an investigation of enclosures by a royal commission that brought no relief, followed in turn by an enclosure riot in Derbyshire in 1569. It was a familiar pattern: "The agrarian riots of 1549 followed upon the government commissions of the previous year for the suppression of enclosures."[137]

Private remedies were no more effective. Tenants' rights turned on uncertain and expensive litigation that they had to initiate and sustain. Further, powerful landowners could make it difficult to obtain justice in local courts. Star Chamber, on the other hand, where proceedings often ended up, was frequently more inclined to recognize the rights of enclosers (as "improvers").[138] Despite the statutes regulating enclosure, the "law's defences could prove frail . . . against an unscrupulous and determined landlord." And determined many were: one enclosure commissioner "accused landowners of taking 'great pains and study' to defeat the laws" designed to protect tenants.[139]

Even if tenants prevailed in court, orders in their favor were often resisted or disregarded. In one instance Sir John Throckmorton, chief justice of Chester, whose tenants complained about his enclosure of the commons and encroachment on their copyholds, was ordered to cease enclosing until the matter could be heard in court. He not only violated that order but also began eviction proceedings against the tenants. A new order had to be issued against him to cease both the violation and the new legal action.[140]

Where tenants shared the costs through a "common purse" they scored some victories. But that joint effort itself exposed them to the charge of maintenance—wrongfully aiding litigation.[141] For a "common purse" to be proper, all those contributing had to have "a joint and equal interest" in the suit, a requirement that divided tenants with different forms of legal title, even though they may all have been injured by encroachment on the commons. The impotence of legal protection prompted alternative remedial action in the form of village revolts.[142] The protesters often appealed to the sanction of the law which was, at least in its letter, on their side, casting themselves as executing law rather than flaunting it.[143]

The interlocking problems of vagrancy, poverty, the futility of legal action, and protest are all explicit in the September eclogue in Diggon's blunt critique of those in authority (104–35, 141–49), in which he promises "playnely to speake of shepheards" (104). If the passage begins as anticlerical satire (106–9), it quickly turns to an examination of the economic practices of the powerful, invoking the authority of religious prophecy in Diggon's declaration that "some sticke not to say, (whote cole on her tongue)" (112), a reference to Isaiah 6. The passage attacks the lavish squandering of wealth by the rich:

All for they casten too much of worlds care,
To deck her Dame, and enrich her heyre.
(114–15)

It is this conspicuous consumption that causes the impoverishment in the countryside:

For such encheason, If you goe nye,
Fewe chymneis reeking you shall espye:
Thc fatte Oxe, that wont ligge in the stal,
Is nowe fast stalled in her crumenall.
(116–19)

This passage describes the depopulation of the countryside ("Fewe chymneis") by landlords through higher rents and enclosures, often at the expense of grazing rights on the commons without which the small farmer could not survive. The working stock for his farm has been turned into money for the landlord, deposited in his "crumenall" (purse). These lines reject the justification mentioned by Lawrence Stone that the landlord raised his rents to maintain "the medieval traditions of generous hospitality." The "fewe chymneis reeking" are not only an image of the depopulation of the countryside; the phrase echoes a sixteenth-century proverb marking the lapse in hospitality: "Many chimnies, but little smoke; faire houses, but small hospitalitie."[144]

It might be objected that Diggon intends to discredit these popular complaints by tracing them to the people, cast as "a Monster of many heads" (121). Certainly this notorious epithet has had a malignant history, and is generally taken, whenever a writer uses it, to signify his contempt for the popular voice, depicting the subordinate classes not as citizens capable and deserving of political participation but as an undifferentiated mass, alien and inimical to civilized society.[145] The epithet would thereby negate any responsibility on the part of the powerful for these "monsters." But while Diggon here uses it to place the complaints he has recited in the context of class relations, the plurality of perspectives and the incisive character of the complaints he presents question the adequacy of this image, promoting instead a view of the nonelite as articulate plain speakers, competent political agents. Rather than discrediting them in the manner this image typically does, its inclusion with the complaints proleptically undermines an important and predictable reaction to them.

The antagonistic character of the class relations the epithet signals is made most explicit in the complaint immediately following, which carries the heaviest weight of all, coming as it does from "they that shooten neerest the pricke" (122). They charge the wealthy with deliberately exploiting the poor, the proverb—"other the fat from their beards doen lick" (123)—referring to cheating someone out of property.[146] The "bigge Bulles *of Basan* [that] brace hem about" (124) was an important biblical image for those who exploited the poor.[147] The specific allusion is to Psalm 22, in which the speaker calls upon God "for *there is* none to helpe *me*": "Manie yong bulles have compassed me: mightie bulls of Bashan have closed me about" (Psalm 22:12). But the psalm offers assurance to the powerless: "For [God] hath not despised nor abhorred the affliction of the poore: neither hathe he hid his face from him, but when he called unto him, he heard. . . . The poore shal eat and be satisfied" (vv. 24, 26). Diggon's allusion enlists this divine assistance, aligning religious authority with those who are oppressed, against the "mightie."[148]

Diggon next addresses the legal situation surrounding the erosion of common rights (127–35). He decries the ineffectiveness of the laws against enclosure, so that "to seeke redresse mought little boote" (127). The expense and effort required to sustain litigation in general and the vulnerability to either eviction or a countersuit made legal proceedings the "foule wagmoire" of Diggon's complaint (130), in which:

. . . if thy galage once sticketh fast,
The more to wind it out thou doest swinck,
Thou mought ay deeper and deeper sinck.
(131–33)

It is no surprise that many were persuaded that

. . . better leave of with a little losse,
Then by much wrestling to leese the grosse.
(134–35)

If we now take Diggon's unmistakably economic critique back with us to the beginning of the eclogue, what at first looked like conventional ecclesiastical satire acquires a different significance. Utilizing the common device of the rustic returning from city and court, Diggon describes the corruption in the "farre countrye" he visited.[149] This description certainly includes not just ecclesiastical hierarchy but also the system of court patronage, where everything, it would seem, was for sale:

They setten to sale their shops of shame,
And maken a Mart of theyr good name.[150]
(36–37)

The competition for favor recalls the brier's attack on the oak in February in its ruthlessness:

The shepheards there robben one another,
And layen baytes to beguile her brother.
(38–39)

The status sought "there" was a scarce commodity, flowing out of a mutually exploitative, zero-sum relationship, "from other men" (43). The powerful futilely try to cover over with religion the contention and hostility this competition bred, "to quench [it] / With holy water" (88–89).

This competitive culture is evidently linked to the exploitation of which Diggon later complains. Describing the powerful "shepheards" of this "countrye" as "bigge as Bulls" (44) identifies them with the "bigge Bulles of Basan" who oppress the rural peasants. Diggon tightens the knot between that exploitation and the powerful when, in answer to Hobbinol's inquiry "howe done the flocks creepe?" (140), he declares: "Sike as the shepheards, sike bene her sheepe" (141). Social injustice so discredits those in authority in the eyes of the people that "they nill listen to the shepheards voyce" (142). Instead, "they wander at wil, and stray at pleasure" (144). With these words Diggon borrows the terms that were used to disparage vagrancy. Significantly, however, he casts it not as a moral defect but as the end result of the exploitation he has just elaborated. The repetition of *stray* (144), earlier used to describe the wealthy who "strayen abroad" (93), underscores the bond between the corruption of the elite and poverty in the countryside.

In severing the question of vagrancy from the moral distinction between deserving and undeserving poor, defining poverty instead as the product of oppressive class conflict, Diggon squarely contradicts the dominant model of socioeconomic analysis. While he affirms the need for authority in society to which people are responsive ("they had be better come at their cal" [146]) and the need for obedience (people who are "buxome and bent" [149]), he de-emphasizes the personal responsibility of the vagrants themselves, instead laying the erosion in those qualities at the doors of the powerful. In a vicious circle, however, the effects of that erosion are most sharply felt among the poor, who are further victimized by it:

. . . many han into mischiefe fall,
And bene of ravenous Wolves yrent.
(147–48)

Wolves, Foxes, and Bandogs

In the process of carefully anatomizing the "disorders" in the "forraine countryes" of which E.K. speaks in his first gloss, Diggon brings them home to English society. Hobbinol, however, resists assimilating the disorders represented by "ravenous Wolves" (148). Looking to history for reassurance, he tries to deport them:

> Well is knowne that sith the Saxon king,
> Never was Woolfe seene many nor some,
> Nor in all Kent, nor in Christendome:
> But the fewer Woolves (the soth to sayne,)
> The more bene the Foxes that here remaine.
>   (151–55)

E.K. supports him by affirming there are no wolves, "unlesse they were brought from other countryes" (455). Their strategy not only denies tensions at home; it also dissolves them in the face of the common menace of Catholicism. In admitting there are foxes—a common reference to papists—Hobbinol acknowledges only religious tensions, which, given the marginalized status of Catholics, was far from controversial, unlike the economic exploitation Diggon recounts.[151] While the fox image was most firmly associated with religious debate, the wolf was not similarly restricted.[152] The wolf's predatory character was frequently employed in political discussion, going back to the Middle Ages. John Bromyard, chancellor of Cambridge and a popular fourteenth-century preacher, declared: "The poor for their good works are not rewarded, but are so oppressed by the rich and powerful that however true a cause a poor man may have against a rich man in this world, it will none-the-less happen to him as it did to the lamb at the hands of the wolf." The image was at the heart of Robert Crowley's pamphlet about economic exploitation and the social order, *The way to wealth, wherein is plainly taught a most present remedy for Sedicion* (1550). Referring to the great farmers, graziers, lawyers, merchants, gentlemen, knights, and lords, he said: "They take our houses over our headdes, they bye our growndes out of our handes, they reyse [our] rentes, they leavie great (yea unreasonable) fines, they enclose oure commens. No custome, no lawe or statute can kepe them from oppressyng us, in such sorte, that we knowe not whyche waye to turne us to lyve. . . . [Addressing a poor man] If thy shepherde had bene a diligent watchman, and had espied the woulfe comyng upon the,

before thou hadst bene . . . in his reach, he wold have steppeth betwene
thee and thine enemi."[153]
    The wolves Diggon describes are dangerously elusive:

They walke not widely as they were wont
For feare of raungers, and the great hunt:
But prively prolling two and froe,
Enaunter they mought be inly knowe.
                                        (158–61)

E.K. helps out here with his gloss on "great hunt" as the "executing of
lawes and justice" (455). Because the wolves do not appear as wolves, law
enforcement and judicial proceedings are impotent against them. This
passage reinforces Diggon's claim that while vagrancy may be associated
with crime, it should not be the focus in trying to repair the social order.
Because vagrants, lacking permanent shelter, necessarily inhabited public spaces, they could be rounded up in a sweep of those areas. They were
the targets of frequent searches, as in the campaign of 1569–72.[154] But
because the threat Diggon perceives is not public but concealed, such a
"great hunt" will not work.
    Hobbinol does not understand this but believes that the same solution
will serve whatever the nature of the threat:

Or privie or pert yf any bene,[155]
We han great Bandogs will teare their skinne.
                                        (162–63)

His reference to bandogs—used as watchdogs, they were notorious for
their violent tendencies (they were the pit bulls of their day)—is telling, because it recalls the growing Elizabethan reliance on quasi-military
force to maintain internal order.[156] During Elizabeth's reign, provost-
marshals, associated with military discipline, became important for their
role in suppressing vagabonds.[157] Many supported these efforts, feeling,
like Harrison, that vagrancy required even more severe measures than
the law provided: "The punishment that is ordained for this kind of
people is very sharp, and yet it cannot restrain them from their gadding;
wherefore the end must needs be martial law, to be exercised upon
them as upon thieves, robbers, despisers of all laws, and enemies to the
commonwealth and welfare of the land." Concern about internal order
following the 1569–70 rebellions prompted the Crown to organize a

national system of military training. In 1573 a system of "bands" was established. These men received military training, including instruction in the use of firearms, as a regular part of peacetime musters.[158] This militarization sparked opposition based on the cost, the increased control it gave to the Crown, and the danger of reliance on military force.[159] Resistance went back at least as far as 1549, when Sir Thomas Smith wrote against the proposal for a standing army in his *Discourse of the Commonweal:* "I would not have a small sore cured by a greater grief, nor for avoiding of sedition popular, which happens very seldom and soon quenched, to bring in a continual yoke and charge both to the king and his people."[160] Hobbinol's "bandogs" would have prompted the same concerns about the possible misuse of such military force.

But Diggon goes beyond the danger of abuse, questioning the reliance on force per se as the means of securing order in the realm: "not good Dogges hem needeth to chace" (166). Lowder, the dog in his story, is himself alert—"so kene a kurre, / That waketh, and if but a leafe sturre" (182–83)—so that his inability to catch the wolf reflects not on him but on the means used to restore order itself. Diggon's rejection of force questions the identification of the strength of the realm with its military capacity, an identification the Crown itself promoted by a medal struck in 1569 or 1570, which had Elizabeth's portrait and the motto *What are we without you!* on one side, and on the reverse the motto *What is this without arms!*[161] Diggon's story of Roffyn removes the reassurance military strength seems to provide, dramatizing the internal vulnerability of even a well-armed realm.

Unlike the fables in February and May, this story bears the marks of historical report rather than fiction. Diggon tells "what my selfe knowe" (170), and E.K. says the tale "seemeth to coloure some particular Action of his" (455).[162] The name Roffyn, readily identified with Rochester through the Latin *Roffensis* and underscored by the reference to Colin Clout as "his selfe boye" (176), probably referred to Spenser's tenure as secretary to John Young, bishop of Rochester, in 1578–79.

While we know relatively little about John Young's life, there is one episode that Diggon's account echoes. In the late 1570s cathedral land in Rochester (one of the poorest sees) and elsewhere was the target of a claim of "concealment." Some unnamed persons claimed that the lands that supported Chatham Hospital in Young's diocese were "concealed" property that should have gone to the Crown on the dissolution of the monasteries.[163] The hospital was originally founded by Gundolf, bishop of Rochester, in 1078, for lepers.[164] Young vigorously resisted the claim, complaining to William Cecil about the lawsuit against the property pending in the Court of Exchequer. He emphasized the service this institution provided, not only to lepers but also to "other poor aged and impotent persons, there resiant [resident] at this present." He urged Cecil to "stand good lord, so far forth as justice would permit, to the same poor people." This situation thus pitted Young, pleading on behalf of the poor, against appropriation of the church's resources to enrich members of the court and the Crown.[165]

Because royal authority lay behind the commission to search for concealment, as well as the legal claim of the Crown's title, this episode echoes in salient respects the kind of exaction that Diggon recounts in his story. In it the wolf does not come as a wolf, easily recognizable by Lowder, but plays all the other parts—dog, sheep, and shepherd.[166] In the climactic passage, he adopts the voice of the shepherd—"eke had he cond the shepherds call. . . . As if it the old man selfe had bene" (215, 218)—using this authority to exploit the helpless while enriching himself. He thereby inverts, while drawing on, the New Testament story of the shepherd whose person and authority are recognized by his voice: "The sheep hear his voice, and he calleth his own sheep by name, and leadeth them out. And when he hath sent forth his own sheep, he goeth before them, and the sheep follow him, for they know his voice."[167]

It is precisely the trust in authority this story exemplifies that makes the abuse of that authority by the wolf so dangerous and pernicious to the social order. Hobbinol's question may even suggest the form that abuse takes:

> Marry Diggon, what should him affraye,
> To take his owne where ever it laye?
> (208–9)

The antecedent of the pronouns is unclear, but if it is the wolf, "his owne" suggests the claim of right that would justify expropriation, precisely the claim asserted on behalf of the Crown against Chatham Hospital.

To combat the subterfuge the wolf represents, it is not force (Lowder) that is needed but the ability to see through the disguises cloaking such claims. Because exploitation comes concealed, speaking the voice of authority, what is required is "heedy shepheards to discerne [its] face" (167), shepherds like Roffyn. He is "wise, and as Argus eyed" (203), and thus he is paradigmatic of those "heedy shepheards" who, in detecting and flushing out the wolves, "doen so carefully theyr flocks tend" (179).

Although the monetary impact of this single incident in Rochester may have been much more significant locally than it was in the national picture, it represents a pervasive strategy of enrichment the *Calender* challenges: the depredation of the church by the Crown and its clients at the expense of the weak, for whom the church ideally should provide. Drawing attention to the authoritative voice the exploiters hide behind dramatizes the need for church officials, who still had the power, regardless of the corruption of some of their colleagues, to stand up for those in their charge. For the *Calender* and its author, such advocacy held the key to religious leadership.

"Content" versus Reform

As with the other moral eclogues, Spenser incorporates into this one an important response to the kind of social protest Diggon mounts: the silent patience Hobbinol recommends. He tells Diggon:

. . . cleanly cover, that cannot be cured.
Such il, as is forced, mought nedes be endured.
(139–40)

This patience is an aspect of the contentment he had urged earlier:

Content who lives with tryed state,
Neede feare no chaunge of frowning fate.
(70–71)

Hobbinol's view of the world as benign or unchangeable, or both, was a part of the ideology that worked to solidify the hierarchical structure. An important manifestation of this view was the Elizabethan doctrine of vocation, which counseled resignation to one's station in life, however lowly. A representative statement of this doctrine appears in the introduction to Aegremont Ratcliffe's translation of *Politique Discourses, treating of the differences and inequalities of vocations etc.* (1578): "There is nothing more decent, commendable, or yet more beneficiall to man, than to be contented, and constantly stande to his calling: without coveting, as ofte as his fond affection shall egge him, to be other

The woodcut from the September eclogue
(Huntington Library).

than he is, by chaunging of his manner of living. . . . There is no change
more dangerous, and more to be eschewed of every wise and warie man,
then the chaunging of his calling or the manner of living, he is in."
Like Hobbinol, Ratcliffe sees social reform as inimical to the desired acquiescence. It is, in fact, the impulse to change that is responsible for
contemporary disorders: "For, who ever sawe so many discontented persons: so many yrked with their owne degrees: so fewe contented with
their owne calling: and such a number desirous, & greedie of change, &
novelties? Who ever heard tel of so many reformers, or rather deform-
ers of estates, and Common weales: so many controllers of Princes, and
their proceedings: so few imbracing obedience?" Against the "greed of
change," vocation holds together a social structure that offers the dignity and security of providence against the mutability of fate. In that
structure each person is "by the incomprehensible ordinaunce of God,
called & appointed eche one in his degree, to some assured particular
estate, & honest maner of living, by his secrete providence: and not by
happe, or fortune." Hobbinol echoes this assurance, extolling the "tryed
state" in which one "neede feare no chaunge of frowning fate." This was,

in fact, official doctrine. The *Homilies* urged "that we take in good part our estate and condition, and content ourselves with that which God sendeth, whether it be much or little."[168]

Diggon's critical attitude challenges the ideal of contentment by probing the human practices that produced and fashioned those conditions, rather than relegating them to a distant divine providence.[169] In doing so, his complaints reveal the bitter irony of Hobbinol's outlook: dramatic change was taking place in the countryside, but it was fueled by the greed of the powerful, not the discontent of the peasants. Regardless of their attitude, those peasants were being pushed out of their places, many into a life as transients. For them "the world [was] much war then it wont" (108).

Diggon's emblem, *Inopem me copia fecit*, must be considered in light of these problems. In what sense does "plenty make poor"? Diggon's account suggests the straightforward claim that the shepherds' plenty produces the people's poverty. E.K.'s gloss gives some support for this reading, reiterating the words *plenty* and *penury* from the eclogue, the one identifying the "forrein costes" to which Diggon traveled (28), and the other the condition of his sheep after his trip there (65).

At the same time, the Narcissus story in Ovid, from which the emblem is taken, evokes the dangers of becoming wedded to a particular image or representation of one's self or, as in this eclogue, one's society. It is a warning against the self-satisfying but debilitating contemplation of a congratulatory self-image, a fixation that engenders complacency about social and economic injustice.

September embodies a strategy to counter that complacency. In reporting the complaints of "the people," Diggon gives attention to the perspectives of those who would otherwise remain obscure. He gives voice to the voiceless. He sums up this strategy of speaking "from below" when he comments, "I dare undersaye" (91). But to "undersaye" is also to contradict, to call into question. Adopting the terms of the Narcissus myth, one might say of Diggon that it is "through his troubling of the Well" that the smooth image of a harmonious, prosperous social order "gan to fade."[170] Against that image is set September's own zodiacal sign, the scales, clearly visible in the woodcut for the eclogue. Those scales, an acknowledged symbol for justice, are dangerously out of balance.[171]

6

"Rurall Musick Scorned"

Poetry in the Poem

Though previous criticism has recognized, however dimly and incompletely, that the moral eclogues contain some sociopolitical dimension, it would quarantine this aspect, separating it from the text's aesthetic discussion. But even E.K. resists this insulation by including October—universally acknowledged to be about poetry— among these moral eclogues and thus "mixed with some Satyrical bitternesse" (419). Far more than philosophical theorizing, the *Calender's* treatment of aesthetic matters interrogates the social affiliations and functions promoted for poetry by court critics like Puttenham. Their perspective did not provide either a compelling rationale for the poetic practice represented by the *Calender* or a viable strategy for securing an audience. Spenser's problem was to develop each, to establish legitimacy for this poetry that could engender the needed material support as well as recognition, without compromising its reformist imperatives. Though these two elements—audience and sanction—often overlap, the June eclogue focuses more closely on poetry's association with the court, while October continues that critique as part of its exploration of how poetic practice can be authorized.

This "Pleasaunt Syte": June and the Politics of Delight

What previous criticism has taken for a psychological discussion of the aesthetics of pleasure in the June eclogue—Nancy Jo Hoffman says it deals with "poetry's power to create autonomous places in the mind"—takes on a specific social registration when viewed in the context of courtly poetics, in particular the emphasis on pleasure that is so evident in Puttenham.[1] The *Calender's* critique of that orientation, however, raised the problem of how the alternative poetry represented by Spenser's work would be received. June dramatizes this problem in the Colin-Rosalind narrative.

"Pleading Pleasant Causes": Puttenham on Poetry

To win the prince's favor, the courtier was urged by courtesy literature to gratify him, "in his wil, maners and facions, to be altogether pliable to please him." The emphasis on pleasing promotes flattering deceit, and Puttenham advises his reader "to play many parts" and "by his many moodes of skill to serve the many humors of men."[2] Indulging the prince's varying humor required adroit self-fashioning—Castiglione calls it "slightenesse" (sleightness)—a talent summed up in Puttenham's oft-discussed "courtly figure *Allegoria* . . . which for his duplicitie we call the figure of [false semblant or dissimulation]."[3] It has been noted how Puttenham's work starts out full of moral purpose, with its model poet patterned after Amphion and Orpheus—the founders of civilization—but is gradually transformed to a catalog of rhetorical strategies, its poet a "cunning Princepleaser[ ]."[4] Though there are references to poetry's profitability, sanctioning it as grave and serious, "princepleasing" comes to dominate the discussion, wedding the practice of poetry so closely with pleasing as to exclude instruction: "Our maker or Poet is appointed not for a judge, but rather for a pleader, and that of pleasant & lovely causes and nothing perillous, such as be those for the trial of life, limme, or livelyhood, and before judges neither sower or severe, but in the eare of princely dames, yong ladies, gentlewomen, and courtiers . . . and . . . all his abuses [of speech in figurative language] tende but to dispose the hearers to mirth and sollace by pleasant conveyance and efficacy of speech." Puttenham's work becomes a handbook for the aspiring courtier, teaching him how to entertain—"to utter with pleasure and delight"—with content, form, and technique all governed by this aim.[5]

Because poetry's ancient function of instructing by communicating blunt advice, complaint, or critique, at best, is a distraction from giving pleasure or, worse, risks hostile reactions, it is repeatedly repudiated by Puttenham. He thus disparages epigrams as the outlet for those who compulsively need to "utter their splenes" and condescends to "the Satyr [satire] of Piers Ploughman" as authored by "a malcontent," with "termes hard and obscure, so as in them is litle pleasure to be taken." In drama he works to ensure audience approval by bowdlerizing sensitive, topical material, applauding the shift away from the specific targeting of "the old *Comedy*" to the more general tone of "the new *Comedy*." The former was "somwhat sharpe and bitter after the nature of the *Satyre*, openly & *by expresse names* taxing men more maliciously and impudently then became," while the latter was "more civill and pleasant a great deale, and not touching any man by name, but in a certaine *generalitie* glancing at every abuse, so as from thenceforth fearing none illwill or enmitie at any bodies hands."[6]

While Puttenham exemplifies court poetics, he does not, contrary to the impression conveyed by recent scholarship's focus on him, represent all Elizabethan criticism.[7] In fact, the attitude he represented was contested. Sir Philip Sidney, for one, responding in his *Defence of Poetry* both to the moralistic criticism represented by Stephen Gosson's *School of Abuse* (1579) and to the cynicism of ingratiating courtly poetics, tried to recuperate pleasure by integrating it into poetry's moral function.[8] In this quality resides poetry's capacity for inspiring virtuous action, "mov[ing] men to take that goodness in hand, which without delight they would fly as from a stranger." The poet, he continues, "doth not only show the way, but giveth so sweet a prospect into the way, as will entice any man to enter into it."[9] Sidney's reorientation of pleasure toward moral utility rejects the emphasis on self-promotion in court culture, replacing it with a commitment to instruction that his own career reflected. Conspicuous for his refusal to "tune" himself to the queen's wishes, he was, in Louis Montrose's words, "downright audacious in the giving of unsolicited advice." In arguing against the Alençon match in his letter to the queen, for instance, a union he well knew Elizabeth favored, he threw himself on her mercy—"laying . . . myself at your feet"—but at the same time asserted her need for such counsel, "because your own eyes cannot see yourself." The role Sidney adopts here is the one he prescribes for the poet. It is patterned after the prophet Nathan, cited in the *Defence* as telling a story "which made David . . . as in a glass, to see his own" conduct, an "application most divinely true."[10]

Spenser himself would later be blunt in criticizing, in *Colin Clouts*

Come Home Againe, poetry's betrayal to the arts of courtly self-advancement.[11] Incorporating the vocabulary of Castiglione and Puttenham in order to indict it, Colin lamented how the rhetorically skillful dissembler prospered at Elizabeth's court:

> . . . he doth soonest rise
> That best can handle his deceitfull wit,
> In subtil shifts, and finest sleights devise,
> . . . .
> Masked with faire dissembling curtesie,
> A filed toung furnisht with tearmes of art,
> No art of schoole, but Courtiers schoolery.
> (ll. 692–94, 700–702)

That "schoolery" was devoted to insinuation through pleasure:

> Ne is there place for any gentle wit,
> Unlesse to please, it selfe it can applie.
> (ll. 707–8)

The *Calender* clearly foreshadows this critique in its disparaging treatment of pleasure, pointedly linked to the court. It is central to the June eclogue and is echoed by important motifs throughout the moral eclogues. Thenot's fable in February, for example, condemns the culture represented by the brier, "puffed up with pryde and vaine pleasaunce" (223). The royal rhetoric of the fable—"King of the field" (108), "trees of state" (146), "my liege Lord" (150), "my soveraigne" (163), and "your Coronall" (178)—locates it in a courtly milieu, drawing attention to the use of rhetorical skill in the competition for advancement there. The oak, whose inferiority on this score is indicated by his inept responses to the brier's charges against him—first "little him answered" (140), then he "cast him to replie / Well as he couth" (189–90)—is no match for his accuser, who used "painted words" (160),

> (As most usen Ambitious folke:)
> His colowred crime with craft to cloke.
> (161–62)

The oak is "overcrawed" (142), literally "outtalked." The brier's "vaine pleasaunce" is part of a contest over aesthetic preferences that surrounds the fable. Thenot praises the tale for its potential to instruct: "none fitter then this to applie" (100). But Cuddie, tasting "little ease" (245) from the tale, rejects the fable—and Thenot's aesthetic of instruction—in favor of entertainment.

In May the figure of Palinode is similarly aligned with pleasure and play, celebrating the season "when all is ycladd / With pleasaunce" (6–7) and envying the "great sport [the outgoing shepherds] gaynen with little swinck" (36). He accuses Piers of a puritanical aversion to pleasure—"I see thou speakest of spight, / All for thou lackest somedele their delight" (55–56)—while he promotes it by conferring on it religious status:

What shoulden shepheards other things tend,
Then sith their God his good does them send,
Reapen the fruite thereof, that is pleasure,
The while they here liven, at ease and leasure?
(63–66)

Piers does not discredit pleasure, however, because of the personal immorality inherent in it but because of the shepherds' neglect of their social responsibility: they "little regarden their charge" (39).[12]

The pleasure principle ingrained in court culture complicated the poet's effort to articulate and justify an alternative to court poetry. As the central cultural as well as political institution in Elizabethan England, the court had to be included in the audience for any poetry that aspired to national status and influence. At the same time, the colonization of pleasure by the parochial aim of ingratiation espoused in poetics like Puttenham's was inimical to a socially responsible poetics like Sidney's and a politically engaged poetry like the *Calender*'s. Represented in the *Calender* as a rejection of its own poetry, this disability figures in the debates of the moral eclogues and in the Colin-Rosalind narrative, each of which in different ways imagines the poem's reception at court.

"Working Delyte": June's Debate

The subtle debate that takes place in the June eclogue revolves around the metaphor of place: where should Colin locate his art? The question is at once an aesthetic and a political one. Hobbinol's opening lines celebrate the "site" he urges on Colin:

Lo, *Colin,* here the place, whose pleasaunt syte
From other shades hath weand my wandring mynde.
Tell me, what wants me here, to worke delyte?
(1–3)

His unqualified emphasis on pleasure, to the exclusion of the didactic pole of the Horatian formula, aligns him with the court poetics I traced earlier. Other elements press the focus of the eclogue away from abstract aesthetic discussion to the more specific location in court. These opening lines, for example, evoke Virgil's first eclogue, namely the radically different relationships of each of its shepherds to state power, Meliboeus on his way to exile, Tityrus sheltered by patronage. While a number of critics have noted the parallel to Virgil, they have not pursued the startling implications of Spenser's reversal of the poet's position: Colin is not the protégé but an outsider, invited to court by Hobbinol in both text (17–22) and woodcut.[13] This reversal introduces the problem the eclogue develops.

When Hobbinol invites Colin to "forsake the soyle" (18), reiterating the familiar court-country dichotomy but adding a distinct element of class, E.K. removes any lingering doubts about the setting with his gloss on the motive for the move—"for his more preferment" (443)—emphasizing the opportunity for material advancement where there are "shepheards ritch" and "fruictfull flocks" (ll. 21–22). The palpable echoes of the April eclogue also underscore the identification of Hobbinol's "pleasaunt syte" with the court. Colin's presence in this eclogue, of course, recalls his song in April, "tuned . . . unto the Waters fall" (36; like the birds' songs in June 8). And Hobbinol borrows the cultural apparatus employed there in celebration of the queen to extol this place. Singled out for special attention in both eclogues is Calliope, the Muse of heroic poetry, whose subject is, in Puttenham's words, "the noble gests of kings & great Princes."[14]

The product of all the cultural accoutrements Hobbinol cites (25–31) is "pierlesse pleasures" (32), a pun on the name of the critical figure of Piers in May. Hobbinol's juxtaposition of this figure to the "pleasures" of this place (which are virtually conditioned on his absence) is a tacit rejection of the vernacular literary tradition traced back to *Piers Plowman* and a punning, if grim, shorthand for a poetic practice void of the sociopolitical commentary characteristic of the *Calender* and its models.

The woodcut from the June eclogue
(Huntington Library).

The narrative Colin recounts in response to Hobbinol's invitation is a
capsule commentary on the courtly poetic practice Hobbinol seems to
espouse. In "carelesse yeeres" (33)—the word *carelesse*, too, marks the
exclusion of social responsibility—the poet happily participated in the
culture of entertainment: "In such delights did joy amongst my peeres"
(35). He refers to both his audience's and his own response. Of particular importance was the "verbal courtship" of the queen and other court
members so thoroughly elaborated by Puttenham.[15]

> Tho would I seeke for Queene apples unrype,
> To give my *Rosalind*, and in Sommer shade
> Dight gaudy Girlonds, was my comen trade,[16]
> To crowne her golden locks.
>   (43–46)

Using the common practice of encoding political dynamics in Petrarchan figures, the lines evoke the exchange whereby the poet offers his
skill "to create symbolic forms . . . which sanctify political power" in
return for "material benefit."[17] The reciprocal character of this patronage is highlighted by the rhyme of *shade* (alluding to Virgil's *lentus in
umbra*) with *trade*. But this alignment of Colin with Tityrus is only mo-
mentary, a thing of the past, as "yeeres more rype" (46) and the loss of

Rosalind's love—the relation of the two is as yet unspecified—lead him to repudiate court poetry as "weary wanton toyes" (48).

Hobbinol attempts to recuperate the practices that Colin rejects with one of their own central strategies—flattery—extolling the appeal of Colin's "silver sound" (61) and seductively offering him superiority in the "highest" of poetic genres (Calliope's heroic poetry):

> But when [the Muses] came, where thou thy skill didst showe,
> They drewe abacke, as halfe with shame confound,
> Shepheard to see, them in theyr art outgoe.
>   (62–64)

Utilizing one of the central modes of this milieu, display (there one is encouraged his "lovely layes . . . [to] freely boste" [13]), Colin could overcome his low social status and secure advancement.

Colin's rejection of Hobbinol's overture is the heart of the eclogue. In disclaiming the Muses as sponsors for his art, he alludes to the contempt by the devotees of "high" culture for a poetic associated with humble genres and classes: they "holden scorne of homely shepheards quill" (67). His allusion to the song contest between Pan and Phoebus underscores the mutual exclusion of these alternative practices. Their competition echoes Hobbinol's emphasis on pleasure (1, 3, 29, 32). It was the "sweetenesse" of Phoebus's songs that garnered the verdict in his favor from the judge who "did so . . . of them delyght."[18]

Prompted by the threat of retaliation—"rebuke and Daunger" (69)—made real in Pan's banishment and Midas's punishment, Colin forsakes the high culture represented by "Parnasse hyll" (70) and with it the judgment of the powerful who promote aesthetic conventions congruent with their privilege. He favors instead pastoral "pyping lowe in shade of lowly grove" (71), disclaiming any pretensions—"I never lyst presume" (70)—the precondition of pastoral critique.

It might appear, however, that, in place of that critique, Colin installs an aesthetic of self-expression: "I play to please my selfe, all be it ill" (72). But his declaration is not a generalized avowal of what Paul Alpers calls "the lyric authority of [Spenser's] pastoral self-representation" but a specific repudiation of the courtly strategy of ingratiation.[19] He chooses not to frame himself according to the "humors" of his audience—"Nought weigh I, who my song doth prayse or blame" (73)—and he forgoes the competitive economy that Hobbinol assured him would produce success:

"Ne strive to winne renowne, or passe the rest" (74). Yet this rejection of the dynamics of court culture is not an assertion of solipsism but the affirmation of an art guided by social responsibility:

> With shepheard sittes not, followe flying fame:
> But feede his flocke in fields, where falls hem best.
> (75–76)

The important element in this passage is not the poet's putative autonomy but the recognition of the social and political pressure brought to bear on his art (in part through court patronage) and the implication that such pressure detracts from an authentic poetic practice, a "song [that] doth prayse or blame" (73) according to the social ethics operative in the moral eclogues.

Those ethics govern style as well:

> I wote my rymes bene rough, and rudely drest:
> The fytter they, my carefull case to frame:
> Enough is me to paint out my unrest,
> And poore my piteous plaints out in the same.
> (77–80)

This espousal of a plain style—rough and rude rhymes—for "plaints" stands in marked contrast to the court preference for ornamentation, reflected in Puttenham's disparagement of Skelton as "a rude rayling rimer" and the style of *Piers Plowman* as "hard and obscure, so as in [it] is litle pleasure to be taken."[20] Echoing E.K.'s alignment of the *Calender's* "hard" language, "most used of country folke," with the vernacular literary tradition—the "most excellent Authors and most famous Poetes" (416)—Colin validates the rude style by locating it in the lineage of Chaucer, "who taught me homely, as I can, to make" (l. 82).

These lines also bring the love narrative together with the poet's social responsibility, "plaints" and "carefull case" (contrasting with the "carelesse" quality of immature poetry [33]) hovering between lovers' lament and social critique. The two are more intimately related than previous criticism has recognized, for the Colin-Rosalind narrative, which has spawned so much fruitless biographical speculation, in fact dramatizes the question of poetry's reception.[21] Rosalind's rejection of Colin, the

The woodcut from the January eclogue
(Huntington Library).

poet figure, is focused on his poetic practice. As he complains in the
January eclogue,

> . . . Of my rurall musick [she] holdeth scorne.
> Shepheards devise she hateth as the snake,
> And laughes the songes, that *Colin Clout* doth make.
>
> (64–66)

In reaction, as January's woodcut shows, Colin "broke his oaten pype"
(72). Rosalind's "discurtesee" (97) in June reiterates this rejection with
the same result, the woodcut again depicting Colin's broken pipe. In
this eclogue, so redolent with images of competition, Colin has a rival.
"Forsaking" Colin, E.K. tells us, Rosalind "hadde chosen another" (443),
Menalcas. E.K.'s allusion to Virgil's character of the same name also
points us to the aesthetic implications of Rosalind's choice, for in Virgil
Menalcas actually provokes a song contest by insulting Damoetas for his
song's rudeness:

> You [Damoetas] beat [Damon] singing? Whenever did panpipes
> Belong to you?—street-corner bard, whose skill's to
> Murder on scrannel straw a wretched song.[22]

Rosalind's "infidelity" thus reenacts the conflict between Pan's "country pype of reedes . . . his rude and homely song" and Phoebus's royal aesthetic represented by "his viol . . . of precious stones and Ivorye intermixt."[23]

Folding this aesthetic choice into the love narrative highlights the problem Colin confronts: while the culture of the court is hostile to his poetry, its social impact rests to a significant extent on its favorable reception there. A tentatively hopeful note is struck, however, by Colin's appeal to an audience that shares his values: "Ye gentle shepheards, which your flocks do feede" (106). The pervasiveness of the court culture of pleasure, however, casts doubt on the extent, even the existence, of this audience and on the *Calender*'s ability to engender it. Colin's rejection here (and elsewhere) augurs a ruling elite "voide of grace" (115) in its support—both rhetorical and material—for poetry that calls their own social responsibility to account.[24]

"Heavenly Instinct" and "Commen Capacitie": October's Debate over Sanctioning Poetry

The October eclogue is in some respects the most difficult in the *Calender*, yet much modern commentary has ignored the important conflicts the eclogue exposes, reading it as an unqualified statement of "Spenser's poetic ideals," what John King calls a "climactic hymn to poetry." The locus of those ideals is the Neoplatonic theory of inspiration these critics see in the eclogue, the concept of the poet as, in the words of J. B. Fletcher, the "mouthpiece of divinity." Gary Waller, for example, reads in the eclogue "the articulation of . . . a theory . . . [that] combines Neoplatonism and traditional Horatianism along with a Christian emphasis on divine inspiration."[25] This perspective treats E.K.'s argument as a transparent explanation of the eclogue's message that poetry is "no arte, but a divine gift and heavenly instinct not to bee gotten by laboure and learning, but adorned with both: and poured into the witte by a certaine [*enthousiasmos*] and celestiall inspiration" (456).

Viewing the eclogue in this fashion, as monologic, suppresses its troubled concern over the status and function of poetry. While there is an apparently idealistic strain in the poem (identified with Piers and even more so with E.K.), it is not neatly affirmed but, following the *Calender*'s common procedure, problematized by being subjected to debate. What is striking about E.K.'s argument, for example, is that, while he bestows on Cuddie the title of "perfecte paterne of a Poete," thus apparently associating him with the divine status of poetry, it is Piers who voices that view. Cuddie challenges it and its implications at every turn.[26]

What is at stake here is one of the central problems of Elizabethan poetics, namely the need to authorize, to sanction, poetic practice: "Of what estimation," in William Webbe's formulation, poetry "hath alwayes beene and ought to be among al sorts of people."[27] Two major strategies for promoting that "estimation" were audience approval and the authority of inspiration. It is these two strategies, which are at times intertwined, that the eclogue tests and, though offering no comprehensive alternative, rejects as inadequate.

The eclogue opens with an echo of June's stress on pleasure in Piers's exhortation to Cuddie to use his song for amusement: "let us cast with what delight to chace" the long day (2). Recalling Cuddie's former popularity—"Whilome thou wont the shepheards laddes to leade" (4)—Piers implies he can regain that status by using his ability to entertain. Cuddie admits this talent was, in fact, the basis of his popular regard:

> The dapper ditties, that I wont devise,
> To feede youthes fancie, and the flocking fry,
> Delighten much.
> (13–15)

But unlike June, where the delight-for-success model is criticized on moral grounds, here Cuddie complains that it has not served to provide the poet with material support:

> . . . What I the bett for thy?
> They han the pleasure, I a sclender prise.
> (15–16)

He lacks an audience that will sustain him *as a poet*, the necessary precondition to a significant public role for poetry. "The flocking fry" are, potentially, an alternative to royal or noble patronage, but their failure to supply the necessary support reflects the inadequacy of the emergent publishing trade to furnish a social role for the poet.

Piers attempts to compensate for this lack of material support with fame—"prayse" and "glory"—and the satisfaction of moral influence, achieved, much as it is in Sidney, by integrating pleasure into poetry's moral function:

O what an honor is it, to restraine
The lust of lawlesse youth with good advice:
Or pricke them forth with pleasaunce of thy vaine,
Whereto thou list their trayned willes entice.
(21–24)

Piers describes the poet's almost magical power over his audience—"Seemeth thou dost their soule of sence bereave" (27)—what E.K. calls "the secrete working of Musick . . . in the myndes of men," exclaiming, "Such might is in musick" (458). To clinch his argument Piers alludes to Orpheus, who was commonly cited in Renaissance defenses of poetry as the model for the civilizing capacity of poetic art.[28] But when Piers refers to the descent into hell as the emblem of Orpheus's power, the notorious failure of that venture creates a curious dissonance, heightened by E.K.'s blandly erroneous declaration that Orpheus "recovered his wife Eurydice from hell" (458).

Cuddie dismisses this poetic ideology as irrelevant to his concern for an audience that will materially support the poet: "But who rewards him ere the more for thy?" (33). He also suggests that the power Piers refers to is nothing more than appreciation for technique, not translated into the moral impact Piers claims for it. The audience praises the beauty of the peacock's tail (31)—"wondren at bright *Argus* blazing eye" (32)—but without any indication that they will emulate the model of diligent watchfulness Argus represents.[29] E.K. widens the gap Cuddie has opened between aesthetic impact and moral behavior with a gloss reminding us that the power of song can be applied to undermine that watchfulness: "Mercury wyth hys Musick lulling Argus aslepe" (458).[30] The power Piers promotes is both uncertain and ambivalent.

Piers next proposes an altogether different audience, implying that Cuddie's problem is the unfitness of the present one, "the base and viler clowne" (37). He advises Cuddie: "Turne thee to those, that weld the awful crowne" (40), cataloging the various modes available to the practitioner in such a milieu (40–53). Heroic poetry, for instance, provides vicarious, ideological compensation for the lapse of a martial life-style:

Sing of bloody Mars, of wars, of giusts.

. . . .

[Turn to] doubted Knights, whose woundlesse armour rusts,
And helmes unbruzed wexen dayly browne.

(39, 41–42)

Lawrence Stone has captured the cultural significance of this chivalric discourse: "As [the nobility's] utility in war declined, they tried to protect their position by a romantic and artificial revival of the chivalric ideal," utilizing "calls for a spiritual regeneration in military prowess to justify social and economic privilege."[31] Piers would enlist the poet in this ideological project. The other avenues Piers sees as open to the court poet are praise for the queen (45), advancing important factions like Leicester's at court (47–48), celebrating love (51), and, recalling Hobbinol's dance scene in June (25–32), adorning courtly entertainments (52–53). Each case provides the opportunity for the poet to advertise himself: "There may thy Muse display her fluttryng wing" (43).

Significantly, Piers in this passage altogether abandons his earlier stress on the poet's moral power over the audience, focusing so exclusively on the possibilities for insinuation that he leaves aside any ethical dimension. His nimble movement from moral force to court politics— replicating his own transformation from the sharp critic of the May eclogue to the voice of accommodation here—suggests the pressures the latter exerts on the former.[32] Moreover, the insular character of his responses—isolating the moral from the material dimension by focusing on each separately—dramatizes an issue central to forging a socially responsible poetics: how does one achieve social status while maintaining the moral integrity of poetic practice?

The obvious means of support available through court is patronage, and Cuddie, seemingly swayed by Piers's proposal, refers to this model:

Indeede the Romish *Tityrus*, I heare,
Through his *Mecœnas* left his Oaten reede.

(55–56)

E.K.'s gloss describes the collaborative, mutually supportive relationship between poetry and political power that patronage often implies, recounting how Virgil "was brought into the favour of the Emperor Augustus, and by him moved to write in loftier kinde" (459).[33] But Cuddie, despite the force of the Virgilian paradigm, repudiates this model decisively, first and most subtly by representing pastoral as the genre practiced prior to the installation of poetry at court (56–57) and, implicitly, not easily transferable there (Virgil "left" it behind). More bluntly, he declares that the model is no longer available:

> But ah *Mecœnas* is yclad in claye,
> And great *Augustus* long ygoe is dead:
> And all the worthies liggen wrapt in leade.
> (61–63)

What made the union of political position and moral purpose in the Virgilian model possible, and tolerable, was the virtue of the powerful themselves,

> That matter made for Poets on to play:
> For ever, who in derring doe were dreade,
> The loftie verse of hem was loved aye.
> (64–66)

The decisive difference between that bygone era and the present is precisely the moral character of the elite. Their decline has rendered the model unavailable:

> But after vertue gan for age to stoupe,
> And mighty manhode brought a bedde of ease:
> The vaunting Poets found nought worth a pease,
> To put in preace emong the learned troupe.
> (67–70)

As is true throughout the eclogue, Cuddie here challenges E.K.'s view, flatly contradicting his claim that "there be many Noble and valiaunt men, that are . . . worthy of [the poet's] payne in theyr deserved prayses" (458).

The corruption Cuddie charges to the court shows up in its inadequacy as an audience as well. Any vestiges of the poetry formerly practiced— "any buddes of Poesie, / Yet of the old stocke" (73–74)—are there effaced. The alternative practices available to the poet are now sharply limited: either he "mens follies mote be forst to fayne" (74)—*fayne* meaning not just "dissimulate" as in Puttenham's injunction but also "celebrate"—

or he must "rolle with rest in rymes of rybaudrye" (75).[34] Only a debased form of poetry can be popular there. True poetry finds no support: "as it sprong, it wither must agayne" (77).

Cuddie's reference to "rymes of rybaudrye" is especially significant because it echoes the moralistic critique frequently leveled against popular cultural forms, as in Thomas Lodge's disparagement of "foolishe ballets" as "savoring of ribaldry."[35] In applying the word *rybaudrye* to the court poetry lauded by Piers, Cuddie audaciously reverses the canons of evaluation. Instead of aligning poetry with social class and political power, he sets them at odds. This upending is completed by his declaration that "Tom Piper makes us better melodie" (78). Most critics acquiesce in E.K.'s assertion that this line is "an Ironicall Sarcasmus, spoken in derision of these rude wits" (459).[36] But this reading ignores the intended target of the line, which is not the popular songs represented by Tom Piper but poetry that adapts to court pressures, "fayning mens follies." For Cuddie it is not vulgarization that threatens poetry, as Puttenham would have it, but the culture of the court itself, with its indolence and self-congratulation. The woodcut dramatizes his attitude, showing Cuddie walking away from the palace (while Piers seems to be suggesting that he return).[37] The implication that popular poetry was morally superior to its counterpart at court punctures the pretension of the latter built on the disparagement of "low" culture. It would certainly have been more than a little scandalous, but squarely in line with the rest of the passage.

Piers, doubtless frustrated by Cuddie's refusal of all his suggestions, asks:

O pierlesse Poesye, where is then thy place?
If nor in Princes pallace thou doe sitt:
(And yet is Princes pallace the most fitt)
Ne brest of baser birth doth thee embrace.
(79–82)

The problem Cuddie has raised is whether there is any fit audience for poetry, any institutional context that can give poetry material shape without compromising its moral purpose. Piers answers his own question by shifting to a different strategy, seeking refuge in an ideology of divine inspiration—"whence thou camst, flye backe to heaven apace" (84)—one that seems to distance itself from concern with audience but

The woodcut from the October eclogue
(Huntington Library).

whose ultimate aim is to recapture it by the sheer weight of its moral
authority, its access to extraordinary power and profound wisdom. This
ideology was a common trope in Elizabethan defenses. Thomas Elyot
describes "celestiall instinction" as pivotal to true poetry, while Lodge,
citing Homer as "no les accompted than *Humanus deus*," asserts "that
poetry is a heavenly gift, a perfit gift."[38]

Cuddie laments that contemporary poetry does not measure up to
Piers's exhortation—"it is all to weake and wanne" (85)—except for the
potential found in Colin, unrealized because he is handicapped by love
(88–90). This last comment sparks the shepherds' debate about the role
of love as a motive force for art (91–102). Given the eclogue's central concern with the social location of poetry, Piers's vertical imagery ("climbe
so hie," "lyftes him up," "rayse ones mynd," "cause . . . to aspire," and
especially "lofty love doth loath a lowly eye" [91–96]), so much a part
of Elizabethan social and political discussion, cannot be confined to the
philosophical or psychological. The coincidence between aesthetic and
social dynamics would not have been surprising coming from Piers, as
he first introduced class terms into the eclogue with his injunction to
Cuddie to forsake the popular audience—"Lyft up thy selfe out of the

lowly dust" (38)—and he expressly favors an aristocratic audience for poetry: "And yet is Princes pallace the most fitt" (81). Recalling Hobbinol's invitation in June, his counsel more than hints at the upward social mobility poetic skill can make possible.

Cuddie reinforces the social registration by using political metaphors to describe the constraints that love imposes on poetic practice:

> All otherwise the state of Poet stands,
> For lordly love is such a Tyranne fell:
> That where he rules, all power he doth expell.
> (97–99)

Recalling his earlier reference to the pernicious influence the aristocracy has on poetry (73–77), Cuddie sees in Piers's paean to love only a disempowering relationship in which the poet must give up critical reflection for mindless praise: "The vaunted verse a vacant head demaundes" (100).[39] Cuddie thus rejects E.K.'s glorification of the "might . . . in musick" (458), exemplified by the poet's sway over Alexander, lamenting instead the submission of the poet to power. He fears the equivocal position of the court poet that Richard McCoy describes: "His creative autonomy diminished as his proximity to power increased."[40]

The alternative inspiration Cuddie offers, "*Bacchus* fruite" (106)— especially appropriate to October, the month of the wine harvest—is a witty rejoinder to the common charge leveled against professional writers, especially ballad makers, of excessive reliance on drink.[41] But the humor turns more pointed with Cuddie's assertion that this "lowly" inspiration could produce the "highest" of literary forms: tragedy, "the Muse on stately stage . . . in bus-kin fine" (112–13).[42] This incongruity disturbs the decorum E.K. promotes between high genres and divine inspiration. He tries to contain the critical implications of the shepherds' debate by framing it within the doctrine of poetic inspiration (at the beginning in his argument and at the end in his final gloss on the emblem). Weightier poetry ("fine verses") is the sign of inspiration "from above," meriting its authors the title of *vatem*, while "lighter matter of Poesie" warranted only the title of "maker" (458). This subordination of the text's own model (the poet as "maker") is accompanied by the altogether different orientation of the *vatem* toward power. The fact that those in this group "sing . . . in prayse" gives them a generic affiliation with princes, reflected in Elizabeth, who provides the substance of "Heroicall argument" (458), and Augustus, who moved Virgil to write "in loftier kinde" (459).[43]

E.K. rebukes Cuddie's alternative as a presumptuous aesthetic and political transgression, chastising him because "he hath forgot the meanenesse of shepheards state and stile" (459). He moves to reestablish the hierarchy his decorum implies, reading Piers's nonexistent emblem as summing up the meaning of the entire eclogue, "that Poetry is a divine instinct and unnatural rage passing the reache of comen reason" (459). This declaration echoes the very similar language he used in the introductory epistle to Gabriel Harvey to complain about "the rakehellye route of our ragged rymers" who write "as if some instinct of Poeticall spirite had newly ravished them above the meanenesse of commen capacitie" (417–18). His consistent subordination of "common capacitie" to inspiration is congruent with the social and political status he associates with "divine instinct." The very fact of his earlier complaint, however, and what he in the October glosses describes as Cuddie's "Poetical furie" (459), an example of his nemesis, shows the instability of his structure of aesthetic privilege.

The conspicuously fragmentary character of the emblem E.K. purports to interpret—only Cuddie has one, and it is missing the antecedent that would identify by whose "movement we are kept warm"—both qualifies E.K.'s enthusiasm and expresses the unfinished nature of the shepherds' debate. Piers's efforts to resolve the questions of audience and motivation by invoking moral power, court rewards, and inspiration have each prompted forceful challenges from Cuddie, exposing the social affiliations and implications of Piers's (and E.K.'s) perspective. Although no fully developed alternative is presented, by qualifying the authority of these rationales, Cuddie opens a space within which such an alternative practice could emerge.

What, then, does the text's own sanction of Cuddie, as "the perfecte paterne of a Poete," signify? The woodcut provides the most helpful guide here, with its striking incongruity that, while the poet has turned his back on the halls of power, with the prestige and support they offer, he retains the crown of laurels, the sign of public status and influence. The scene could well be taken as an emblem of Spenser's own situation. Though his class largely ruled out conventional political avenues to influence, his talent and education prepared him for alternative public roles available in cultural activity. The woodcut affirms this potential. Unlike those of January and June, the singer's pipe here is intact, and central, signifying the durability and potency of the poet's art. In the face of the threat of official retaliation, audience inertness or misunderstanding, and antagonistic poetic ideologies, the strength of the woodcut's figure attests this art's endurance and vitality.

Epilogue

Inventing Society

In criticizing the ruling elite of Elizabethan society, Spenser was by no means alone. Dissent was voiced in a number of different arenas, and though the protest took different shapes in response to the particular issues addressed, unquestionably loyal subjects challenged the regime's authority to prescribe the terms of public debate by transgressing the royal commands to remain silent. When they engaged public issues, they asserted the right to participate in the making of policy and the shaping of Elizabethan institutions. In one fashion or another, their action constituted a call for more inclusive governance, which goes far in explaining why the regime suppressed them. Besides Archbishop Grindal's challenge to the queen, several other important episodes indicate how widespread the spirit of that call was, issuing as it did from institutional contexts as disparate as the church, Parliament, the popular press, the university, and the court itself.

Adopting the role of preacher as prophet, Edward Dering censured the Crown for its abuses of the church, in the most famous instance declaring to the queen's face that "the hands of the Princes and Rulers, are chiefe in this trespasse."[1] Though Dering's popularity inhibited retaliation for a time, the queen finally barred him from preaching anywhere in the realm.

The contest over competing versions of governance—exclusive or collaborative—was most dramatic in Parliament. The long-simmering dispute over its role in formulating religious policy came to a head in 1576 with Peter Wentworth's eloquent defense of the liberty of Commons:

"There is nothing soe necessary for the preservacion of the prince and state as free speech, and without it it is a scorne and mockery to call it a parliement house for in truth it is none, but a very schoole of flattery and dissimulacion." He was summarily dispatched to prison for over a month, his confinement punctuating the declaration by one Privy Council member that free speech did not mean "a man in this Howse may speake what, and of whom he lyst.... the contrary ... by the punishment of such inconsiderate and disorderly speakers, hath appeared."[2]

In 1569, lectures on the book of Acts by Thomas Cartwright, Lady Margaret Professor of Divinity at Cambridge, raised disturbing questions about church polity. In order to neutralize the protection Cartwright's popularity gave him, the government responded first by revising the university statutes to prohibit saying anything against the established religion, and then by expelling him for doing so.

Despite the rank of its author, Sir Philip Sidney's letter to the queen to dissuade her from the Alençon match seems to have provoked her animosity, leading to his withdrawal from court for almost a year.[3] His exile precluded any effective political influence, as he complained in a letter to the earl of Leicester in August 1580: "My only service is speeche and that is stopped" by the lack of access to the queen.[4]

Public dissent was treated even more harshly. For publishing the pamphlet against the Alençon match, John Stubbs, his publisher, and his printer, Hugh Singleton, were convicted of sedition and sentenced to maiming. But public disapproval of the Crown's action is suggested by the jury's refusal to convict the defendants on a more serious charge (sought by the queen for its penalty of hanging). A lawyer and a judge even questioned the legality of the prosecution itself, brought as it was under a Marian statute enacted for the protection of the queen's husband.[5] After his sentence—the amputation of his right hand—had been executed, Stubbs doffed his hat with his remaining hand and declared loudly, "God save the queen." The audience remained silent, out of horror or pity, the historian William Camden speculates, "or else out of hatred of the marriage."[6]

The *Calender* and its author have affiliations with this party of silenced speakers. The connection to Singleton and the role of Grindal have already been discussed. Spenser would have been well aware of Cartwright, because he entered Cambridge just as Cartwright began lecturing there. The controversy over Cartwright's deprivation was a celebrated feature of Spenser's tenure. While it is impossible to specify what effect that controversy had on Spenser, it must have made some impression. Spenser was also associated with Sidney in 1579, when the latter was an increasingly obstreperous dissenter from both the decorum of court life and the substance of royal policy. The *Calender*'s affiliation with him is conspicuously declared in a dedication that may well have been written when Sidney was in exile from the court.

Reading Spenser's poem in a way that reveals its affinities with this pattern of resistance to authoritarian royal power does more than just highlight the public significance of the work. Recapturing the prominence of such criticism in Elizabethan society requires us to reevaluate understandings of that society that posit such protest as either unnecessary (because Elizabeth's own popularity, genial demeanor, and/or sound policy removed the soil from which it could spring) or impossible (because the regime's hegemony was so effective that no one dared, or could even conceive, such opposition).

Similarly, if we take seriously the text's own markers of social position, treating them as more than a literary pose (another version of the humility trope), then we must rethink the exclusion of class as an integral element of the Elizabethan social order. Preempting the question of class by generalized references to the spirit of national unity or the aristocratic character of cultural activity or the preindustrial character of Elizabethan England cannot be persuasive without some account of palpable traces of its presence: the insistent, even obsessive, enforcement of hierarchical differences and the political exclusion they entailed; the effort to neutralize the abiding impulse to inclusiveness in Protestantism's emphasis on the equal status of all believers before God; and the persistent consciousness of and resistance to marginalization expressed in the artifacts of popular culture.

It should be clear that the questions of critique and class around which this study revolves are not simply subjects of textual interpretation but entail issues of historical investigation that are equally complex if not more so. Historical perspective has traditionally been an important component of readings of the *Calender*, but the norms of relevance have channeled it into the by now well-worn paths of religious controversy, the poet's relationship to the queen, and specific events like the Alençon match. My claim is for a new topicality, an expanded sense of the historically pertinent that does not reject earlier paradigms so much as extend their sociopolitical significance (by, for example, elaborating the ineluctable political dimension of religious debate and the dilemma posed by the poet's public and critical role), as well as adding to, under the rubric of "institutions," the referents the poem intends.

The justification for any interpretive account can only be that it is plausible, coherent, and explicative.[7] How these criteria apply to literary interpretation will never be a matter of absolute precision, but at a minimum, historicist accounts of literature must claim a fidelity to historical conditions, achieved by elaborating the local contexts in which those conditions resonated most resoundingly. Instances in which Spenser's language intersects nonliterary usage constitute an important set of those contexts (e.g., the husbandry image in February, the phrase *motherly care* in May), for that rhetorical engagement is of prime significance in this poem. It signals the work's sociopolitical intention, initiating for the percipient reader then and now the interrogation of institutional dynamics and the historical inquiry that interrogation requires.

The parameters of the inquiry cannot be dictated in advance. Indeed, doing justice to the distinctiveness of the past requires us to recapture the ignorance of how the historical episode, as well as our account of it, will turn out. But it will surely entail, as it has here, extensive investigation into nonliterary sources, such as records of all kinds and other histories. The technique found in some new historicist work of describing a coincidence between a work of "high" culture and an apparently far different text will not be sufficient by itself to reconstruct the social ground in which literary texts are embedded.[8] That the process of understanding a society, which is the object of historicist inquiry, is provisional, partial, or incomplete does not warrant short-circuiting it. Nor does the recognition that our understanding is mediated through texts mean that all texts make equally important contributions. It is no longer sufficient, now that the object of our attention has shifted to "culture," to substitute it for more traditional aesthetic concerns as the central subject of literary texts while proceeding to read them very much as we did before.[9] The material conditions of social life, what Lee Patterson refers to as their "palpable force . . . and intentional purposiveness," are generally more fully available to us in records other than poems and plays, records for which the protocols of literary analysis are not appropriate.[10] We must learn how to enlist this material in the process of uncovering literature's historicity.

It is surely valid to warn against the accumulation of detail as sufficient warrant for generalization about the character of an entire culture.[11] But neither can a serious historicist perspective ignore the concrete particulars in which social experience is incarnated. The copious notes in this book offer one indication of my effort to incorporate that experience into a reading of Spenser's poem. In particular, by including varied resources such as official documents, church papers, and the products of popular culture, I have tried to show the fluidity of the languages, images, and ideas through which social life in Elizabethan England was imagined and represented. An analysis of early modern texts using insular categories derived from our experience as twentieth-century American intellectuals (e.g., religion as a discrete discourse and set of experiences) prematurely forecloses fruitful avenues of interpretation. Rather than an aggregate of separate strands, public speech in Elizabethan England was a tapestry whose interwoven discourses gave it a rich allusiveness the depths of which we have not yet fully plumbed.

One cannot go far in delineating the elements of a historicist approach without engaging the question of the local and the global, the particular and the general, if only because the history of our profession has so privileged certain forms of comprehensiveness. Authority in critical explanation often rested on the articulation of a universal or essential human nature in literary works or on assimilation of all the important works of a period or genre to a single descriptive scheme.[12] While it is easy enough to dismiss these perspectives as dehistoricizing idealizations that ignore or repress the social specificity (and even the formal distinctiveness) of literary works, we need to ask more explicitly what historicism has to offer—what explanatory credentials it can present—to replace these approaches.

Little guidance is offered by the polar notions that the local is simply an instance, one more example whose significance rests wholly in the structure or pattern to which it points, or that the particular is trapped in its own discreteness, intrinsically resistant to or even at odds with any sort of generalization. Topical allusion is a lever that opens up the interplay between text and society to broader questions and larger cultural patterns, crystallizing social formations while maintaining focus and intensity by anchoring those forms in the local sites in which they were embodied. Their concrete specificity gives them critical purchase, revealing what is at stake, what determinate interests larger themes entail. Spenser's thinly concealed allusions to Grindal's challenge to

Queen Elizabeth do not merely give a knowing nod to readers that the author was *au courant*, but they make available the fundamental issues of polity with which that historical episode was charged. Topicality that functions in this way calls for an approach that melds literary interpretation with sociopolitical analysis (itself, of course, interpretive) into a narrative of textual significance. The process need not entail a claim of univocal or homogenous meaning, but instead it elucidates the spectrum that interpretation traverses, the nodes around which the text's meaning circulates. Nor does the element of indeterminacy in our work deny our capacity to draw distinctions between accounts in their fidelity to both literary and historical material or relieve us from our responsibility to invent (in both rhetorical senses, "to find" and "to make") the society that constitutes and is constituted by those texts.

All historical work is vulnerable to the charge of antiquarianism, the accumulation of disparate facts about the past for its own sake apart from any narratives conveying those elements in an intelligible form, and projection, denying the authentic status of the past by reading it solely as it relates to contemporary concerns. The question implied, though begged, by each is how historical work bears on our contemporary situation. Borrowing Sir Walter Ralegh's famous dictum, exactly how is it "that in speaking of the past, [we] point at the present"?[13] That bearing itself is historically contingent, varying with time and place, but we have inherited a valuable tradition that prizes history as a source of moral guidance and social understanding. We need not resort to the premise of universal human nature or other totalizing mechanisms to warrant our connection with past societies. It is sufficient to recognize that features of social organization and personal identity recur in such a way to give history pertinence. It is the very situatedness of historical actors and structures then and now, which the extraction of universals would occlude, that grounds and animates that pertinence.

Perhaps the most salutary aspect of the revived interest in historicism is the renovated sense of history's contemporary bearing. To fully exploit it requires us to exercise our social imagination, to ask what it means to live with and among others, how the affiliations among persons and groups are mediated by conventions and institutions, how personal identity is fashioned and public resources allocated. While accountability to the records we have is essential, any illusion of a view of history "untainted" by contemporary concerns needs to be discarded, not just

because it is an illusion but also because it inhibits us from asking forthrightly how history can respond to those concerns while retaining the
integrity of its otherness. This process need not become projection, but
it would allow history to interrogate us, to show us facets of the historical situation, and our own, to which we are blinded by the partiality
(in both senses) of our own experience and tradition.[14] Nor does viewing
the process of historical investigation in this way preordain or dictate its
outcome. Contrary to Stephen Greenblatt's pronouncement that "there
is subversion, no end of subversion, only not for us"—premised as it is
on a view of our profession as radically homogeneous—because our concerns are sumptuously protean, our accounts will be too.[15] Some will see
in the past strains that others do find subversive.

   Historicism has already generated a vigorous and healthy conversation
over the sociopolitical dimension of various interpretations. It presents
the further prospect that literary criticism will once again become a
participant in the ongoing debate over the character and destiny of our
own society. Already cultural resources are being impressed in the service of various visions of the social order. The *Calender*'s critique of
political and cultural authority can be instructive in that debate, working as it did to make Spenser's society more visible and accessible to
understanding and critical judgment. The actual conduct of institutions
and individual agents, and its social ramifications, are often hidden,
only relatively rarely becoming the subject of individual reflection or
collective deliberation. And the practice is widespread—in Elizabethan
society and ours—of taking the representation for the event or process
itself.[16] Historical study can illuminate social practices and structures
that would otherwise remain veiled and thus provides one means of ex-
ploring the gaps between the representations of those practices and their
material foundation.

   My effort to situate Spenser's *Shepheardes Calender* historically grows
out of the belief that this form of criticism—uncovering as it does what
artists have revealed to us about the conditions and possibilities of common life—can and should participate in the debate over the terms of our
collective life. There is an urgency to this claim: I am writing weeks
after the April 1992 Los Angeles riots. Public problems are more dramatically visible at the same time that the conceptual, linguistic, and
affective resources available for dealing with them seem threadbare. It is
not grandiose to believe that literary criticism can contribute to revital-

izing the languages and ideas that reveal and shape our common life. The literature we produce, both the literary and the critical texts, will help fashion the world it recounts. We can only accomplish the society we can conceive. What we construct will be as free or constrained, mean or magnanimous, just or exploitative, as what we imagine. It is not just a cliché that in making our past we are choosing our future. Far from over, the past is always just beginning.

Notes

Introduction: Literature and Society

1 All references to Spenser's poems are to J. C. Smith and E. de Sélincourt, eds., *Spenser: Poetical Works* (London: Oxford University Press, 1912). References to the eclogues indicate line numbers; references to other parts of *The Shepheardes Calender* (e.g., emblems, epilogue, E.K.'s commentary) provide page number. Throughout, I have silently amended the letters *u, v, i, j,* and other obsolete orthographic usages, where necessary, to accord with modern practice.

2 The phrase is from J. Hillis Miller's 1986 presidential address to the Modern Language Association (*PMLA* 102 [1987]: 283).

3 M. P. Tilley, *A Dictionary of the Proverbs in England in the Sixteenth and Seventeenth Centuries* (Ann Arbor: University of Michigan Press, 1950), 203; *OED*, s.v. "lick" 1.

4 Virgil, eclogue 3, and Theocritus, idyll 1. The repeated word *warre* (26, 28) merges the artifactual character of poetry (a *warre* was a knot in timber) with the conflict that is its subject.

5 The author refers to himself as a "shepheards swaine" in his introductory poem, as does Colin Clout, the poem's most important poet figure (April 98).

6 Edward Said, *The World, the Text, and the Critic* (Cambridge: Harvard University Press, 1983), 290–92; Frank Lentricchia, *After the New Criticism* (Chicago: University of Chicago Press, 1980), xiii; Annabel Patterson, *Censorship and Interpretation: The Conditions of Writing and Reading in Early Modern England* (Madison: University of Wisconsin Press, 1984), 23; Terry Eagleton, *The Function of Criticism: From the Spectator to Post-Structuralism* (London: Verso, 1987), 7. These critics also suggest the unsuspected costs to our society of an essentialist aesthetic, however distant it might seem from "real life" concerns. Delegitimating the social and political, this perspective reinforces "the

177

privatized condition of social life" and "the depoliticization of [our] citizenry," remarks Edward Said (292, 25), a condition evident in the takeover of public functions by private interests, the appropriation of public resources for private purposes, and public opinion produced by media maneuvering rather than the deliberation of citizens. By locating cultural authority in a purely personal realm, the essentialist perspective, inadvertently or not, aligns itself with this trend toward the erosion of the public sphere, depriving us of resources that could assist us in understanding and acting on social and political reality. For a concrete example of how such criticism works against social understanding, see Richard Ohmann with Carol Ohmann, "A Case Study in Canon Formation: Reviewers, Critics, and *The Catcher in the Rye*," chapter 4 of Richard Ohmann, *Politics of Letters* (Middletown, Conn.: Wesleyan University Press, 1987).

7   I have borrowed the word *negotiation* from Lee Patterson (*Negotiating the Past: The Historical Understanding of Medieval Literature* [Madison: University of Wisconsin Press, 1987]), who uses it to refer to engaging the oppositions inherent in historical study between "the otherness of the past" and the historian's contemporary situation and between "the particularity and detail" of the past and the larger context that affords that detail significance (ix–x). This is somewhat different from Ann Rosalind Jones (*The Currency of Eros: Women's Love Lyric in Europe, 1540–1620* [Bloomington: Indiana University Press, 1990]), who focuses on the response of the sixteenth- and seventeenth-century women writers to the dominant and dominantly male literary genres available to them (5). My use is rather more different from that of Stephen Greenblatt (*Shakespearean Negotiations: The Circulation of Social Energy in Renaissance England* [Berkeley: University of California Press, 1988]), who refers to exchanges whereby "cultural capital" of various sorts is impersonally transferred from one discourse, institution, or other social location to another (7, 12).

8   Michael Murrin, *The Veil of Allegory: Some Notes Toward a Theory of Allegorical Rhetoric in the English Renaissance* (Chicago: University of Chicago Press, 1969), 121, 163.

9   Nancy Jo Hoffman, *Spenser's Pastorals: "The Shepheardes Calender" and "Colin Clout"* (Baltimore: Johns Hopkins University Press, 1977), 120, 54. She writes, "The grandeur of Spenser's generalizations contradict and overshadow the particular facts of any single character's life" (127).

10   Paul Alpers, "Pastoral and the Domain of Lyric in Spenser's *Shepheardes Calender*," *Representations* 12 (1985): 94, 95, 96–97. The objection Alpers attempts to refute is that of the new historicist Louis Montrose. Alpers writes, "I think 'domain' takes cultural and ideological elements into account, because it conceives 'aesthetic space' in terms of rule and authority" (94).

11   "The vision . . . turns out to be primarily a fixture of pastoral art, not political life" (Hoffman, *Spenser's Pastorals* x).

12   Ibid., x, ix. When, in *Colin Clout*, Spenser "brings the unaccommodated poor into view and expresses some bitterness about his own situation . . . [t]hese seemingly unselfconscious intrusions ruin the aesthetics of the mode" (xi).

13   Ibid., xi, 3.

14 Murrin, *Veil of Allegory* 14, 13.

15 Allan Bloom, *The Closing of the American Mind* (New York: Simon and Schuster, 1987), 381, 264. "Men may live more truly and fully in reading Plato and Shakespeare than at any other time, because then they are participating in essential being and are forgetting their accidental lives" (380).

16 "The regime of philosopher-kings is usually ridiculed and regarded as totalitarian, but it contains much of what we really want. Practically everyone wants reason to rule, and no one thinks a man like Socrates should be ruled by inferiors or have to adjust what he thinks to them" (Bloom, *Closing* 266).

17 Ibid., 49, 372, 289.

18 Yuri Afanasiev, "The Past and Ourselves," in *Kommunist* (Sept. 1985), quoted in the *Nation*, Oct. 24, 1987, p. 448.

19 Paul McLane, *Spenser's "Shepheardes Calendar": A Study in Elizabethan Allegory* (Notre Dame, Ind.: University of Notre Dame Press, 1961). Louis Montrose describes this criticism as the "detective work" of assembling and analyzing clues to determine the "*real*" identity of poetic figures ("Renaissance Literary Studies and the Subject of History," *ELR* 16 [1986]: 6).

20 Montrose, "Renaissance Literary Studies" 8, 6.

21 I have in mind particularly Stephen Greenblatt's essay "Invisible Bullets: Renaissance Authority and Its Subversion, *Henry IV* and *Henry V*," in *Political Shakespeare: New Essays in Cultural Materialism*, ed. Jonathan Dollimore and Alan Sinfield (Ithaca, N.Y.: Cornell University Press, 1985), 18–47.

22 See Frank Lentricchia, *Ariel and the Police: Michel Foucault, William James, Wallace Stevens* (Madison: University of Wisconsin Press, 1988), 86–102; James Holstun, "Ranting at the New Historicism," *ELR* 19 (1989): 189–225; and David Norbrook, "Life and Death of Renaissance Man," *Raritan* 8 (1989): 89–110.

23 While the creative process I am describing may not be completely within the control of rational consciousness, that does not detract from the status and significance of Spenser's agency, the intention to create a text whose meaning can be traced, at least theoretically, to that intention.

24 Montrose, "Renaissance Literary Studies" 8. See Patterson, *Negotiating the Past* 62.

25 See Alan Liu's criticism of new historicism for linking the two only through the suggestiveness of metaphor, which posits an analogy between text and context ("an intertextuality of culture") without spelling out the precise connections ("reference") between them or the role of historical evidence in articulating those connections ("The Power of Formalism: The New Historicism," *ELH* 58 [1989]: 743–44). The result is, in Liu's view, a new formalism that allows for, even encourages, a narcissistic projection of the desire for "a refuge of intellect" onto history (752). Though his analysis of new historicism is provocative and often incisive (e.g., he explores the centrality of theatricality and the subsuming of action by the subject in its accounts), he fails to examine the predispositions about society that those features embody or generate. As a result, his reliance on a greater self-awareness among new historicists about assumptions and method does not seem the most profitable corrective. Rather, addressing more openly the

question that underlies much of Liu's discussion—why has it proven so difficult to get history into literary studies—would point simultaneously to philosophical inheritance and social situation, whose interwoven character historicism postulates.

26 For a different kind of reading animated by a similar concern for the *Calender*'s social and political dimension, see *The Shepheardes Calender: An Introduction* (University Park: Pennsylvania State University Press, 1990), by Lynn Staley Johnson, who views the moral eclogues as "explor[ing] the conflicts inherent in the institutions and relationships of [Spenser's] own day" but articulates those relationships in abstract philosophical terms, through "subjects like ambition, desire, greed, luxury, folly, laziness, and duty" (53, 59).

27 Pastoral was, according to Louis Montrose, "dominantly aristocratic in values and style" ("Of Gentlemen and Shepherds: The Politics of Elizabethan Pastoral Form," *ELH* 50 [1983]: 426).

28 See, for example, Louis Montrose, " 'Eliza, Queene of shepheardes,' and the Pastoral of Power," *ELR* 10 (1980): 153–82. See also Gary Waller's emphasis on the control of culture by the court in *English Poetry of the Sixteenth Century* (London: Longman Group, 1986), 13–22, 108, 267–68.

29 Waller, *English Poetry* 15 (the phrase "instrument of state" is Sir Henry Wotton's), 41; Louis Montrose, " 'The perfecte paterne of a Poete': The Poetics of Courtship in *The Shepheardes Calender*," *TSLL* 21 (1979): 42; Waller, 178, describing Spenser.

30 Louis Montrose, "The Elizabethan Subject and the Spenserian Text," in *Literary Theory / Renaissance Texts*, ed. Patricia Parker and David Quint (Baltimore: Johns Hopkins University Press, 1986), 317. He cites as examples "the dynamic relationships among various status, occupational, and age groups, [and] among numerous political factions, religious sects, and regional loyalties" (317).

31 See Annabel Patterson's criticism of Montrose on these grounds in *Pastoral and Ideology: Virgil to Valéry* (Berkeley: University of California Press, 1987), 130–31. See also David Norbrook, *Poetry and Politics in the English Renaissance* (London: Routledge and Kegan Paul, 1984), 3. Norbrook's work is a striking exception to the historicist overemphasis on patronage.

32 Montrose rules out "any concerted program of sedition, of political opposition or subversion," allowing only for "the text registering . . . felt but perhaps not consciously articulated contradiction[s]" between poet and social or political conditions ("Elizabethan Subject," 323). See also Waller, *English Poetry* 10–12.

33 Montrose, "Of Gentlemen and Shepherds" 427.

34 Montrose at one point refers to "the inevitable collusion between scholarship and power" ("Of Gentlemen and Shepherds" 438). While the specific reference is to Puttenham, the phrase resists confinement to that context.

35 Montrose suggests as much when he identifies as an important motivation for their work "a questioning of our very capacity for action . . . a nagging sense of professional, institutional, and political impotence" ("Renaissance Literary Studies" 11–12).

36 My point is distinct from, though it has affinities with, the convergence James Holstun points out between old and new historicisms in their focus on canoni-

cal works as revelatory of cultural totalities ("Ranting" 189–225). In specifying the convergence between these critical approaches in their treatment of the aristocratic character of culture and the phenomenon of class in general, my analysis shows how much less distinct the lines between high culture and popular culture, canonical and noncanonical works, are than critics have assumed.

37   See Montrose, "Elizabethan Subject" 318.

38   "While Spenser lacks the acumen and clarity . . . to designate the *source* of exploitative human relations . . . his largeness of mind allows him . . . to demonstrate that the psychological questions of how to live most interest him" (Hoffman, *Spenser's Pastorals* 118). See also p. 114.

39   Patrick Cullen, *Spenser, Marvell, and Renaissance Pastoral* (Cambridge: Harvard University Press, 1970), 62, 66. In contrast, Hobbinol's "pragmatic ideal . . . of moderation" (31), his "practical understanding of human nature, his realization that the shepherd is a man like other men, is a useful qualification of the Mantuanesque Diggon Davie's wild-eyed, lofty but unrealistic demand for perpetual vigilance" (32). Cullen does comment on Hobbinol's limitations, but the preference for his character over Diggon's is palpable.

40   For case studies of historical accounts "psychoanalyzing the dissenter," see the essay of that name in Howard Zinn, *The Politics of History* (Urbana: University of Illinois Press, 1990), 153–66. "Psychological explanations are comforting," according to Zinn, "because they emphasize the irrationality of the protester rather than the irrationality of that which produces protest" (165).

41   R. H. Tawney, *The Agrarian Problem in the Sixteenth Century* (New York: Harper and Row, 1967), 271.

42   Paul L. Hughes and James F. Larkin, eds., *Tudor Royal Proclamations*, vol. 2, *The Later Tudors* (New Haven: Yale University Press, 1969), 115.

1   Historicisms and 1579

1   The social theorist Roberto Unger sees this as characteristic of all social conflict: "The endless, petty practical and imaginative quarrels . . . may escalate at any time into structure-subverting fights" (*Social Theory: Its Situation and Its Task* [Cambridge: Cambridge University Press, 1987], 6).

2   Statute of Silence, 23 Eliz. 1, c. 2; Paul L. Hughes and James F. Larkin, eds., *Tudor Royal Proclamations*, vol. 2, *The Later Tudors* (New Haven: Yale University Press, 1969), 501, 506, 488. The religious dissenters were Robert Browne and Robert Harrison.

3   Ralph Houlbrooke, "The Protestant Episcopate, 1547–1603: The Pastoral Contribution," in *Church and Society in England: Henry VIII to James I*, ed. Felicity Heal and Rosemary O'Day (London: Macmillan, 1977), 83.

4   Wallace T. MacCaffrey, *Queen Elizabeth and the Making of Policy, 1572–1588* (Princeton, N.J.: Princeton University Press, 1981), 105 and 107 (quoting Whitgift), 105, 109; Patrick Collinson, *Archbishop Grindal, 1519–1583: The Struggle for a Reformed Church* (London: Jonathan Cape, 1979), 288.

5   See MacCaffrey, *Queen Elizabeth* 110–15. The Crown also confiscated the bill

and supporting book of church discipline; Patrick Collinson, *The Elizabethan Puritan Movement* (Berkeley: University of California Press, 1967), 310–12.

6   Collinson, *Elizabethan Puritan Movement* 274, 397. See J. B. Black, *The Reign of Elizabeth, 1558–1603* (Oxford: Clarendon, 1936), 165–66.

7   35 Eliz. 1, c. 1.

8   The copious literature on this subject includes Frances A. Yates, *Astraea: The Imperial Theme in the Sixteenth Century* (London: Routledge and Kegan Paul, 1975); Roy Strong, *The Cult of Elizabeth: Elizabethan Portraiture and Pageantry* (London: Thames and Hudson, 1977), and *Gloriana: The Portraits of Queen Elizabeth I* (New York: Thames and Hudson, 1987); Philippa Berry, *Of Chastity and Power: Elizabethan Literature and the Unmarried Queen* (London: Routledge, 1989); Jean Wilson, *Entertainments for Elizabeth I* (Totowa, N.J.: Rowman and Littlefield, 1980); David Bergeron, *English Civic Pageantry, 1558–1642* (Columbia: University of South Carolina Press, 1971); and E. C. Wilson, *England's Eliza* (Cambridge: Harvard University Press, 1939).

9   Strong, *Cult of Elizabeth* 120. "By the end of [her] reign," according to Penry Williams, "the tone of public acclamation was pitched high and shrill" (*The Tudor Regime* [Oxford: Clarendon, 1979], 370).

10   Strong, *Cult of Elizabeth* 115.

11   Roberto Unger, *Passion: An Essay on Personality* (New York: Free Press, 1984), 106.

12   "The primary purpose of a state portrait," as Strong notes, "was . . . not to portray an individual as such, but to invoke through that person's image the abstract principles of their rule" (*Gloriana* 36). See also Williams, *Tudor Regime* 361f.

13   Strong finds that the queen's portraits reflected "a policy of deliberate rejuvenation" traceable to this anxiety. The Privy Council's 1596 order that unseemly portraits of the queen be destroyed was a further attempt to dampen it (*Gloriana* 20, 14).

14   Louis Montrose, "The Elizabethan Subject and the Spenserian Text," in *Literary Theory / Renaissance Texts*, ed. Patricia Parker and David Quint (Baltimore: Johns Hopkins University Press, 1986), 320–23.

15   John Frederick Nims, ed., *Ovid's Metamorphoses: The Arthur Golding Translation, 1567* (New York: Macmillan, 1965), 6. 185–399. Further citations of this edition are in the text.

16   Jonathan Goldberg calls it "a troubled center" accountable by the fact that April's praise "is founded on elegiac strains" (*Voice Terminal Echo: Postmodernism and English Renaissance Texts* [New York: Methuen, 1986], 52–53). Thomas H. Cain calls it "an odd sour note" explainable by the "inappropriateness" of "too great comparison to the virgin Diana" (*Praise in "The Faerie Queene"* [Lincoln: University of Nebraska Press, 1978], 18).

17   Montrose, "Elizabethan Subject" 337. The destruction of Niobe's "children" would also have suggested the common belief that the people suffered for their sovereign's faults.

18   Latona complains about just this conduct: "Most railing words hath Niobe to my defacing rackt" (*Met.* 6.268).

19   John Phillips, *The Reformation of Images: Destruction of Art in England, 1535–1660* (Berkeley: University of California Press, 1973), 120.

20   George Gascoigne, "The Princely Pleasures at Kenilworth Castle," in *The Complete Works of George Gascoigne*, vol. 2, ed. John Cunliffe (Grosse Pointe, Mich.: Scholarly Press, 1969), 93.

21   Jean Wilson, *Entertainments* 22. The illustration is discussed in Strong, *Gloriana* 65–69. George Puttenham invoked the same myth as a vehicle for compliment, declaring: "I have vowed while I live, / T'addore all three godheads [Juno, Venus, and Minerva] in your own starre" (from his *Partheniades* [1579], in *Ballads from Manuscripts*, ed. W. A. Morfill [Hertford, Eng.: Stephen Austin and Sons, 1873], 76).

22   Cain, *Praise* 16. He characterizes the references to Elizabeth as "without spotte" (50) and with "no mortall blemishe" (54), as "making Eliza's birth a variety of Immaculate Conception" (16). See also Wilson, *England's Eliza* 200–229.

23   Those who were sensitized to representations of divinity objected to the implications of Elizabeth's cult. One Puritan was imprisoned in 1581 for opposing the elevation of her Accession Day to a holy day because it would make the queen "a god" (Strong, *Cult of Elizabeth* 125–26).

24   In describing a general feature of Spenser's poetry, Montrose says, "It is precisely by calling attention to its own processes of representation that Spenser's art calls into question the status of the authority it represents" ("Elizabethan Subject" 331).

25   Ibid., 307. Niobe would not have fallen "had she not / So thought hir selfe" (*Met.* 6.195–96).

26   As is often true at moments in the text heavily charged with political potential, E.K.'s gloss is misleading. First, Himera was Stesichorus's "native town, not his mistress," which invalidates E.K.'s suggestion of a female rivalry as Stesichorus's motive; William A. Oram et al., eds., *The Yale Edition of the Shorter Poems of Edmund Spenser* (New Haven: Yale University Press, 1989), 78. Moreover, rather than criticizing Helen on the aesthetic grounds of her inferior beauty, Stesichorus in all likelihood leveled a moral criticism against her for her role in igniting the Trojan War. The speculation of *The Oxford Classical Dictionary* (Oxford: Clarendon, 1970) is suggestive: "Perhaps the truth behind this [legend] is that Stesichorus outraged opinion which regarded Helen as a goddess, as it did in Sparta" (1013).

27   Plato, *Phaedrus* 243, from *The Dialogues of Plato*, trans. Benjamin Jowett (Chicago: Encyclopaedia Britannica, 1952), 123.

28   See June 25–31, 57, and April 38, 64–65, 100–112, and 121.

29   Less pointed but still disturbing are the overtones of April in the February eclogue. The destructive competition of the earlier eclogue, accomplished chiefly through a rhetoric of praise for a royal figure (often cast in flower imagery, following the common sixteenth-century metaphor for rhetorical adornment), creates an uneasiness about such rhetoric, so central to April's song.

30   13 Eliz. 1, c. 1. See Jonathan Crewe, *Hidden Designs: The Critical Profession and Renaissance Literature* (New York: Methuen, 1986), 67.

31 Phillips, *Reformation of Images* 120. The motto is associated with the phoenix, the embodiment of immortality (Yates, *Astraea* 65).

32 A number of critics have noted the connection. See Edwin A. Greenlaw et al., eds., *The Works of Edmund Spenser: A Variorum Edition*, 11 vols. (Baltimore: Johns Hopkins University Press, 1932–57), vol. 7, pt. 1, pp. 398–402; S. K. Heninger, Jr., ed., *Selections from the Poetical Works of Edmund Spenser* (Boston: Houghton-Mifflin, 1970), 33, 93; and Ruth Samson Luborsky, "The Illustrations to *The Shepheardes Calender*," *SSt* 2 (1981): 38. The link is underscored by the elements the two eclogues share: the same dialogue and song structure (*Yale* 185) with similar verse forms introducing the songs; the figures of Thenot and Colin, the latter of whom is referred to in both as a shepherd's swain; and the presence of water nymphs, Graces, and garlands of flowers, bays, and olives.

33 The identification is reinforced by a number of allusions: Dido's other name (in the *Aeneid* Dido was also "Elisa"); her description as the daughter of "the greate shepehearde" (38), harking back to April's identification of Pan as Elisa's father; and E.K.'s references in his argument to "some mayden of greate bloud" and, mistakenly, to Marot's poem "which he made upon the death of Loys the frenche Queene" (460). Marot's poem was not for the queen but for the queen mother. See Paul McLane, *Spenser's "Shepheardes Calender": A Study in Elizabethan Allegory* (Notre Dame, Ind.: University of Notre Dame Press, 1961), chap. 4; and Mary Parmenter, "Spenser's *Twelve Aeglogues Proportionable to the Twelve Monethes*," *ELH* 3 (1936): 214–16.

34 Elizabeth, Parmenter suggests, "had of late been 'dead' indeed to the Earl of Leicester, to the Sidneys, to all who saw her true self lost and gone by reason of her policy of marrying the heir to the throne of France" ("Spenser's *Twelve Aeglogues*" 214). This is McLane's reading: "In the last five months of 1579 the group of English statesmen led by Leicester, Walsingham, and the Sidneys regarded the Alençon marriage as threatening the real and actual death of England, Elizabeth, and themselves" (*Spenser's "Shepheardes Calender"* 50).

35 *The Dutchy of Lancaster's Case* (1562) in *The Commentaries or Reports of Edmund Plowden, Part I* (London: S. Brooke, 1816), 213. See Ernst H. Kantorowicz, *The King's Two Bodies: A Study in Medieval Political Theology* (Princeton, N.J.: Princeton University Press, 1957).

36 See Marie Axton, *The Queen's Two Bodies: Drama and the Elizabethan Succession* (London: Royal Historical Society, 1977), chaps. 2 and 3. *The Dutchy of Lancaster's Case* 217.

37 This effect had its roots partly in the affinities the political theory had with the theological doctrine of the twofold nature of Christ as God and man. See Kantorowicz, *King's Two Bodies* 15–19.

38 Quoted in Axton, *Queen's Two Bodies* 38. See the discussion in Leah Marcus, *Puzzling Shakespeare: Local Reading and Its Discontents* (Berkeley: University of California Press, 1988), 53–66.

39 Quoted in Axton, *Queen's Two Bodies* 14. The prince's decease was not even called a death, but rather a "demise" (Kantorowicz, *King's Two Bodies* 13, from a 1561 case).

40   The queen's near-fatal attack of smallpox in 1562 was a dramatic demonstration of the fragility of her reign.

41   Elizabeth wanted to eliminate parliamentary participation in determining the succession, trying unsuccessfully to remove a provision the Commons added to the treason statute cited above that made it treasonous to assert that the queen *with Parliament* could not determine the succession by statutes "of suffycyent force and valyditie to lymit and bynd the Crowne of this Realme" (in MacCaffrey, *Queen Elizabeth* 475–76).

42   The temporal segregation is reinforced by a spatial one. "*There* lives shee" sums up the pattern of references to the other place Dido now inhabits (187, 188, 191, 195).

43   H. Oskar Sommer, ed. *The Kalender of Shepherdes*, 3 vols. (London: Kegan Paul, Trench, Trübner and Co., 1892), 3:19. [Note: three volumes published in a single binding. Each volume is paginated separately.]

44   Quoted in Collinson, *Grindal* 244.

45   Strong, *Cult of Elizabeth* 114; Christopher Haigh, introduction to *The Reign of Elizabeth I*, ed. Christopher Haigh (Athens: University of Georgia Press, 1985), 4; Roy Strong, "The Popular Celebration of the Accession Day of Queen Elizabeth I," *JWCI* 21 (1958): 91. According to Strong, this celebration was a central element in the diversion of religious energy to the Crown's political purposes.

46   November is the only eclogue in which Colin's appearance is unequivocal. In both January and December another voice brackets his appearance.

47   The repeated rhyme of *herse*—referring not only to the bier but also to the funeral eulogy—with *verse* points to the potential of Colin's poetry: to *make* Elizabeth's fame ("The honor now of highest gods she is" [197]) and thereby to provide the continuity her mortality disrupts.

2   "Emongste the Meaner Sorte": The Social Orientation of the *Calender*

1   Count Annibale Romei, *Courtiers Academie*, trans. John Kempers (London, 1598), 267.

2   The phrase is from a royal proclamation. Paul L. Hughes and James F. Larkin, eds., *Tudor Royal Proclamations*, vol. 2, *The Later Tudors* (New Haven: Yale University Press, 1969), 449.

3   William Harrison, *The Description of England*, ed. Georges Edelen (Ithaca, N.Y.: Cornell University Press, 1968), 94; Richard Mulcaster, *Positions* (1581), quoted in David Cressy, "Describing the Social Order of Elizabethan and Stuart England," *Literature and History* 3 (1976): 30–31.

4   Raymond Williams, *Marxism and Literature* (Oxford: Oxford University Press, 1977), 110; Richard Ohmann, *Politics of Letters* (Middletown, Conn.: Wesleyan University Press, 1987), 205; Louis Montrose, "Renaissance Literary Studies and the Subject of History," *ELR* 16 (1986): 9.

5   Hannah Arendt, *Between Past and Future: Six Exercises in Political Thought*

(Cleveland: World Publishing Company, 1963), 97. Royal proclamations routinely described religious dissenters as working to "break," "burst asunder," or "impeach and subvert the universal quietness and peace of this realm" (Hughes and Larkin, *Proclamations* 2: 347, 343, 376–77).

6   Claire Cross, *The Royal Supremacy in the Elizabethan Church* (London: Allen and Unwin, 1969), 129; Hughes and Larkin, *Proclamations* 2: 99; *Certain Sermons or Homilies Appointed to Be Read in Churches* (London: Society for Promoting Christian Knowledge, 1899), 590–91, hereinafter cited as *Homilies*.

7   Hughes and Larkin, *Proclamations* 2: 99. Official prayers, including Elizabeth's own, reiterate this theme, referring to "thy [God's] chosen servant Elizabeth," who was "by thy mighty hand brought to reign over us," and offering thanks for this selection of God's. See John E. Booty, ed., *The Book of Common Prayer, 1559: The Elizabethan Prayer Book* (Washington, D.C.: Folger Shakespeare Library, 1976), 250; William Keatinge Clay, ed., *Private Prayers Put Forth by Authority During the Reign of Queen Elizabeth* (Cambridge: Cambridge University Press, 1851), 480; William Keatinge Clay, ed., *Liturgical Services of the Reign of Queen Elizabeth* (Cambridge: Cambridge University Press, 1847), 457f.; Elizabeth I, *A Book of Devotions Composed by Her Majesty*, with translations by Adam Fox (Gerrards Cross, Eng.: Colin Smythe, 1970), 23.

8   Reinhard Bendix, *Kings or People: Power and the Mandate to Rule* (Berkeley: University of California Press, 1978), 221.

9   Claiming Constantine was born the son of an Englishwoman, Foxe presents him in his dedication as the model for Elizabeth to emulate (*Actes and Monuments* [London: John Day, 1563], B.i.). See also S.R. Cattley, ed., *The Acts and Monuments of John Foxe*, 8 vols. (London: R.B. Seeley and W. Burnside, 1837–41), 1:280–304, 312; and John Jewel, *An Apology of the Church of England*, ed. John E. Booty (Ithaca, N.Y.: Cornell University Press, 1963), 116–19. In 1578 Richard Cox, bishop of Ely, also praised Elizabeth as "truly godly, that comest so near to the example of Constantine the Great"; John Strype, *Annals of the Reformation* (Oxford: Clarendon, 1824; reprint, New York: Burt Franklin, n.d.), vol. 2, pt. 2, 182. Foxe's dedication repeated the language of the Act of Supremacy in extolling Elizabeth as "next under the Lorde, as well in causes ecclesiastical, as also to the temporall state appertaining" (*Actes and Monuments* [London: John Day, 1563], B.i).

10   The frequent dedications of religious works such as Foxe's and various editions of the Bible (both the Bishops' Bible and the Geneva Bible) testify to the vitality of Elizabeth's image as patroness of the reformed church. Felicity Heal and Rosemary O'Day describe how "Elizabeth was able to take advantage of her bishops' fervent belief that she alone could protect the Protestant faith: a variety of unpalatable policies were accepted by them as *adiaphora*, things indifferent," not required by Scripture and thus subject to royal command; introduction to *Church and Society in England: Henry VIII to James I*, ed. Felicity Heal and Rosemary O'Day (London: Macmillan, 1977), 12.

11   Bendix, *Kings or People* 219–20.

12   Sir Fulke Greville Brooke, *The Life of Philip Sidney* (Oxford: Clarendon, 1907), 67–68.

13   *Homilies* 109, 326, 626. The Geneva Bible glosses *pride* in Proverbs 11:2 as "when man forgetteth himself, and thinketh to be exalted above his vocation." (*The Geneva Bible: A Facsimile of the 1561 Edition* [Madison: University of Wisconsin Press, 1969].)

14   *Homilies* 612; John Ayre, ed., *The Works of John Whitgift*, 3 vols. (Cambridge: Cambridge University Press, 1851–53), 3:579. All quotations from Whitgift are from these volumes.

15   *Calendar of State Papers, Domestic* 7:172, 221; Anthony Fletcher, *Tudor Rebellions* (London: Longmans, Green and Co., 1968), 100–101.

16   According to Patrick Collinson, "the physical arrangement at church assemblies, and especially the seating, were a deliberate demonstration of social difference. . . . Wooden pews and stalls froze the orders of society in a static and visually edifying representation of hierarchy" (*The Religion of Protestants: The Church in English Society, 1559–1625* [Oxford: Clarendon, 1982], 194–95). It was not so static as to eliminate contention, however, for "disputes over seating were endemic in parish life and they normally reflected contests for social precedence" (141).

17   Jewel, *Apology* 24.

18   Whitgift, *Works* 1:344; 2:399; and 3:537. See also 1:478; 2:239, 280–81, 384. The section on church hierarchy is by far the longest in Whitgift's *Defence of the Answer to the Admonition*. Hierarchy was not just religious and political doctrine, of course. Degree constituted a pervasive social reality embodied in important institutions and everyday conventions, down to bodily gestures, dress, and forms of address. Whitgift, for example, considered it anti-Christian to omit titles, whose function was to teach "us to acknowledge our duty towards our superiors, and their authority over us" (2:189–90). Perhaps the most visible sign of degree was dress, on which Elizabeth's regime focused intense attention, issuing no fewer than ten proclamations for enforcement of the sumptuary laws regulating apparel according to social status. Lawrence Stone, *The Crisis of the Aristocracy, 1558–1641* (Oxford: Clarendon, 1979), 29; see the discussion of sumptuary legislation in Frank Whigham, *Ambition and Privilege: The Social Tropes of Elizabethan Courtesy Theory* (Berkeley: University of California Press, 1984), 155–69. There was also a homily directed specifically "Against Excess of Apparel," which declared: "All may not look to wear like apparel, but every one according to his degree, as God hath placed him" (*Homilies* 326). The "vulgar people" were held particularly culpable: "No sort of people have so much exceeded," another proclamation declared, "or do daily exceed in the excess of apparel . . . than such as be of the meaner sort" (Hughes and Larkin, *Proclamations* 2:187; reiterated in a further proclamation later that same year [193]). Specifying rank among the elite was important, but differentiating them from the commons (itself considered undifferentiated) was crucial.

19   James I's declaration "No bishops, no king, no nobility," encapsulates this inter-

dependence of social, political, and religious hierarchy. Godfrey Goodman, *The Court of King James the First*, vol. 1 (London: Richard Bentley, 1839), 421.

20 Alexander Nowell, *A Catechism* (Cambridge: Cambridge University Press, 1853), 130. The alignment of this work with government policy is indicated by Nowell's letter to Cecil, promising not to publish it without Cecil's approval (vi).

21 Ibid., 131. As the queen succinctly put it: "All in authority ought to be credited" (speech on the opening of Parliament, 1562, from George P. Rice, Jr., *The Public Speaking of Queen Elizabeth: Selections from Her Official Addresses* [New York: Columbia University Press, 1951], 120). Offenses against different authorities were frequently defined in the same terms, so that the murder of a master by a servant was a form of "treason," though hierarchy was preserved by labeling it "petty treason"; Keith Thomas, "Work and Leisure," *Past and Present* 29 (1964): 52.

22 *Homilies* 110. This passage implies the innate lawlessness of the people, held in check only by rule, as Bishop Edwin Sandys declared in 1573: "Take away authority, and the people will rush headlong into everything that is bad" (quoted in Cross, *Royal Supremacy* 161).

23 In the catechism in *The Book of Common Prayer* the communicant vows "to submit myself to all my governors, teachers, spiritual pastors, and masters" (286).

24 Sir Thomas Smith, *De Republica Anglorum*, ed. L. Alston (Cambridge: Cambridge University Press, 1906), 46; Whitgift, *Works* 3:275; Stone, *Crisis* 51; Smith 46.

25 In Elizabeth's England "the expression of personal opinions—and in matters of policy, the very possession of personal opinions" constituted, according to Louis Montrose, "a privilege granted . . . to a very few" (" 'The perfecte paterne of a Poete': The Poetics of Courtship in *The Shepheardes Calender*," *TSLL* 21 [1979]: 48).

26 While some useful recent work has emphasized the political importance of "the middling sort" (see Theodore B. Leinwand, "Negotiation and the New Historicism," *PMLA* 105 [1990]: 477–90), this group's political role as defined and constrained by the ideology of hierarchy was confined to executing others' laws, rather than initiating policies or policy changes or, as we see here, even exercising "judgment" on the policies forged by others.

27 Hughes and Larkin, *Proclamations* 2:449.

28 *Homilies* 593. Shakespeare's bishop of Carlisle puts it more succinctly: "What subject can give sentence on his king?" (*Richard II* 4.1.121). Official doctrine preempted the subjects' censure of wrongful government by depicting the prince's injustice as God's judgment on *them* and, as such, a trial to be borne patiently and penitently. "God," the *Homilies* declared, "maketh a wicked man to reign for the sins of the people" (594–95, citing Job 34:30). Foxe frequently reiterates this theme, citing examples of "what mischief and inconvenience groweth in commonweals . . . where the subjects forget the office of christian patience in suffering their prince's injuries by God's wrath inflicted for their sins" (*Acts* 2:539). This claim diverts attention from the responsibility of those in power to

the moral condition of those who suffer at their hands, a sophisticated version of the "blame the victim" strategy. Using God to thus ratify even the injustice of the powerful, it works to deprive criticism of moral authority, a strategy rationalized by the claim that "a rebel is worse than the worst prince, and rebellion worse than the worst government of the worst prince" (*Homilies* 594).

1 Peter 2:13–15 and Romans 13:1–6 were frequently cited in support of the doctrine of nonresistance because the duty of obedience they prescribe is unconditional. This doctrine is in sharp contrast with other Protestant views stressing the provisional character of obedience, views occasioned in large part by exile during Mary's reign and the St. Bartholomew's Day Massacre in 1572. See A. F. Scott Pearson, *Church and State: Political Aspects of Sixteenth-Century Puritanism* (Cambridge: Cambridge University Press, 1928), chap. 4; and Quentin Skinner, *The Foundations of Modern Political Thought*, vol. 2, *The Age of Reformation* (Cambridge: Cambridge University Press, 1978), pt. 3.

29 Whitgift, *Works* 2:241, 1:570. He acknowledges that the people may, at times, decide correctly, but only "most rarely" and only by coincidence (570).

30 Ibid., 3:568–70. "They be not able to judge of controversies according to learning and knowledge, and therefore are ruled by affection, and carried headlong with blind zeal into divers sinister judgments and erroneous opinions" (1:49). The common image of this trait was "the monster of many heads," incorporated into the September eclogue of the *Calender*. See Christopher Hill, "The Many-Headed Monster," in his *Change and Continuity in Seventeenth-Century England* (Cambridge: Harvard University Press, 1975), 181–204.

31 Whitgift, *Works* 3:578, 574, 573. Typically, even when commoners engage in political action, through rebellion or other sedition, they are not presented as agents initiating that activity, but as the passive targets of others' inducements, mobilized only by *their* energy, "seduced," as Whitgift put it, "by false prophets and contentious teachers" (3:569) and "easily brought by ambitious persons to give their consent to unworthy men" (1:467). Incapacitated by their lack of judgment in the minds of the authorities, the people are rendered vulnerable to such "abuse." The regime frequently justified its repressive action as providing needed protection for the people against such mistreatment.

32 John Bruce and Thomas Perowne, eds., *Correspondence of Matthew Parker* (Cambridge: Cambridge University Press, 1853), 223–25. According to *The Book of Common Prayer* God is the "lover of concord" (59). Dire consequences resulted from going against that nature. Elizabeth's lord keeper, Nicholas Bacon, spelled out the causal chain: "Diversity of minds maketh seditions, seditions bring in tumults, tumults make insurrections and rebellions, insurrections make depopulations and bring in utter ruin and destruction of mens bodies, goods and lands" (quoted in D. M. Loades, "The Theory and Practice of Censorship in Sixteenth-Century England," *Transactions of the Royal Historical Society*, 5th ser., 24 [1974]: 142).

33 *Book of Common Prayer* 16.

34 *Homilies* 110, 588. It is in the discussion of obedience in the "Homily Against

Disobedience and Wilful Rebellion," occasioned by the Northern Rebellion of
1569, that the convergence of religious injunction with this political duty is most
dramatic. The obedience owed to God, which is the centerpiece of "the original
kingdom of God," merges with that owed to the prince through an identification
of the two based on "that similitude of government" between them (587–92).
Political obedience thus becomes a central religious doctrine, its model, oddly
enough, Jesus, "an eternal example . . . to teach us to obey princes" (608). Con-
versely, rebellion is not just an attack on the prince but also a sin against God
for which the model is Lucifer, "the first author and founder of rebellion" (588).

35   *Homilies* 589.

36   Ohmann, *Politics of Letters* 81; Parker to William Cecil, Lord Burghley, July 18,
1573 (*Correspondence* 437). The emphasis on obedience went well beyond external conformity, encompassing the inner self as well. According to the *Homilies*,
the injunction to obedience extended to speech and even to inward complaint—
"murmuring"—recalling "the heavy wrath and dreadful indignation of Almighty
God against such subjects as do only but inwardly grudge, mutter, and mur-
mur against their governors; though their inward treason, so privily hatched
in their breasts, come not to open declaration of their doings" (617). Any impulse to dissent, however private and interior, was deemed a violation of the
subject's duty.

37   George Puttenham, *The Arte of English Poesie*, in *Elizabethan Critical Essays*,
ed. G. Gregory Smith, 2 vols. (Oxford: Clarendon, 1904), 2:1–193; unless otherwise indicated, all passages cited are to this volume. According to Puttenham's
editors, the composition of his work extended as far back as the mid-1560s,
even though it was not published until 1589 (*The Arte of English Poesie*, ed.
Gladys Doidge Willcock and Alice Walker [Cambridge: Cambridge University
Press, 1936], xliv–liii).

38   Puttenham, *Arte* 87, 164.

39   Ibid., 4. Her aesthetic prowess "easily surmounteth all the rest . . . even by as
much oddes as her owne excellent estate and degree exceedeth all the rest of her
most humble vassalls" (66).

40   Ibid., 158, 155, 177–78.

41   Queen Elizabeth's comment on Shakespeare's play, "I am Richard II, know ye
not that," reveals how sensitive she was to this pertinence (*The Life and Death
of Richard II*, ed. Matthew W. Black [Philadelphia: Lippincott, 1955], 582).

42   Puttenham, *Arte* 35, 36, 177, 35. Only extreme instances of princes' "wick-
ednes"—"the vanities of *Nero* [or] the ribaudries of Caligula"—qualified this
decorum of style. Everything else touching those who ruled—"their birth, alli-
aunces, governement, exploits in warre and peace, and other publike affaires"
(157)—required lofty rhetoric.

43   Jonathan Crewe sees Puttenham's discussion of tragedy in the context of the
hegemonic function of the institution of the theater (*Hidden Designs: The
Critical Profession and Renaissance Literature* [New York: Methuen, 1986]),
suggesting that Puttenham anticipates the model of subversion always already

contained by power found in much new historicist writing. See, for example, Stephen Greenblatt, "Invisible Bullets: Renaissance Authority and its Subversion, *Henry IV* and *Henry V*," in *Political Shakespeare: New Essays in Cultural Materialism*, ed. Jonathan Dollimore and Alan Sinfield (Ithaca, N.Y.: Cornell University Press, 1985), 18–47. Crewe, however, overlooks the persistent effort Puttenham has to mount to contain the critical impulses of all dramatic genres. He even discredits the specific character of the satire of "the old *Comedy*," preferring the generality of "the new *Comedy*" because it will avoid provoking antagonism that would threaten social peace (*Arte* 33–34). Far from revealing any inherent quality of the institutional theater, Puttenham works very hard to shape a theory consonant with the interests of those in power, with whom he saw himself as affiliated. It should be obvious that I reject Crewe's claim that Spenser wrote Puttenham's work. Regarding E.K. as providing support for that argument, see the discussion in chapter 3 about his function in the *Calender*.

44 Puttenham, *Arte* 142–43, 150, 62–63. This is the silence to which, according to John B. Thompson, "those dispossessed of the official language are condemned. . . . lacking the means of legitimate expression, they do not speak but are spoken to" (*Studies in the Theory of Ideology* [Berkeley: University of California Press, 1984], 46).

45 See Richard Foster Jones, *The Triumph of the English Language: A Survey of Opinions Concerning the Vernacular from the Introduction of Printing to the Restoration* (Stanford, Calif.: Stanford University Press, 1953), 13, 22. While the opposition that Richard Helgerson elaborates between the Gothic or vernacular and the classical humanist models of culture has explanatory force (especially when applied to the change in regimes on Elizabeth's death), in Spenser's case it is based largely on the slender evidence of the letters, leaving out the *Calender* altogether ("Barbarous Tongues: The Ideology of Poetic Form in Renaissance England," in *The Historical Renaissance: New Essays on Tudor and Stuart Literature and Culture*, ed. Heather Dubrow and Richard Strier [Chicago: University of Chicago Press, 1988], 273–92). Helgerson does not give enough attention here to the serious divisions among those associated with the humanist perspective, divisions that had a substantial bearing on writers' affiliations, imagined or real, with social and political power.

46 From Ascham's dedication to *Toxophilus*: "To All Gentle Men and Yomen of Englande," in *English Works*, ed. William A. Wright (Cambridge: Cambridge University Press, 1904), xiv.

47 *Fitzharberts Booke of Husbandrie* (1598), quoted in Jones, *Triumph* 174–75; Holinshed, *The Firste Volume of the Chronicles*, quoted in Jones 189.

48 William Webbe, for example, thought the language had been established, preserved, and improved "by men of great authoritie and judgement" (*A Discourse of English Poetrie*, in Smith, *Elizabethan Critical Essays* 1:227).

49 Puttenham, *Arte* 86, 91.

50 "The common peoples judgments of Poets is seldome true," Webbe declared, "and therefore not to be sought after" (*Discourse* 298), while the preface to

Tottel's Miscellany promoted its "statelinesse of stile removed from the rude skill of common eares"; Hyder E. Rollins, ed., *Tottel's Miscellany (1557–1587)*, vol. 1 (Cambridge: Harvard University Press, 1928), 2.

51 In his edition of Phoebe Sheavyn's *The Literary Profession in the Elizabethan Age* (Manchester: Manchester University Press, 1967), J. W. Saunders describes the competitive pressures that led, in part, to this early instance of "product differentiation" (142–47).

52 Quoted in Sanders, *Literary Profession* 143. See Smith, *Elizabethan Critical Essays* 1:141; 2:197. William Webbe believed his *Discourse of English Poetrie* (1586) would go a long way toward defining what he regarded as the divide between elite and popular culture: "Whereby I thinke wee may not onelie get the meanes . . . to discerne betweene good writers and badde, but perhappes also challenge from the rude multitude of rusticall Rymers, who will be called Poets, the right practise and orderly course of true Poetry" (227).

53 See Whigham, *Ambition and Privilege*, chap. 3; and Peter Burke, *Popular Culture in Early Modern Europe* (London: Temple Smith, 1978), 272–78.

54 Stone, *Crisis* 36.

55 Katherine Duncan-Jones and Jan van Dorsten, eds. *Miscellaneous Prose of Sir Philip Sidney* (Oxford: Clarendon, 1973), 105, 76, 87, 93–94. All references to Sidney, *Prose*, are to this volume.

56 Ibid., 121, 81. One Sidney critic considers the former passage lightheartedly ironic: Kenneth O. Myrick, *Sir Philip Sidney as a Literary Craftsman* (Cambridge: Harvard University Press, 1935), 80–81.

57 Sidney, *Prose* 83. Many recommended concealing wisdom with figurative language to ensure that literary practice would remain the exclusive domain of the elite. But this counsel was aimed at forestalling comprehension by commoners, the same commoners whose "naturall ignoraunce" should have precluded that comprehension in the first place. The inconsistency reveals how strong the impulse was to protect culture from "contamination" by the multitude.

58 Puttenham, *Arte* 150.

59 Richard Mulcaster, *The First Part of the Elementarie*, ed. E. T. Campagnac (Oxford: Clarendon, 1925), 274. The animus against such usage is also reflected in critical comment on the *Calender* itself, especially by those preferring classical and Continental traditions. Sidney declared, "That same framing of his style to an old rustic language I dare not allow, sith neither Theocritus in Greek, Virgil in Latin, nor Sannazzaro in Italian, did affect it" (*Prose* 112), while Jonson said that "Spenser, in affecting the ancients, writ no language" (George Parfitt, ed., *Ben Jonson: The Complete Poems* [New Haven: Yale University Press, 1982], 428).

60 Robert Kinsman, "The Voices of Dissonance: Patterns in Skelton's *Colyn Cloute*," *HLQ* 26 (1963): 305. On shepherds as courtiers see Louis Montrose, "Of Gentlemen and Shepherds: The Politics of Elizabethan Pastoral Form," *ELH* 50 (1983): 431–33; and as poets see Paul Alpers, "Pastoral and the Domain of Lyric in Spenser's *Shepheardes Calender*," *Representations* 12 (1985): 86.

61 See Bruce Robert McElderry, Jr., "Archaism and Innovation in Spenser's Poetic

Diction," *PMLA* 47 (1932): 144–70; Edwin A. Greenlaw, "The Shepheardes Calender," *PMLA* 26 (1911): 427–28; and Patricia Ingham, "Spenser's Use of Dialect," *ELN* 8 (1971): 164–68.

62   E.K. plays on the last word, using it to refer to "the usual" while its other meaning of "the nonelite" accents with irony the fact that the speech involved does not "differ from the comen" but is precisely theirs.

63   David Richardson, "Duality in Spenser's Archaisms," *Studies in the Literary Imagination* 11 (1978): 83. Some of September's dialect words noted by McElderry and Ingham are *her, han, cote, ken, crag, mirk, mister, gar, crancke, gang, thilke,* and *dirke.*

64   In the first two—February and May—E.K. points out the kinship with Aesop (426, 440).

65   Louis S. Friedland, "Spenser as a Fabulist," *Shakespeare Association Bulletin* 12 (1937): 87. Describing the continuing reappropriation of Aesop, Joseph Jacobs refers to "the law that Aesop always begins his career as a political weapon in a new home" (*The Fables of Aesop*, vol. 1, *The History of the Aesopic Fable* [1889; reprint, New York: Burt Franklin, 1970], 218). See also David G. Hale, "Aesop in Renaissance England," *Library* 27 (1982): 125.

66   F. J. Furnivall, ed., *Political, Religious and Love Poems* (London: Oxford University Press, 1903), 39. Arnold Henderson traces the trend in Britain from the twelfth through the fifteenth centuries "toward more explicit social commentary" in fables, culminating in Robert Henryson's fables, which contained the "most striking defence of the poor" since the Middle Ages ("Animal Fables as Vehicles of Social Protest and Satire: Twelfth Century to Henryson," in *Third International Beast Epic, Fable and Fabliau Colloquium*, ed. Jan Goosens and Timothy Sodmann [Cologne: Böhlau, 1981], 172).

67   On the political registration of Aesop's fables, see Annabel Patterson, *Fables of Power: Aesopian Writing and Political History* (Durham, N.C.: Duke University Press, 1991), esp. 59–64 (a discussion of the fables in the *Calender*).

68   Sidney, *Prose* 87; Thomas Wilson, *Wilson's Arte of Rhetorique, 1560*, ed. G. H. Mair (Oxford: Clarendon, 1909), 197–98.

69   Friedland, "Spenser" 90; Hale, "Aesop" 117; see also F. J. Furnivall, ed., *Robert Laneham's Letter* (London: Kegan Paul, Trench, Trübner and Co., 1887), 61.

70   Annabel Patterson, "Fables of Power," in *Politics of Discourse: The Literature and History of Seventeenth-Century England*, ed. Kevin Sharpe and Steven N. Zwicker (Berkeley: University of California Press, 1987), 274.

71   Ben Edwin Perry, *Babrius and Phaedrus* (Cambridge: Harvard University Press, 1965), xx; Friedland, "Spenser" 88.

72   Michael Mullett, *Popular Culture and Popular Protest in Late Medieval and Early Modern Europe* (London: Croom Helm, 1987), 73; Archer Taylor, *The Proverb* (Cambridge: Harvard University Press, 1931; reprint, Hatboro, Pa.: Folklore Associates, 1962), 169; Charles Smith, *Spenser's Proverb Lore: With Special Reference to His Use of the "Sententiae" of Leonard Culman and Publilius Syrus* (Cambridge: Harvard University Press, 1970).

73   See M. P. Tilley, *A Dictionary of the Proverbs in England in the Sixteenth and Seventeenth Centuries* (Ann Arbor: University of Michigan Press, 1950), 203, for instances of the proverb's quotation.

74   See Bernard Capp, *English Almanacs, 1500–1800* (Ithaca, N.Y.: Cornell University Press, 1979), 27; Keith Thomas, *Religion and the Decline of Magic* (New York: Charles Scribner's Sons, 1971), 295–96.

75   H. Oskar Sommer, ed., *The Kalender of Shepherdes*, 3 vols. (London: Kegan Paul, Trench, Trübner and Co., 1892), 1:38–39 (1518 ed.).

76   See W. L. Edgerton, "The Calendar Year in Sixteenth-Century Printing," *JEGP* 59 (1960): 439–49; Charles Phythian-Adams, *Local History and Folklore: A New Framework* (London: Bedford Square Press, 1975), 21.

77   Ruth Samson Luborsky, "The Allusive Presentation of *The Shepheardes Calender*," *SSt* 1 (1980): 41. The *Calender*'s illustrations were also "the last depictive woodblocks specially made to accompany new imaginative poetry until . . . 1795"; Ruth Samson Luborsky, "The Illustrations to *The Shepheardes Calender*," *SSt* 2 (1981): 18.

78   Luborsky, "Illustrations" 16, 3. Relevant here is Roger Chartier's discussion of the publication history of Molière's comedies, in which he notes the impact of the illustrations added to later editions as "constitut[ing] a protocol of reading for the text" ("Text, Printing, Readings," in *The New Cultural History*, ed. Lynn Hunt [Berkeley: University of California Press, 1989], 162–63).

79   The poem also followed the broadsides' convention of printing the text in black letter, but proper names in roman; Leslie Shephard, *The Broadside Ballad: A Study in Origins and Meaning* (London: Herbert Jenkins, 1962), 59. The experience in publishing broadside ballads that Hugh Singleton, Spenser's printer, brought to his work on the *Calender* must have proven useful; H. J. Byrom, "Edmund Spenser's First Printer, Hugh Singleton," *Library*, 4th ser., 14 (1933): 152.

80   Bernard Capp, "Popular Literature," in *Popular Culture in Seventeenth-Century England*, ed. Barry Reay (New York: St. Martin's Press, 1985), 231; Hale, "Aesop" 118; Jacobs, *Fables* 1: 187, 195; Friedland, "Spenser" 87–88; Luborsky, "Presentation" 30, 43; Luborsky, "Illustrations" 19.

81   Friedland, "Spenser" 87–88. Two of the four fables in the moral eclogues are depicted in the woodcuts.

82   Luborsky, "Illustrations" 3, quoting Richard Morison's *Discourse Touching the Reformation of the Lawes in England*.

83   See Bruce R. Smith, "On Reading *The Shepheardes Calender*," *SSt* 1 (1980): 79–85; and Theodore K. Rabb, "Sebastian Brant and the First Illustrated Edition of Vergil," *Princeton University Library Chronicle* 21 (1960): 187–99.

84   Annabel Patterson, *Pastoral and Ideology: Virgil to Valéry* (Berkeley: University of California Press, 1987), 93–94. See also 104–5; Luborsky, "Illustrations" 18–19.

85   34 & 35 Hen. 8, c. 1; Mulcaster, *Mulcaster's Elementarie* 20.

86   Foxe, *Acts* 6: 361.

87   Puttenham himself has difficulty accommodating pastoral's mixed character to

his decorum, as evidenced by his inability to assess the style of Virgil's fourth eclogue because he cannot tell whether its subject was "th'Emperour" or Pollio, who was "of no great nobilitie" (*Arte* 156–57).

88 Raymond Williams, *Sociology of Culture* (New York: Schocken Books, 1981), 204. According to Edwin Miller, "By 1600 patronage like many other medieval institutions was obsolescent," though it was not fully recognized as such for "almost another century and a half" (*The Professional Writer in Elizabethan England* [Cambridge: Harvard University Press, 1959], 94). Puttenham recognized the value of publishing to celebrity, expressing regret that courtiers were so "loath to be a knowen of their skill" in poetry (*Arte* 22). See J. W. Saunders, "The Stigma of Print: A Note on the Social Bases of Tudor Poetry," *Essays in Criticism* 1 (1951), 141; and Jan van Dorsten, "Literary Patrons in Elizabethan England: The Early Phase," in *Patronage in the Renaissance*, ed. Guy Fitch Lytle and Stephen Orgel (Princeton, N.J.: Princeton University Press, 1981), 192.

89 Lawrence Stone, "The Educational Revolution in England, 1560–1640," *Past and Present* 28 (1964): 42; Stephen J. Greenberg, "Elizabeth I and the Control of Printing in Tudor England," unpublished, p. 6; Foxe, *Acts* 3: 720. E.K. echoes Foxe's indictment: "Friers and knavish shavelings . . . soughte to nousell [rear or foster] the comen people in ignorounce, least being once acquainted with the truth of things, they woulde in tyme smell out the untruth of theyr packed pelfe and Massepenie religion" (443).

90 Harrison, *Description* 76. See Lawrence Stone, "The Size and Composition of the Oxford Student Body, 1580–1909," in *The University in Society*, vol. 1, *Oxford and Cambridge from the Fourteenth to the Early Nineteenth Century*, ed. Lawrence Stone (Princeton, N.J.: Princeton University Press, 1974), 17, 19; see also Stone, "Educational Revolution" 50, 60, 67–68, and graph 1. See Richard Mulcaster, *Positions Wherein Those Primitive Circumstances Be Examined, Which Are Necessarie for the Training Up of Children . . .* (London: Thomas Vautrollier, 1581), 134f., 141f.; David Cressy, "Educational Opportunity in Tudor and Stuart England," *History of Education Quarterly* 16 (1976): 301–20.

91 David Cressy, *Literacy and the Social Order: Reading and Writing in Tudor and Stuart England* (Cambridge: Cambridge University Press, 1980), 159–63, also 72. These figures measure literacy as of the age when it would have been acquired (ten years), which is why I have referred to 1570: by 1579 this population would have become a part of the potential reading public. In an earlier essay Cressy found even higher rates for the 1570s, reflecting the "strong gains" made by all classes from 1560 to 1580: 70 percent for yeomen, 30 percent for husbandmen, and 60 percent for tradesmen ("Educational Opportunity" 315). Margaret Spufford shows that seventeenth-century rural boys would generally start agricultural work after the age reading was learned but before writing was taught, underscoring the "possibility that reading was a much more socially diffused skill than writing" ("First Steps in Literacy: The Reading and Writing Experiences of the Humblest Seventeenth-Century Spiritual Autobiographers," *Social History* 4 [1979]: 434).

92 Marjorie Plant, *The English Book Trade: An Economic History of the Making*

and Sale of Books (London: Allen and Unwin, 1965), 83. Arthur Marotti points out how the occasional character of court poetry limited its audience to the court ("The Transmission of Lyric Poetry and the Institutionalizing of Literature in the English Renaissance," in *Contending Kingdoms: Historical, Psychological, and Feminist Approaches to the Literature of Sixteenth-Century England and France*, ed. Marie-Rose Logan and Peter Rudnytsky [Detroit: Wayne State University Press, 1991], 21–31). He also notes "the treatment of lyric poems as ephemera, encouraged by the circumstances of their original production and reception" (25), with which Spenser's concluding description of the *Calender* is squarely at odds: "made . . . for every yeare, / That steele in strength, and time in durance shall outweare" (467).

93 Though J. W. Saunders's description of this stigma ("Stigma of Print") was challenged by Steven May ("Tudor Aristocrats and the Mythical 'Stigma of Print,'" in *Renaissance Papers, 1980*, ed. A. Leigh DeNeef and M. Thomas Hester [Durham, N.C.: Southeastern Renaissance Conference, 1981], 11–18), May acknowledges its validity as far as lyric poetry was concerned: "It was poesy, not the printing press, which our ancestors viewed with suspicion: the 'stigma of print' should give place to the 'stigma of verse'" (17). He claims this stigma "dissolved" during Elizabeth's reign, but his evidence does not support this claim, especially for the first two decades of the reign. On *Tottel's Miscellany*, see Saunders, "Stigma of Print" 139.

94 Saunders, "Stigma of Print" 155. The *Calender* also registers the conventional ranking of anonymous works at the bottom of the scale of prestige (reflected in the ordering of the poems in *Tottel's Miscellany*) in its self-description as "base begot with blame" (416).

95 See Keith Wrightson, *English Society, 1580–1680* (New Brunswick, N.J.: Rutgers University Press, 1982), 64–65; Peter Laslett, *The World We Have Lost Further Explored* (New York: Charles Scribner's Sons, 1984), chap. 2; Mullett, *Popular Culture and Popular Protest* 2–3.

96 Vernon Hall, *Renaissance Literary Criticism* (Gloucester, Mass.: Peter Smith, 1959), 10, 168; Robert Weimann, *Shakespeare and the Popular Tradition in the Theater: Studies in the Social Dimension of Dramatic Form and Function* (Baltimore: Johns Hopkins University Press, 1978), 24–25.

97 Mikhail Bakhtin, *Rabelais and His World*, trans. Helene Iswolsky (Bloomington: Indiana University Press, 1984), 6. See Frank Lentricchia's similar criticism of Foucault's "saturnalian rebellion" (*Ariel and the Police: Michel Foucault, William James, Wallace Stevens* [Madison: University of Wisconsin Press, 1988], 45–46).

98 E. P. Thompson, *The Making of the Working Class* (New York: Pantheon Books, 1963), 9–10, 13; E. P. Thompson, *The Poverty of Theory and Other Essays* (London: Merlin Press, 1978), 295.

99 Indeed, as Joel Samaha argues, some of the best evidence of that voice comes from criminal court records, which graphically document its political insubordination ("Gleanings from Local Criminal-Court Records: Sedition Amongst the

'Inarticulate' in Elizabethan Essex," *Journal of Social History* 8 [1975]: 61–79].

100   Thomas Churchyard praised the "reverence and humilitie . . . towardes all the [queen's] trayne" by the rural crowds on her progress to Suffolk and Norfolk in 1578, in stark contrast to the "unmannerly disordered boldnesse" he attributed to the lower classes in London, who had "long familiaritie" with nobility (*A Discourse of the Queenes Majesties entertainement in Suffolk and Norfolk* [London: Henry Bynneman, n.d.], B–B.2).

101   Victor Neuberg, *Popular Literature: A History and Guide From the Beginning of Printing to the Year 1897* (London: Woburn Press, 1977), 38. See also Miller, *Professional Writer* 194–95; Albert Friedman, *Ballad Revival* (Chicago: University of Chicago Press, 1961), 68, 70; C. H. Firth, "Ballads and Broadsides," in *Shakespeare's England*, vol. 2 (Oxford: Clarendon, 1932), 513, 522f; Hyder Rollins, *Old English Ballads, 1553–1625* (Cambridge: Cambridge University Press, 1920), introduction and 23; Henry's "Acte for thadvauncement of true Religion" (34 & 35 Hen. 8, c. 1), and Mary's sedition statute (1 & 2 Phil. and M., c. 3), reenacted early in Elizabeth's reign (1 Eliz. 1, c. 6); 5 Eliz. 1, c. 15; Rupert Taylor, *Political Prophecy in England* (New York: Columbia University Press, 1911), 105–6; Bernard Capp, "Popular Literature," in Reay, *Popular Culture in Seventeenth-Century England* 200; Capp, *English Almanacs* 29; Thomas, *Religion and the Decline of Magic* 397; Mary Parmenter, "Spenser's *Twelve Aeglogues Proportionable to the Twelve Monethes*," *ELH* 3 (1936): 197; and Penry Williams, *The Tudor Regime* (Oxford: Clarendon, 1979), 243.

102   A. L. Beier, *Masterless Men: The Vagrancy Problem in England, 1560–1640* (London: Methuen, 1985), 92, 98. The regime's comprehensive efforts to regulate public speech will be discussed in chapter 3.

103   Louis B. Wright, *Middle-Class Culture in Elizabethan England* (Ithaca, N.Y.: Cornell University Press, 1958), 424; Shephard, *Broadside Ballad* 48, 51, 55; Firth, "Ballads and Broadsides" 524.

104   James K. Lowers, *Mirrors for Rebels: A Study of Polemical Literature Relating to the Northern Rebellion, 1569* (Berkeley: University of California Press, 1953), 47–48; Conyers Read, "William Cecil and Elizabethan Public Relations," in *Elizabethan Government and Society*, ed. S. T. Bindoff, J. Hurstfield, and C. H. Williams (London: University of London, 1961), 29.

105   Fletcher, *Tudor Rebellions* 44; see M. H. Dodds and Ruth Dodds, *The Pilgrimage of Grace, 1536–1537* (Cambridge: Cambridge University Press, 1915; reprint, London: Frank Cass and Co., 1971), 1: 80–86. Puttenham warned against the political potency of prophecies, declaring that "by the comfort of those blind prophecies many insurrections and rebellions have been stirred up in this Realme," citing the Peasants' Revolt of 1381 and Kett's Rebellion (*Arte*, ed. Willcock and Walker, 260). This apprehension accounts for the legislation against these works. See Carroll Camden, Jr., "Elizabethan Almanacs and Prognostications," *Library*, 4th ser., 12 (1931–32): 88–90; and Taylor, *Political Prophecy* 92, 104–7.

106   The home production of broadside ballads made them a "major challenge" to

198 Notes to Pages 52–57

the government's apparatus of censorship (Loades, "Censorship" 150–51).

107 James C. Scott, *Weapons of the Weak: Everyday Forms of Peasant Resistance* (New Haven: Yale University Press, 1985), xv, xvii.

108 Ibid., 319, 320; Roberto Unger, *Social Theory: Its Situation and Its Task* (Cambridge: Cambridge University Press, 1987), 28.

109 See Mullett, *Popular Culture and Popular Protest* 7–8, for a description of this barrier and its absence from popular culture.

110 Roger Chartier, *The Cultural Uses of Print in Early Modern France*, trans. Lydia G. Cochrane (Princeton, N.J.: Princeton University Press, 1987), 179.

3 "Labouring to Conceale It": The Hermeneutics of Protection

1 W. R. Matthews and W. M. Atkins, *A History of St. Paul's Cathedral* (London: John Baker, 1964), 134. The monarch was so intimidating that Nowell "completely lost his nerve [and was] unable to continue" (134).

2 John Ayre, ed., *The Works of John Whitgift*, 3 vols. (Cambridge: Cambridge University Press, 1851–53), 1:122.

3 See Paul L. Hughes and James F. Larkin, eds., *Tudor Royal Proclamations*, vol. 2,: *The Later Tudors* (New Haven: Yale University Press, 1969), 120; Patrick Collinson, *Archbishop Grindal, 1519–1583: The Struggle for a Reformed Church* (London: Jonathan Cape, 1979), 240; John Strype, *Annals of the Reformation* (Oxford: Clarendon, 1824; reprint, New York: Burt Franklin, n.d.), vol. 1, pt. 1, p. 225; 1 Eliz. 1, c. 1, quoted in Claire Cross, *The Royal Supremacy in the Elizabethan Church* (London: Allen and Unwin, 1969), 129; David Cressy, *Education in Tudor and Stuart England* (London: Edward Arnold, 1975), 122; Patrick Collinson, "John Field and Elizabethan Puritanism," in *Elizabethan Government and Society*, ed. S. T. Bindoff, J. Hurstfield, and C. H. Williams (London: University of London, 1961), 139; R. B. McKerrow, ed., *A Dictionary of Printers and Booksellers in England, Scotland and Ireland, and of Foreign Printers of English Books, 1557–1640* (London: Bibliographical Society, 1968), x; Edward Arber, ed., *A Transcript of the Registers of the Company of Stationers of London, 1554–1640*, vol. 1 (London, 1875), xxxviii–xxxix, 393–94; Cyprian Blagden, "Book Trade Control in 1566," *Library*, 5th ser., 13 (1958): 287–92; and John H. Primus, *The Vestments Controversy* (Amsterdam: J. H. Kole N. V. Kampan, 1960), 107.

4 Montaigne, "Of the Institution and Education of Children; to the Ladie Diana of Foix, Countesse of Gurson," in *The Essays of Montaigne: John Florio's Translations* (New York: Modern Library, n.d.), 140; John E. Booty, ed., *The Book of Common Prayer, 1559: The Elizabethan Prayer Book* (Washington, D.C.: Folger Shakespeare Library, 1976), 372. See the 1559 injunctions (Hughes and Larkin, *Proclamations* 2: 123) and *Book of Common Prayer* 247.

5 These sermons bore directly on the subjects' attitude toward the government (such as the "Exhortation to Obedience"), social practices ("Against Excess of Apparel"), and the interpretation of important current events ("An Homily Against

Disobedience and wilful Rebellion," issued after the Northern Rebellion of 1569).
Just how carefully the sermons were fashioned with their political impact in
mind is indicated by the excision from Elizabethan editions of a passage in the
1547 version of "An Exhortation to Obedience" that delineated the Crown's
responsibilities to its subjects, because it could be taken to sanction civil disobedience by implying that the subject's duty was conditioned on conscientious
performance by the prince of his (or her) own responsibilities. See Philip Styles,
"The Commonwealth," in *Shakespeare in His Own Age*, ed. Allardyce Nicoll,
Shakespeare Survey 17 (Cambridge: Cambridge University Press, 1964), 104, 109.

6 *Certain Sermons or Homilies Appointed to be Read in Churches* (London: Society for Promoting Christian Knowledge, 1899), 174. Promoting certain public
gatherings entailed excluding others that, as alternative forums, could generate
political energy not subject to the Crown's control. Such "unlawful assemblies"
were considered "mothers of rebellion" and were suppressed as such by the
regime. Important among these were religious meetings like those of the Family
of Love, outlawed as "privy assemblies," which constituted a threat precisely
because they were beyond the reach of official regulation (Hughes and Larkin,
Proclamations 2:350, 474). In the case of the prophesyings—public conferences
of preachers—not only was it difficult for the Crown to control what was said,
but their format—several preachers explicating the same text—embodied an
image of diversity in interpretation inimical to the orthodoxy of prescribed doctrine.

7 See Conyers Read, "William Cecil and Elizabethan Public Relations," in *Elizabethan Government and Society*, ed. Bindoff, Hurstfield, and Williams, 21–55;
and Gladys Jenkins, "Ways and Means in Elizabethan Propaganda," *History*, n.s.,
26 (1941): 105–14.
    William Cecil, Lord Burghley, described by one historian as "a master in the
management of positive propaganda" (D. M. Loades, "The Theory and Practice
of Censorship in Sixteenth-Century England," *Transactions of the Royal Historical Society*, 5th ser., 24 [1974]: 154), was particularly adept at ensuring that
the regime's perspective was prominently represented. He sponsored a number
of publications justifying the Crown's policies at home and abroad, even engaging in a disinformation campaign in 1588 through a series of "deliberately
misleading . . . pamphlets to confuse England's enemies and encourage her
friends" (Stephen Jay Greenberg, "Elizabeth I and the Control of Printing in
Tudor England," unpublished, 10); see Denis B. Woodfield, *Surreptitious Printing in England, 1550–1640* (New York: Bibliographical Society, 1973), 10, 24–37.
Burghley may also have had a hand in the production of various purportedly unofficial publications denouncing the Northern Rebellion; see James K. Lowers,
*Mirrors for Rebels: A Study of Polemical Literature Relating to the Northern
Rebellion, 1569* (Berkeley: University of California Press, 1953), 36–37. And he
caused Bishop John Jewel's *Apology of the Church of England* (1564) to be written "in the name of the whole clergy," presenting a united front to rebut rumors
of a split in the church; John Jewel, *An Apology of the Church of England*, ed.

John E. Booty (Ithaca, N.Y.: Cornell University Press, 1963), xiv. See also Read, "Cecil" 25.

8 Christopher Hill, *Economic Problems of the Church from Archbishop Whitgift to the Long Parliament* (Oxford: Clarendon, 1956), xi. According to Hill, the pulpits were "the main source of information and ideas on political subjects [and] of instruction on economic conduct" (xi).

9 George P. Rice, Jr., *The Public Speaking of Queen Elizabeth: Selections from Her Official Addresses* (New York: Columbia University Press, 1951), 125; John Stubbs, *Gaping Gulf*, ed. Lloyd E. Berry (Charlottesville: University Press of Virginia, 1968), xxx.

10 See 5 Eliz. 1, c. 1; and Hughes and Larkin, *Proclamations* 2:312, 341, 376, 379. A 1563 statute outlawed prophecies (5 Eliz. 1, c. 15). For the history of censorship generally, see Loades, "Censorship"; Fredrick S. Siebert, *Freedom of the Press in England, 1476–1776* (Urbana: University of Illinois Press, 1952); and Frederick J. Youngs, "The Tudor Government and Dissident Religious Books," in *The Dissenting Tradition*, ed. C. Robert Cole and Michael E. Moody (Athens: Ohio University Press, 1975), 167–90.

11 For the history of the law of treason, see John Bellamy, *The Tudor Law of Treason: An Introduction* (London: Routledge and Kegan Paul, 1979).

12 1 Eliz. 1, c. 6, reenacting 1 & 2 Phil. & M., c. 3. As expansive as were the definitions of proscribed speech, Elizabeth's government went beyond them, charging defendants in such general terms as "disturbing the tranquillity of the realm" or "alter[ing] or subvert[ing] established religion or government" (Bellamy, *Tudor Law of Treason* 252, 80).

Accusations of seditious talk, which were not uncommon and became more frequent in the first two decades of Elizabeth's reign, included calling the queen "a rascal" and "an arrant whore" and her church service "paltry," alleging she was pregnant by Dudley, asking if she were a papist, speaking against lords, and lamenting the taking of preachers' licenses. F. G. Emmison, *Elizabethan Life: Disorder* (Chelmsford: Essex County Council, 1970), 41–48, 54. Religious criticism was a chief target: the "tendency to associate sedition with religious dissent became an official habit of mind"; Roger B. Manning, "The Origins of the Doctrine of Sedition," *Albion* 12 (1980): 102. But the expression of social discontent was also considered dangerous. Four unemployed laborers were hanged in 1567 for voicing complaints about economic conditions coupled with equivocal references to a "remedy[,] for the commons will rise" (Emmison 63–64).

13 Matters of state included "war, peace, all foreign relations, royal marriage, the succession, and, for the Queen, most certainly, religion"—every important public issue; Wallace T. MacCaffrey, *Queen Elizabeth and the Making of Policy, 1572–1588* (Princeton, N.J.: Princeton University Press, 1981), 466. This "new constitutional rule" was without precedent, "invented" by Elizabeth, according to Geoffrey Elton, because "she always wanted to keep Parliament out of the act"; see G. R. Elton, "Parliament," in *The Reign of Queen Elizabeth I*, ed. Christopher Haigh (Athens: University of Georgia Press, 1985), 97, and *The Par-*

liament of England, 1559–1581 (Cambridge: Cambridge University Press, 1986), 343. It produced continual tension and occasional open conflict.

14 Hughes and Larkin, *Proclamations* 2: 115. Because historical material provided an important avenue for reflection and discussion of these issues, the government was particularly wary of its circulation. This wariness helped generate what Annabel Patterson describes as "the belief that the history of the realm, not only in terms of access to state documents but in terms of interpretation, belonged to the monarch" (*Censorship and Interpretation: The Conditions of Writing and Reading in Early Modern England* [Madison: University of Wisconsin Press, 1984], 129). Acting on this policy, the Privy Council ordered changes in both the 1577 and 1587 editions of Holinshed's *Chronicles*. Passages ordered deleted related to the Crown and prominent nobles, Scottish politics, and the Babington conspiracy of 1586; see *DNB* and Elizabeth Story Donno, "Some Aspects of Shakespeare's Holinshed," *HLQ* 50 (1987): 229–48.

15 G. R. Elton, ed., *The Tudor Constitution: Documents and Commentary* (Cambridge: Cambridge University Press, 1982), 17. Elton calls *prerogative* "the great Tudor word" (17). Even when writers advocated what was the Crown's policy on forbidden topics they were punished, as was the author of a 1567 tract opposing settlement of the succession, who was "fined £500 and imprisoned in the Tower for fifteen months"; John Neale, "Peter Wentworth," *English Historical Review* 39 (1924): 185–86.

16 T. E. Hartley, ed., *Proceedings in the Parliaments of Queen Elizabeth I*, vol. 1 (1558–1581) (Wilmington, Del.: Michael Glazier, 1981), 238; Neale, "Wentworth" 39.

17 MacCaffrey, *Queen Elizabeth* 48; Patrick Collinson, "A Mirror of Elizabethan Protestantism: The Life and Letters of 'Godly Master Dering,'" in Collinson, *Godly People: Essays on English Protestantism and Puritanism* (London: Hambledon Press, 1983), 311–12.

18 Stubbs, *Gaping Gulf* 31; see also 16, 91–92.

19 Patterson, *Censorship and Interpretation* 40; Frank Whigham, *Ambition and Privilege: The Social Tropes of Elizabethan Courtesy Theory* (Berkeley: University of California Press, 1984), 145.

20 See Steuart A. Pears, ed., *Correspondence of Sir Philip Sidney and Hubert Languet* (London: William Pickering, 1845), 187; Roger Howell, *Sir Philip Sidney: The Shepherd Knight* (London: Hutchinson and Co., 1968), 67–74; Malcolm William Wallace, *The Life of Sir Philip Sidney* (Cambridge: Cambridge University Press, 1915), 213–19. For the view that the letter was written later, see H. R. Fox Bourne, *Sir Philip Sidney* (New York: G. P. Putnam's Sons, 1901), 182.

21 William Nicholson, ed., *The Remains of Edmund Grindal* (Cambridge: Cambridge University Press, 1843), 387, 388, 389. Translations are from the *Remains*. The memorandum is quoted in Collinson, *Grindal* 238.

22 Though convicted at Stubbs's trial, Singleton was apparently pardoned before execution. See H. J. Byrom, "Edmund Spenser's First Printer, Hugh Singleton," *Library*, 4th ser., 14 (1933): 121–56.

23 See Hughes and Larkin, *Proclamations* 2:343, 378; Roger Ascham, *English Works*, ed. William Wright (Cambridge: Cambridge University Press, 1904), 200; Hughes and Larkin 2: 446–49 (see also 323, 332, 342–43, 400); Rice, *Public Speaking* 125, 132.

24 The lord keeper Nicholas Bacon warned the Commons in 1571 that they "should do well to meddle with no matters of state but such as should be proposed unto them and to occupy themselves in other matters concerning commonwealth" (quoted in MacCaffrey, *Queen Elizabeth* 465–66). At the close of the same session the queen rebuked those who supported bills for church reform for "their audacious, arrogant and presumptuous folly . . . meddling with matters neither pertaining unto them nor within the capacity of their understanding" (Cross, *Royal Supremacy* 87; Hartley, *Proceedings* 1:171, 188). See also Strype, *Annals*, vol. 1, pt. 2, p. 239.

25 Patterson, *Censorship and Interpretation* 189. See also Janet E. Halley, "Heresy, Orthodoxy, and the Politics of Religious Discourse: The Case of the English Family of Love," *Representations* 15 (1986): 109f.

26 George Puttenham, *The Arte of English Poesie*, in *Elizabethan Critical Essays*, ed. G. Gregory Smith, 2 vols. (Oxford: Clarendon, 1904), 2: 40.

27 Patterson refers to just such an "implicit social contract," the parties to it sharing "the acceptance of encoding as the deference due to political authority" (*Censorship and Interpretation* 17, 12).

28 For a thorough discussion of the development and transmission of this interpretive approach to Virgil's *Eclogues*, see Annabel Patterson, *Pastoral and Ideology: Virgil to Valéry* (Berkeley: University of California Press, 1987), chaps. 1 and 2. According to Helen Cooper, "matters of state concern were not only a right and fitting subject for [medieval and Renaissance] pastoral, but even *the* right and fitting subject" (*Pastoral: Mediaeval into Renaissance* [Ipswich: D. S. Brewer, 1977], 187, 133). See also David Norbrook, *Poetry and Politics in the English Renaissance* (London: Routledge and Kegan Paul, 1984), 59–60, 86.

29 Katherine Duncan-Jones and Jan van Dorsten, eds., *Miscellaneous Prose of Sir Philip Sidney* (Oxford: Clarendon, 1973), 94–95; William Webbe, *A Discourse of English Poetrie*, in Smith, *Elizabethan Critical Essays* 1: 264.

30 John Frederick Nims, ed., *Ovid's Metamorphoses: The Arthur Golding Translation, 1567* (New York: Macmillan, 1965), 425.

31 Robert Crowley, *The Fable of Philargyrie* (1551), preface; S. R. Cattley, ed., *The Acts and Monuments of John Foxe*, 8 vols. (London: R. B. Seeley and W. Burnside, 1837–41), 4: 249–50, referring to *The Plowman's Tale*, thought to be Chaucer's. Many biblical passages were also interpreted as social allegory; see Richard L. Greaves, "Traditionalism and the Seeds of Revolution in the Social Principles of the Geneva Bible," *Sixteenth Century Journal* 7 (1976): 94–109.

32 5 Eliz. 1, c. 15.

33 *DNB* 3:116; Siebert, *Freedom of the Press* 89–90.

34 Puttenham, *Arte* 40; Patterson, *Censorship and Interpretation* 31. Paul McLane, *Spenser's "Shepheardes Calender": A Study in Elizabethan Allegory* (Notre Dame, Ind.: University of Notre Dame Press, 1961), 7.

35 Patterson refers to the "dismemberment" of the author in Virgil, "a wickedly shifting authorial presence" (*Pastoral and Ideology* 4).

36 I will not repeat the many arguments over E.K.'s identity. My thesis is that, whomever E.K. may represent, his apparatus is consonant with Spenser's intention throughout the work, even where that apparatus consists of errors or misleading interpretations.

37 Jonathan Goldberg, *Voice Terminal Echo: Postmodernism and English Renaissance Texts* (New York: Methuen, 1986), 62.

38 This is a paraphrase of James Jackson Higginson, *Spenser's "Shepheardes Calender" in Relation to Contemporary Affairs* (New York: Columbia University Press, 1912), 86.

39 Bruce R. Smith, "On Reading *The Shepheardes Calender*," *SSt* 1 (1980): 89; Edwin A. Greenlaw, "The Shepheardes Calender," *PMLA* 26 (1911): 432; Leigh DeNeef, *Spenser and the Motives of Metaphor* (Durham, N.C.: Duke University Press, 1982), 19.

40 "E.K. is concerned," according to Jonathan Goldberg, "mainly with the linguistic value of the text" (*Endlesse Worke: Spenser and the Structures of Discourse* [Baltimore: Johns Hopkins University Press, 1981], 10 n. 5). Modern criticism has, in varying ways, reiterated both of E.K.'s approaches. See Michael F. Dixon, "Rhetorical Patterns and Methods of Advocacy in Spenser's *Shepheardes Calender*," *ELR* 7 (1977): 131–54; and Nancy Jo Hoffman, *Spenser's Pastorals: "The Shepheardes Calender" and "Colin Clout"* (Baltimore: Johns Hopkins University Press, 1977), chaps. 1–4.

41 Relying uncritically on E.K.'s apparatus, John King reiterates his argument that the moral eclogues are exclusively religious, antipapal satires with a "universal" and "archetypal" dimension ("Spenser's *Shepheardes Calender* and Protestant Pastoral Satire," in *Renaissance Genres: Essays on Theory, History, and Interpretation*, ed. Barbara Kiefer Lewalski [Cambridge: Harvard University Press, 1986], 369–98). Though King places less emphasis on the archetypal in a later discussion of the *Calender* (*Spenser's Poetry and the Reformation Tradition* [Princeton, N.J.: Princeton University Press, 1990]), he reaffirms E.K.'s perspective, downplaying the persistent and vehement controversy over church polity in positing a "broad Protestant consensus" to support a reading of the moral eclogues as solely concerned with Protestant-Catholic conflict. Although Anthea Hume recognizes the serious conflicts within the English church, she overlooks their sociopolitical ramifications, treating the moral eclogues as solely religous in their reference (*Edmund Spenser: Protestant Poet* [Cambridge: Cambridge University Press, 1984]).

42 The historian Peter Lake sees criticism of the Catholic and the established Protestant churches as "expressions of the same protestant world-view and as such . . . but two sides of the same coin" (*Moderate Puritans and the Elizabethan Church* [Cambridge: Cambridge University Press, 1982], 69).

43 See Stephen Batman, *The Golden Booke of the Leaden Goddes* (London, 1577), 16–17; Ovid, Met. 11. 164–202.

44 In the sixteenth century both the viol and the violin were introduced into

England through the court; *Grove Dictionary of Music* 19: 795, 798; E. van Straeten, *The History of the Violin, Its Ancestors and Collateral Instruments* (London: Cassell, 1933), 1: 57. "By 1555 violins were part of the English royal establishment"; David D. Boyden, *The History of Violin Playing from Its Origins to 1761* (London: Oxford University Press, 1965), 57.

45 This pressure, which intensifies as E.K.'s resolutions grow progressively more unsatisfying, prompts us to reread the eclogues "back to front"—interpreting the early parts in light of later ones—an instance of the interpretive labor the work incites.

46 E.K. sees Algrind's injury as "chaunce" and "myshap" (448).

47 DeNeef refers to such mistakes as "literalizing errors" (*Spenser* 41).

4 "The Time Was Once": The Configuration of Authority in the Poem

1 See James Scott, *Weapons of the Weak: Everyday Forms of Peasant Resistance* (New Haven: Yale University Press, 1985), 25–27, and, generally, Scott's *Domination and the Arts of Resistance: Hidden Transcripts* (New Haven: Yale University Press, 1990).

2 Hannah Arendt, *Between Past and Future: Six Exercises in Political Thought* (Cleveland: World Publishing Company, 1963), 97.

3 Scott, *Weapons of the Weak* xvii.

4 David Miller, "Authorship, Anonymity and *The Shepheardes Calender*," *MLQ* 40 (1979): 227; Keith Thomas, *Religion and the Decline of Magic* (New York: Charles Scribner's Sons, 1971), 425.

5 S. R. Cattley, ed. *The Acts and Monuments of John Foxe*, 8 vols. (London: R. B. Seeley and W. Burnside, 1837–41), 1:504; E. J. Hobsbawm, "The Social Function of the Past: Some Questions," *Past and Present* 52 (1972): 4–5.

6 James M. Osborn, ed., *The Quenes Majesties Passage Through the Citie of London to Westminster the Day Before Her Coronation* (New Haven: Yale University Press, 1960), 59.

7 *Theatre for Worldlings* quoted in Frances A. Yates, *Astraea: The Imperial Theme in the Sixteenth Century* (London: Routledge and Kegan Paul, 1975), 113; preamble to 1 Eliz. 1, c. 1, from Claire Cross, *The Royal Supremacy in the Elizabethan Church* (London: Allen and Unwin, 1969), 126; John B. Thompson, *Studies in the Theory of Ideology* (Berkeley: University of California Press, 1984), 186.

8 W. H. Frere and C. E. Douglas, eds., *Puritan Manifestoes: A Study of the Origins of the Puritan Revolt* (London: Church Historical Society, 1959), 10–12; hereinafter cited as *Puritan Manifestoes.*

9 Joseph Lilly, ed., *Black Letter Ballads and Broadsides* (London, 1870), 247–50. A Henrician ballad entitled "Now a Dayes" (c. 1520) similarly criticizes current social ills by invoking "Our auncient customs bolde" that "be clene cast away" (F. J. Furnivall, ed., *Ballads from Manuscripts* [London: Ballad Society, 1868], 93).

10   In "The Generall Argument" Christ himself is represented as part of this re-
storative movement "returning the compasse of expired yeres to theyr former
date and first commencement" (420).

11   Alexander B. Grosart, ed., *The Works of Gabriel Harvey, vol. 1* (London: Hazell,
Watson and Viney, 1884; reprint, New York: AMS Press, 1966), 146.

12   Louis Montrose, "Of Gentlemen and Shepherds: The Politics of Elizabethan
Pastoral Form," *ELH* 50 (1983): 432.

13   Quoted in John Strype, *Memorials of the Most Reverend Father in God Thomas
Cranmer, vol. 1* (Oxford: Clarendon, 1812), 127–28.

14   *Puritan Manifestoes* 5.

15   Cartwright, in John Ayre, ed., *The Works of John Whitgift*, 3 vols. (Cambridge:
Cambridge University Press, 1851–53), 1:372; *Puritan Manifestoes* 126. Cartwright flatly rejected the claim that monarchy was necessary, "for . . . there
are other good commonwealths, wherein many have like power and authority"
(Whitgift, *Works* 2:263).

16   Whitgift, *Works* 1:42, 19, 34; 2:84.

17   Ruth Kelso, *The Doctrine of the English Gentleman in the Sixteenth Century*
(Urbana: University of Illinois Press, 1929; reprint, Gloucester, Mass.: Peter
Smith, 1964), 31. See also Sylvia Resnikow, "The Cultural History of a Demo-
cratic Proverb," *JEGP* 36 (1937): 391–405. According to one contemporary ac-
count, Ball's sermon was attended by two hundred thousand commoners; R. B.
Dobson, ed., *The Peasants' Revolt of 1381* (Basingstoke: Macmillan, 1983), 374.

18   Quoted in Kelso, *Doctrine* 31. The couplet and the proverbial "children of Adam"
were both current in the sixteenth century. See F. P. Wilson, ed., *Oxford Dictionary of English Proverbs* (Oxford: Clarendon, 1970), 3, and M. P. Tilley, *A Dictionary of the Proverbs in England in the Sixteenth and Seventeenth Centuries*
(Ann Arbor: University of Michigan Press, 1950), 3.
    Not only rebels voiced this claim. Similar assertions were made by prominent
medieval churchmen like Thomas Brunton, bishop of Rochester, who declared:
"All Christians, rich and poor alike, without distinction of persons, are from
one father, Adam. . . . In these [citing common religious privileges] and many
other things the rich and the poor are *alike and equal*"; G. R. Owst, *Literature
and Pulpit in Medieval England* (New York: Barnes and Noble, 1961), 291–92.
In 1548 Robert Crowley wrote that "we are all one mans chyldren, and have (by
nature) lyke ryght to the richesse and treasures of thys worlde" (*An Information
and Petition agaynst the oppressors of the pore Commons of this Realme . . .*
[London: John Day, 1548], A.6). And in the allegorical *Complaynt of Scotlande*
(1549), an unknown Scotsman exhorted his fellow countrymen to overcome
their differences and unite against the English who claimed dominion over their
land. Dame Scotia inveighs against the pretensions of "the nobilis ande gentil
men," invoking "the goldin varld" when there "vas na defferens of staitis . . .
amang men" (James A. H. Murray, ed., *The Complaynt of Scotlande* [London:
Trübner and Co., 1872], 144).

19   Dobson, *Peasants' Revolt* 375. The historian is Thomas Walsingham.

20 Helen Cooper emphasizes the "enormous artistic potential" this flexibility gave pastoral. The shepherd figure "was an obvious metaphor for the prince as well as for the common man" (*Pastoral: Medieval into Renaissance* [Ipswich: D. S. Brewer, 1977], 47, 85).

21 See, for example, Psalm 23, John 10, and 1 Peter 2 and 5, each read at various services during the year. John Ayre, ed., *The Sermons of Edwin Sandys* (Cambridge: Cambridge University Press, 1842), 47; Foxe, *Acts* 1:502.

22 *The Geneva Bible: A Facsimile of the 1560 Edition* (Madison: University of Wisconsin Press, 1969), Ezekiel 34:2–4. See also Jeremiah 23:1–4.

23 Ibid., gloss to Ezekiel 34:2. The gloss to the similar denunciation of "pastors" in Jeremiah also includes political leaders.

24 Robert Crowley, *The way to wealth* . . . (London, 1550), A.4v, 5. Diggon alludes to the same default when he declares the need for "heedy shepheards to discerne [wolves'] face" (September 167).

25 Quoted in R. H. Tawney, *Social History and Literature* (Leicester: Leicester University Press, 1958), 22.

26 See also July 187–90.

27 See Cooper, *Pastoral* 76–77.

28 Text and translations are from Peter Happé, ed., *English Mystery Plays: A Selection* (Harmondsworth, Eng.: Penguin Books, 1975), p. 266, ll. 12–18.

29 Ibid., l. 21.

30 See the discussion of the work of "Luke Shepherd" in David Norbrook, *Poetry and Politics in the English Renaissance* (London: Routledge and Kegan Paul, 1984), 33–36, 48–49 (quotation on 33); and John King, *English Reformation Literature: The Tudor Origins of the Protestant Tradition* (Princeton, N.J.: Princeton University Press, 1982), 252–70.

31 This and the subsequent quotations are from Furnivall, *Ballads from Manuscripts*, vol. 1.

32 Louis Montrose, " 'Eliza, Queene of shepheardes,' and the Pastoral of Power," *ELR* 10 (1980): 163.

33 John W. Cunliffe, ed., *The Complete Works of George Gascoigne*, 2 vols. (Cambridge: Cambridge University Press, 1910), 1:142, 143. The poem was published in 1575 in Gascoigne's volume *Posies*.

34 Katherine Duncan-Jones and Jan van Dorsten, eds., *Miscellaneous Prose of Sir Philip Sidney* (Oxford: Clarendon, 1973), 112; George Puttenham, *The Arte of English Poesie*, in *Elizabethan Critical Essays*, ed. G. Gregory Smith, 2 vols. (Oxford: Clarendon, 1904), 2:64–65, 87, 62; John Peter, *Complaint and Satire in Early English Literature* (Oxford: Clarendon, 1956). See also C. W. Previté-Orton, *Political Satire in English Poetry* (New York: Haskell House, 1966).

35 The passages that follow are from John Skelton, *The Complete English Poems*, ed. John Scattergood (New Haven: Yale University Press, 1983), ll. 287–88, 412, 479, 1119–21, 76–79.

36 The modern critical consensus is that Skelton's commentary was born of a social conservatism (evidenced in part by his disparagement of Wolsey's low birth).

Whether or not this view gives an adequate account of his poetry, especially *Collyn Clout*, it is far less germane than sixteenth-century views of Skelton. Then he was frequently praised, with full recognition of the satiric thrust of his poetry, as one in William Webbe's words "of a very sharpe wytte, exceeding bolde, [who] would nyppe to the very quicke where he once sette holde" (*A Discourse of English Poetrie*, in Smith, *Elizabethan Critical Essays* 1:242). Significantly, though Puttenham dissented in his assessment of Skelton's poetry, his description of him as unpolished and base ("rude") and impudently critical ("rayling") accords with his status in Spenser's work. See L. J. Lloyd, *John Skelton: A Sketch of His Life and Writings* (New York: Russell and Russell, 1969), 58, 103; William Nelson, *John Skelton: Laureate* (New York: Columbia University Press, 1939), 138, 228; and Stanley E. Fish, *John Skelton's Poetry* (New Haven: Yale University Press, 1965), 126–35.

37   See Alice S. Miskimin, *The Renaissance Chaucer* (New Haven: Yale University Press, 1975), esp. 18, 97. Webbe says of him, "For such was his bolde spyrit, that what enormities he saw in any he would not spare to pay them home, eyther in playne words, or els in some pretry and pleasant covert, that the simplest might espy him" (*Discourse* 241).

38   In his glosses to February 92 and June 81, E.K. identifies Tityrus as Chaucer.

39   It is relatively easy to assimilate the first in these terms, for he articulates a thoroughgoing critique of church and government officials. Though the second seems incongruous, promoting aristocratic affiliations and rationales for poetry, this transformation may well be intentional, imaging the vulnerability of poetry to the cultural, as well as the political, power of the court. Indeed, the word *pierless* (the spelling, unique in all of Spenser's work, cannot have been coincidental) was used to describe poetry itself in October and court entertainment in June. I discuss these eclogues in chapter 6.

40   G. H. Kingsley and F. J. Furnivall, eds., *Francis Thynne's Animadversions upon Speght's First (1598 A.D.) Edition of Chaucer's Works* (London, 1875; reprint, London: Oxford University Press, 1965), xiv.

41   King, *English Reformation Literature* 51. *The Plowman's Tale* had been printed separately before this prohibition was enacted. It was included as part of Chaucer's works for the first time in the same year the proscription was put into place. It was first added to Chaucer's works by William Thynne, a friend of Skelton's who encouraged him to publish *Collyn Clout* (Miskimin, *Renaissance Chaucer* 245, 256).

42   There are recognizable echoes of *The Plowman's Tale* in February 149, April 99, and July 169–204. See Edwin A. Greenlaw et al., eds., *The Works of Edmund Spenser: A Variorum Edition*, 11 vols. (Baltimore: Johns Hopkins University Press, 1932–57), vol. 7, pt. 1, pp. 263, 284, 334.

43   In her study of the plowman tradition, Barbara Ann Johnson describes the figure as "a popular folk character" ("From 'Piers Plowman' to 'Pilgrim's Progress': The Generic and Exegetical Contexts of Bunyan's 'Similitude of A Dream,'" Ph.D. diss., Brown University, 1983, p. 144).

44 "General Prologue," *The Canterbury Tales*, in *The Riverside Chaucer*, ed. Larry D. Benson (Boston: Houghton Mifflin Co., 1987), ll. 531–38.

45 See, for example, ll. 141–42, 175–80, 259, 287, 355, 481, 733–39, 746, 859–60, 1027, and 1322–23, in Walter W. Skeat, ed., *Chaucerian and Other Pieces* (Oxford: Oxford University Press, 1897).

46 Robert Crowley's three quarto editions of Langland's work in 1550 secured its prominence. Crowley's text of Langland was reprinted in 1561 (King, *English Reformation Literature* 326), as was that of Chaucer.

47 According to Helen White, the anonymous *I Playne Piers Which Can Not Flatter* (c. 1550) "combines a plea for the free circulation of the Scriptures in English with a general attack on the old religious order and on the wealthy" (*Social Criticism in Popular Religious Literature of the Sixteenth Century* [New York: Macmillan, 1944], 32).

48 See Robert L. Kelly, "Hugh Latimer as Piers Plowman," *SEL* 17 (1977): 13–26. Allen G. Chester, ed., *Selected Sermons of Hugh Latimer* (Charlottesville: University Press of Virginia, 1968), 33–34.

49 *Newes from the North* . . . (London: John Allde, 1579), A.5v, B.3, D.1v, K.3. The censure comes near the end of the text, which concludes with the same biblical verse Skelton used as the epigraph to *Collyn Clout*.

50 *Pyers plowmans exhortation* . . . (London, c. 1550), A.ii, B.iii. For other works that incorporate important elements of the plowman tradition, see *A Proper Dyalogue betwene a Gentillman and a Husbandman, eche complaynynge to the other their miserable Calamite through the Ambicion of Clergye* (1530), in which the Husbandman is the voice of the laborers and the poor in society; the Husbandman figure in William Stafford, *A Compendious or briefe Examination of Certayne Ordinary Complaints* (London, 1581); Johnson, "From 'Piers Plowman' to 'Pilgrim's Progress,'" chaps. 3 and 4; and King, *English Reformation Literature* 500.

51 Norbrook reports that Langland was "so alarmed [by the peasants' citation of his work] that he inserted attacks on communism in later versions of the poem" (*Poetry and Politics* 54).

52 Rodney Hilton, *Bond Men Made Free: Medieval Peasant Movements and the English Rising of 1381* (London: Methuen, 1973), 223; see also Dobson, *Peasants' Revolt* 380. Ball quoted in Dobson 381. The similarities between the poem *Vox populi* cited above and the grievances that Kett's rebels voiced a year or two later suggest similar appropriation of a literary vision for immediate political purposes (Furnivall, *Ballads from Manuscripts* 1:147).

53 See M. V. Clarke and V. H. Galbraith, "The Deposition of Richard II," *Bulletin of John Rylands Library* 14 (1930): 164. According to C. S. L. Davies, one revolt that was part of the Pilgrimage of Grace in 1536–37 also "adopted the phraseology of the 'Piers Plowman' tradition" ("The Pilgrimage of Grace Reconsidered," in *Rebellion, Popular Protest and the Social Order*, ed. Paul Slack [Cambridge: Cambridge University Press, 1984], 30).

54 On the incorporation of the revolt into literature, see Dobson, *Peasants' Revolt*

353–62, 383–91, 396–98, 403–4. Not surprisingly, the Peasants' Revolt has received attention as an object of study and debate at times of dramatic social change such as 1789, and 1848 and its aftermath (Dobson 392–96, 399–402).

5 "I Dare Undersaye": The Social Commentary of the Moral Eclogues

1 G. B. Harrison, ed., *The Letters of Queen Elizabeth* (New York: Funk and Wagnalls, 1968), 120–21.

2 Paul McLane, for example, argues they have "no real significance" (*Spenser's "Shepheardes Calender": A Study in Elizabethan Allegory* [Notre Dame, Ind.: University of Notre Dame Press, 1961], 66). Ronald Bond ("Supplantation in the Elizabethan Court: The Theme of Spenser's February Eclogue," *SSt* 2 [1981]: 55–66) and Louis Montrose ("Interpreting Spenser's February Eclogue: Some Contexts and Implications," *SSt* 2 [1981]: 67–74) ignore them altogether.

3 Edwin A. Greenlaw, "The Shepheardes Calender, II," *SP* 11 (1913): 24.

4 Anthony Munday, *Watchward to England* (1584), quoted in E. C. Wilson, *England's Eliza* (Cambridge: Harvard University Press, 1939), 218; Elizabeth quoted in George P. Rice, Jr., *The Public Speaking of Queen Elizabeth: Selections from Her Official Addresses* (New York: Columbia University Press, 1951), 68.

5 27 Hen. 8, c. 27. quoted in Joyce Youings, *The Dissolution of the Monasteries* (London: Allen and Unwin, 1971), 199.

6 27 Hen. 8, c. 28, quoted in Youings, *Dissolution* 155.

7 Youings, *Dissolution* 73.

8 S. R. Cattley, ed., *The Acts and Monuments of John Foxe*, 8 vols. (London: R. B. Seeley and W. Burnside, 1837–41), 5:181.

9 Ruth Samson Luborsky, "The Illustrations to The Shepheardes Calender," *SSt* 2 (1981): 30.

10 Penry Williams, *The Tudor Regime* (Oxford: Clarendon, 1979), 63. See Youings, *Dissolution*; G. W. O. Woodward, *The Dissolution of the Monasteries* (London: Blandford Press, 1966); and Felicity Heal, *Of Prelates and Princes: A Study of the Economic and Social Position of the Tudor Episcopate* (Cambridge: Cambridge University Press, 1980), chaps. 8–11.

11 G. R. Elton, ed., *The Tudor Constitution: Documents and Commentaries* (Cambridge: Cambridge University Press, 1982), 380. See Woodward, *Dissolution* 50–57; Youings, *Dissolution* 118.

12 1 Eliz. 1, c. 19, 24.

13 Claire Cross, *The Royal Supremacy in the Elizabethan Church* (London: Allen and Unwin, 1969), 77; Christopher Hill, *Economic Problems of the Church* (Oxford: Clarendon, 1956), 15.

14 There were twenty-four vacancies of sees that lasted a year or more, the longest being Oxford (forty-one years) and Ely (eighteen); Michael A. R. Graves, *Tudor Parliaments: Crown, Lords, and Commons, 1485–1603* (London: Longman Group, 1985), 132. "First fruits" consisted of "more or less the first year's

210 Notes to Pages 95–97

income in the new post"; David L. Edwards, *Christian England*, vol. 2, *From the Reformation to the Eighteenth Century* (Grand Rapids, Mich.: William B. Eerdmans, 1983), 172. Hill, *Economic Problems* 188, 192.

15 Cross, *Royal Supremacy* 68; Heal, *Of Prelates and Princes* 215.

16 See Reinhard Bendix, *Kings or People: Power and the Mandate to Rule* (Berkeley: University of California Press, 1978), 259; Alan Kreider, *English Chantries: The Road to Dissolution* (Cambridge: Harvard University Press, 1979), 64; Craig R. Thompson, *Schools in Tudor England* (Washington, D.C.: Folger Shakespeare Library, 1958), 7; Woodward, *Dissolution* 168; and A. E. Bland, P. A. Brown, and R. H. Tawney, eds., *English Economic History: Select Documents* (London: G. Bell and Sons, 1915), 251.

17 Joyce Youings, *Sixteenth-Century England* (Harmondsworth, Eng.: Penguin, 1984), 254. David Knowles believes that before the dissolution the church devoted as much as 10 percent of its income to charity. The amount, whatever the percentage, was not replaced from any other source for a long time. Knowles, *The Religious Orders in England*, vol. 3, *The Tudor Age* (Cambridge: Cambridge University Press, 1959), 266.

18 J. M. Cowper, ed., *Henry Brinklow's Complaynt of Roderyck Mors . . . unto the parliament howse of England . . .* (London: N. Trübner and Co., 1874; reprint, Millwood, N.Y.: Kraus Reprint Co., 1975), 34, 48. Crowley's poem is in Robert Crowley, *Select Works*, ed. J. M. Cowper (London: Kegan Paul, Trench, Trübner and Co., 1872), 11–12.

19 Anthony Fletcher, *Tudor Rebellions* (London: Longmans, Green and Co., 1968), 35, 62, 136, 120, 123, 133. Aske's words come from his examination in the Tower. The restoration of church lands was among the demands of those involved in the Western Rebellion of 1549 as well. According to Joan Thirsk, "the monasteries and their farms often constituted the social centre of community life as well as its economic framework" (Joan Thirsk, ed., *Agricultural Change: Policy and Practice* [Cambridge: Cambridge University Press, 1990], 73).

20 M. P. Tilley, *A Dictionary of the Proverbs in England in the Sixteenth and Seventeenth Centuries* (Ann Arbor: University of Michigan Press, 1950), 681; Thirsk, *Agricultural Change* 46–48. As Mulcaster's derogatory reference to "the poets akecorns" cited in chapter 2 indicates, the contrast between acorns and more "civilized" grains and their products as food was common throughout the period. See, for example, Spenser's *Virgils Gnat*, ll. 206–7; Tilley, *Dictionary* 2; Roger Ascham, *English Works*, ed. William Wright (Cambridge: Cambridge University Press, 1904), 289; and William Molesworth, ed., *The English Works of Thomas Hobbes*, 11 vols. (London: 1839–1845; reprint, Aalen, Germany: Scientia Aalen, 1962), 1:1–2 and 3:665. The association of grain with the upper classes was so strong that, at the time of the Pilgrimage of Grace, there were rumors of a tax on the poor for eating white bread; M. H. Dodds and Ruth Dodds, *The Pilgrimage of Grace, 1536–1537* (Cambridge: Cambridge University Press, 1915; reprint, London: Frank Cass and Co., 1971) 1:77.

21 Bendix, *Kings or People* 281. See Guy Fitch Lytle, "Religion and the Lay Patron in

Reformation England," in *Patronage in the Renaissance*, ed. Guy Fitch Lytle and Stephen Orgel (Princeton, N.J.: Princeton University Press, 1981), 65. Patrick Collinson cites the "virulent anticlericalism" of the landowning class in the 1570s and 1580s (*The Religion of Protestants: The Church in English Society, 1559–1625* [Oxford: Clarendon, 1982], 41).

22 Roland Usher, *The Reconstruction of the English Church*, vol. 1 (New York: D. Appleton and Co., 1910), 95–96.

23 William Nicholson, ed., *The Remains of Edmund Grindal* (Cambridge: Cambridge University Press, 1843), 382–83.

24 Norman L. Jones, "Profiting from Religious Reformation: The Land Rush of 1559," *Historical Journal* 22 (1979): 279.

25 D. M. Loades, *Tudor Court* (Totowa, N.J.: Barnes and Noble, 1987), 133; Henry VII quoted in Loades, *Tudor Court* 134; Arthur Marotti, "John Donne and the Rewards of Patronage," in Lytle and Orgel, *Patronage in the Renaissance* 210; William Cecil, Lord Burghley, quoted in Lawrence Stone, *The Crisis of the Aristocracy, 1558–1641* (Oxford: Clarendon, 1965), 464.

26 E.K.'s identification of the brier with youth also indicates the particular importance patronage had as an avenue for the advancement of those relatively new to the scene of power. See Keith Thomas, "Age and Authority in Early Modern England," *Proceedings of the British Academy* 62 (1976): 213, 229.

27 Sir Robert Naunton, *Fragmenta Regalia; or, Observations on the Late Queen Elizabeth Her Times and Favourites*, ed. Edward Arber (London, 1870), 16.

28 See Louis S. Friedland, "Spenser as a Fabulist," *Shakespeare Association Bulletin* 12 (1937): 97; R. T. Lenaghan, ed., *Caxton's Aesop* (Cambridge: Harvard University Press, 1967), 135–6, 185.

29 Luborsky, "Illustrations" 21; Percy W. Long, "Spenser and the Bishop of Rochester," *PMLA* 31 (1916): 732; McLane, *Spenser's "Shepheardes Calender"* 193; Heal, *Of Prelates and Princes* 287. "Aylmer alleged that it was his debts to the queen which had forced him to sell many hundreds of pounds of timber" (Collinson, *Religion of Protestants* 74).

30 F. O. White, *Lives of the Elizabethan Bishops of the Anglican Church* (London: Skeffington and Son, 1898), vii; Collinson, *Religion of Protestants* 27; Wallace T. MacCaffrey, *Queen Elizabeth and the Making of Policy, 1572–1588* (Princeton, N.J.: Princeton University Press, 1981), 39.

31 I am grateful to Professor Valeria Finucci of the Duke University Department of Romance Languages for her assistance in the translation of the emblems.

32 McLane, *Spenser's "Shepheardes Calender"* 61–76. Similarly, Higginson's equation of the oak with the duke of Norfolk runs afoul of Norfolk's close relationship with prominent Protestants, including Dering, Foxe, and Nowell (the last two of whom were with him when he was executed). See Patrick Collinson, *Godly People: Essays on English Protestantism and Puritanism* (London: Hambledon Press, 1983), 300.

33 The fable's "purpose," according to E.K., "is to warne the protestaunt beware, howe he geveth credit to the unfaythfull Catholique" (440).

34   See Anthea Hume, *Edmund Spenser: Protestant Poet* (Cambridge: Cambridge University Press, 1984), 2f.; Edwin A. Greenlaw et al., eds., *The Works of Edmund Spenser: A Variorum Edition*, 11 vols. (Baltimore: Johns Hopkins University Press, 1932–57), vol. 7, pt. 1, pp. 292, 295; James Jackson Higginson, *Spenser's "Shepheardes Calender" in Relation to Contemporary Affairs* (New York: Columbia University Press, 1912), 71–99; and McLane, *Spenser's "Shepheardes Calender"* 121–24.

35   That this concern should be voiced by a figure named Piers, "in Sommer season" (176), firmly situates the May eclogue in the tradition of Piers Plowman, who appeared in a dream that occurred in the same month, recorded in a poem that begins "In a summer season." William Langland, *Will's Vision of Piers Plowman: An Alliterative Verse Translation by E. Talbot Donaldson*, ed. Elizabeth D. Kirk and Judith H. Anderson (New York: W. W. Norton and Co., 1990), 1.

36   Ruth Samson Luborsky, "The *Illustrations to The Shepheardes Calender*," *SSt* 2 (1981): 33.

37   Robert Weimann, *Shakespeare and the Popular Tradition in the Theater: Studies in the Social Dimension of Dramatic Form and Function*, ed. Robert Schwartz (Baltimore: Johns Hopkins University Press, 1978), 24, 25; Frank Fowell, *Censorship in England* (London: Frank Palmer, 1913), 9; John Stow, *A Survey of London*, 2 vols., ed. Charles Kingsford (Oxford: Clarendon, 1908), 1:98–99. See Joseph Strutt, *The Sports and Pastimes of the People of England*, ed. J. Charles Cox (London: Methuen, 1903), 275–81; Robert Withington, *English Pageantry: An Historical Outline*, 2 vols. (Cambridge, Mass.: Harvard University Press, 1918; reprint, New York: Benjamin Blom, 1963), 1:202–3; Loades, *Tudor Court* 99. There was an elaborate May Game at Greenwich in 1559; C. J. Sisson, *Lost Plays of Shakespeare's Age* (Cambridge: Cambridge University Press, 1936), 162.

38   F. J. Furnivall, ed., *Phillip Stubbes's Anatomy of the Abuses in England in Shakespeare's Youth*, 2 vols. (London: New Shakespeare Society, 1877–79), 1:149.

39   Michael McGiffert, "Covenant, Crown, and Commons in Elizabethan Puritanism," *Journal of British Studies* 20 (1980): 39. The Puritans tried to "put [May Games] down throughout the country" (Sisson, *Lost Plays* 162).

40   For discussion of lay patronage in the church, see Rosemary O'Day, "Ecclesiastical Patronage: Who Controlled the Church," in *Church and Society in England: Henry VIII to James I*, ed. Felicity Heal and Rosemary O'Day (London: Macmillan, 1977), 137–55; and Lytle, "Religion and the Lay Patron" 65–114.

41   *Puritan Manifestoes: A Study of the Origin of the Puritan Revolt*, ed. W. H. Frere and C. E. Douglas (London: Church Historical Society, 1907; reprint, New York: Burt Franklin, 1972), 9–10. Strype, *Whitgift* 1:368, 500, quoted in Hill, *Economic Problems* 65.

42   For a discussion of pluralism, see Hill, *Economic Problems*, chap. 10.

43   Parker quoted in Hill, *Economic Problems* 66. See Felicity Heal, "Economic Problems of the Clergy," in Heal and O'Day, *Church and Society in England* 110. In 1584 Whitgift led the opposition in Parliament to the abolition of pluralities (Hill, *Economic Problems* 232–33).

44   Collinson, *Godly People* 162; *Puritan Manifestoes* 10–11; Cartwright in John
Ayre, ed., *The Works of John Whitgift*, 3 vols. (Cambridge: Cambridge University
Press, 1851–53), 1:521, my emphasis. The "continual residence" of the pastor was
essential, both for the "knowledge of [the people's] estate" and for the efficacy of
his example among them: "If the pastor be not amongst his flock, and have not
his conversation there, they cannot follow him" (Whitgift, *Works* 1:514, 518).

45   Furnivall, *Phillip Stubbes's Anatomy of the Abuses* 2:76–77.

46   Youings, *Sixteenth-Century England* 320; Heal, *Of Prelates and Princes* 211–12.
See *Puritan Manifestoes* 102–3.

47   E.K. glosses Pan here as God, citing the priestly Israelite tribe of Levi (439–40).

48   The injunction to live differently grows out of the proverb that encapsulates
Piers's rejection of the powerful as a model: "Who touches Pitch mought needes
be defilde" (74). This proverb is from a section of Ecclesiasticus 13, which is
bluntly glossed by the Geneva Bible: "The companies of the proude & of the
riche are to be eschewed."

49   Heal, *Of Prelates and Princes* 74; *Puritan Manifestoes* 11, 63, 126, 30, 67, 63, 8.

50   Lenaghan, *Caxton's Aesop* 94–95.

51   *Caxton's Aesop* 94.

52   The *yet* of line 233 marks the tension between those warnings and her action.
Recounting the well-known story "of the Lord Hastingues in king Rycharde the
third his dayes," E.K.'s lengthy gloss gives to the ominous interpretations of
such events the credibility of common knowledge, "the like to be marked in all
histories" (440). See Shakespeare's *Richard III* 3.4, which emphasizes Hastings's
arrogance in his supposedly secure position.

53   The *but* again highlights the tension between that concern and her departure.

54   The word is used in this sense more than twice as often as in the other eclogues.

55   T. E. Hartley, ed., *Proceedings in the Parliaments of Queen Elizabeth I*, vol. 1,
1558–1581 (Wilmington, Del.: Michael Glazier, 1981), 173. In the same context
in 1576 she claimed that the depth of the "restles care which I have ever bent to
governe for youre greatest weales" was beyond words (471).

56   Paul L. Hughes and James F. Larkin, eds., *Tudor Royal Proclamations*, vol. 2,
The Later Tudors (New Haven: Yale University Press, 1969), 449. She used the
word *care* six times in this proclamation, four times in the phrase *princely care*.
For other public uses by the queen, see Allison Heisch, "Queen Elizabeth I: Par-
liamentary Rhetoric and the Exercise of Power," *Signs* 1 (1975): 41; John Strype,
Annals of the Reformation (Oxford: Clarendon, 1824; reprint, New York: Burt
Franklin, n.d.), vol. 1, pt. 2, p. 308; and J. E. Neale, "The Commons' Privilege
of Free Speech in Parliament," in *Tudor Studies Presented to Albert Frederick
Pollard* (London: Longmans, Green and Co., 1924), 284.

57   See chapter 2 and *Homilies* 611.

58   Mary used the image as well (see Fletcher, *Tudor Rebellions* 83), but it was not
as central to her regime as it was in the promotion of Elizabeth.

59   William Keatinge Clay, ed., *Private Prayers Put Forth by Authority During the
Reign of Queen Elizabeth* (Cambridge: Cambridge University Press, 1851), 480;

Elizabeth I, A Book of Devotions Composed by Her Majesty, with translations by Adam Fox (Gerrards Cross: Colin Smythe, 1970), 23.

60   Heisch, "Queen Elizabeth I" 32; Hartley, *Proceedings* 1:95.

61   Louis Montrose, " 'Eliza, Queene of shepheardes,' and the Pastoral of Power," *ELR* 10 (1980): 180. As Lawrence Stone notes, "England was particularly insistent upon the subordination of children to parents" (*Crisis* 591).

62   Hayward quoted in Montrose, "Eliza" 180.

63   Richard Mulcaster, *Mulcaster's Elementarie,* ed. E. T. Campagnac (Oxford: Clarendon, 1925), A.2–A.2v.

64   Bishop Edwin Sandys neatly paired the Crown's concern with the disability of its subjects when he declared in 1571: "The care of the commonwealth chiefly appertaineth to the head of the commonwealth, who is *Parens Patriae,* the mother of the sickly child"; John Ayre, ed., *The Sermons of Edwin Sandys* (Cambridge: Cambridge University Press, 1842), 47.

65   Quoted in Neale, "Commons' Privilege" 283.

66   Alexander Nowell, *A Catechism* (Cambridge: Cambridge University Press, 1853), 131. Cartwright, for one, complied, vowing, "We love [magistrates] as our fathers and mothers" (Whitgift, *Works* 1:79).

67   State of the nation address, 1569, in Rice, *Public Speaking* 127. For other examples of the maternal image, see Foxe, *Acts* 8:601–2; Louis Montrose, "The Elizabethan Subject and the Spenserian Text," in Patricia Parker and David Quint, eds., *Literary Theory / Renaissance Texts* (Baltimore: Johns Hopkins University Press, 1986), 316; Rice, *Public Speaking* 117; Thomas Norton, *A Warning Agaynst the Dangerous Practises of the Papistes* (London: John Day, 1569?), N.2v; and Wilson, *England's Eliza.*

68   The queen was, of course, prominently referred to as "governor"—as the "supreme governor" of the realm in the Act of Supremacy, as "queen and governor" in the Communion service (John E. Booty, ed., *The Book of Common Prayer, 1559: The Elizabethan Prayer Book* [Washington, D.C.: Folger Shakespeare Library, 1976], 250), and as "principal Governor" by Foxe (*Acts* 1:502).

69   Thomas Churchyard, *A Discourse of the Queenes Majesties entertainement in Suffolk and Norfolk* (London: Henry Bynneman, n.d.), C.1v. See also the *OED,* s.v. "dame," II.6.

70   E. K. Chambers, *The Elizabethan Stage,* vol. 4 (Oxford: Clarendon, 1923), 75–97; A. L. Rowse, *The England of Elizabeth: The Structure of Society* (London: Macmillan, 1961), 185; William Harrison, *The Description of England,* ed. Georges Edelen (Ithaca, N.Y.: Cornell University Press, 1968), 227.

71   In each woodcut, the sun is on the right, flanked by a tree; on the left two shepherds converse; and in the center there is a festive scene consisting of eleven figures in contemporary dress. (In April's cut there may be another figure hidden behind the third figure from the right, but only eleven stand out.) The lines mentioned are the only two uses of the phrase "Sopps in wine" in Spenser's poetry.

72   Harrison, *Description* 227; Jean Wilson, *Entertainments for Elizabeth I* (Wood-

bridge, Eng.: D.S. Brewer, 1980), 39. Progresses were usually made in wagons like the one depicted in May's woodcut (see Loades, *Tudor Court* 68).

73 Lenaghan, *Caxton's Aesop* 95. See William Meredith Carroll, *Animal Conventions in English Renaissance Non-Religious Prose (1550–1600)* (New York: Bookman Associates, 1954), 104, 119. The wolf in Aesop is not disguised, so the kid can recognize him through the keyhole.

74 Collinson, *Godly People* 162; *Homilies* 110.

75 Spenser uses the word only one other time in his poetry.

76 Letter to James VI in 1590, in Harrison, *Letters of Queen Elizabeth* 204.

77 See McLane, *Spenser's "Shepheardes Calender"* 340; Higginson, *Spenser's "Shepheardes Calender"* 181. In explicating the word *pallinodie*, Puttenham tells the story of Stesichorus (alluded to in E.K.'s glosses on April), a poet who was blinded by Helen for censuring her in one of his poems. To win her favor (and to recover his sight), he wrote a new version—his "pallinodie"—"in which it was not Helen, but her phantom, that accompanied Paris to Troy"; Paul Harvey, ed., *Oxford Companion to Classical Literature* (Oxford: Clarendon, 1962), 406. Puttenham is not concerned with the falsity of the recantation, just its ingratiating function: he recommends such poetry, for it "may suffise for [the poet's] amends" (*The Arte of English Poesie*, in *Elizabethan Critical Essays*, ed. G. Gregory Smith, 2 vols. [Oxford: Clarendon, 1904], 2:49).

78 See Lytle, "Religion and the Lay Patron" 103; and William A. Oram et al., eds., *The Yale Edition of the Shorter Poems of Edmund Spenser* (New Haven: Yale University Press, 1989), 105.

79 This advice was given to a patron, recommending on whom he should bestow his living in *The Return from Parnassus* (1601–2), quoted in Hill, *Economic Problems* 65.

80 For just one important example of the use of *high* and *low,* see the *Homilies'* matter-of-fact description: "Some are in high degree, some in low" (109).

81 Though Morrell is a goatherd, underscoring the demarcation that hierarchy effected between classes, to facilitate the discussion I will refer to both figures as shepherds.

82 For example, Higginson, *Spenser's "Shepheardes Calender"* 99–112; McLane, *Spenser's "Shepheardes Calender"* 188–202.

83 Luborsky, "Illustrations" 36.

84 *Proud* refers to social station as well as to mental attitude (*OED* B.II.6.a).

85 Morrell later points to the medicinal herbs that grow on hills as an example of this social benefit (85–88). Thomalin responds by pointing to the goats' poor food ("frowie fede" and "weedes" [111–12]) as the source of infection, implicitly laying the cause at their herdsman's door.

86 "Standing on the Sinister hindleg, with both forelegs elevated, the Dexter above the Sinister, and the head in profile" (*OED*, s.v. "rampant" A.1.b, quoting John E. Cussans, *The Handbook of Heraldry*).

87 5 Eliz. 1, c. 15, prohibited "any fonde fantasticall or false Prophecye upon or by thoccasion of any Armes Fieldes Beastes Badges or suche other lyke things

accustomed in Armes Cognisaunces [heraldic insignia] or Signettes [seals]."

88 Keith Thomas, *Religion and the Decline of Magic* (New York: Charles Scribner's Sons, 1971), 83. In particular, "pyne, plagues, and dreery death" (23) were among the most commonly cited instruments of that judgment. (*Pyne* meant both physical suffering in general and famine specifically; *OED*, s.v. "pine" *sb.*1 2, 4 (citing *The Faerie Queene*). Thomas further notes that "the *Homilies* taught that penury, dearth and famine were caused by God's anger at the vices of the community. . . . Famine, plague, flood and fire were acts of God, directly provoked by the moral condition of those upon whom they fell" (83–84). John Walter and Keith Wrightson also identify "the three great national judgments" as "dearth, plague and the sword" ("Dearth and the Social Order in Early Modern England," *Past and Present* 71 [1976]: 28). Foxe also treats disease, drought, famine, and pestilence as instruments of God's wrath (*Acts* 1:238–39, 244).

89 Barnaby Googe, *Eglogs, Epytaphes, and Sonettes (1563)*, ed. Edward Arber (Westminster: A. Constable and Co., 1895), 62.

90 "A long roll of English earls, barons and knights wore the lion on their coats." The rampant posture was so common "that the adjective 'rampant' was often dropped" (*Encyclopaedia Britannica* [Chicago: William Benton, 1963], 11:468). See also Charles Boutell, *English Heraldry* (London: Cassell, Petter, and Galpin, 1867), 83; John Woodward, *A Treatise on Heraldry, British and Foreign* (Rutland, Vt.: Charles E. Tuttle Co., 1969), 208. William Berry, ed., *Encyclopedia Heraldica*, 4 vols. (London: Sherwood, Gilbert and Piper, 1828), includes in Glover's "Ordinary of Arms" twenty-one pages of family arms (with fifty to sixty items per page) with the lion on them.

  See Carroll, *Animal Conventions*, chapters 1–3, where Carroll discusses the channels through which animal images circulated in Elizabethan culture.

91 Boutell, *English Heraldry* 83.

92 See, for example, the fables of the lion and his conversation, and the fox and the lion (Lenaghan, *Caxton's Aesop* 119, 130–31). The Reynard stories were widely circulated, in part through the many churches that "contain[ed] parodies on events in the history of Reynard as part of their stone and wood carvings"; Arthur B. Leible, *Conventions of Animal Symbolism and Satire in Spenser's "Mother Hubberds Tale"* (Chicago: University of Chicago Press, 1930), 31. Spenser's poem speaks of the lion: "Lo where they spide, how in a gloomy glade, / The Lyon sleeping lay in secret shade, / His Crowne and Scepter lying him beside" (ll. 951–53). Both Elizabeth and her father, Henry VIII, were depicted as lions; see Thomas, *Religion and the Decline of Magic* 402–3, 405; and Annabel Patterson, "Fables of Power," in *Politics of Discourse: The Literature and History of Seventeenth-Century England*, ed. Kevin Sharpe and Steven N. Zwicker (Berkeley: University of California Press, 1987). In urging subjects to obey the prince, the *Homilies* quote Proverbs 19:12: "The anger and displeasure of the prince is as the roaring of a lion."

93 Sir Thomas Smith, *De Republica Anglorum*, ed. L. Alston (Cambridge: Cambridge University Press, 1906), 46; Stone, *Crisis* 50, 39. Prominent among

Smith's qualifications for gentlemen is the ability "to live idly and without manuall labor" (40). William Harrison emphasizes the "great wealth" that enables men to "live without labour" as the "means to become gentlemen" (*Description* 118). See also Louis Montrose, "Of Gentlemen and Shepherds: The Politics of Elizabethan Pastoral Form," *ELH* 50 (1983):427. Keith Thomas underscores the durability of this stigma: "A contempt for manual labor permeates aesthetic, educational, scientific and religious assumptions until very modern times" ("Work and Leisure," *Past and Present* 29 [1964]: 57).

94   Ayre, *Sermons of Edwin Sandys* 99–100.

95   Quoted in Ruth Kelso, *The Doctrine of the English Gentleman in the Sixteenth Century* (Urbana: University of Illinois Press, 1929; reprint, Gloucester, Mass.: Peter Smith, 1964), 31. Ball himself echoed the medieval churchman who complained that the rich were "fattened from the toil of the poor" (quoted in G. R. Owst, *Literature and Pulpit in Medieval England* [New York: Barnes and Noble, 1961], 299).

96   There is palpable irony, of course, in Morrell's word *rancke*, which had a plethora of pointedly pejorative meanings besides "abundant," including "excessive in amount" and "loathsome."

97   Thomas, *Religion and the Decline of Magic* 89. On the national level, prosperity was frequently taken by apologists for the regime as a sign of divine approval for the regime's policies: "This may be a good token unto us," Whitgift said, "that this church of England is reformed, because the commonwealth doth flourish" (*Works* 1:23–24).

98   Harrison notes its use for "the prince, dukes, marquises, earls, viscounts, and barons" and for "sundry [secular] offices," as well as for bishops (*Description* 94, 97).

99   Whitgift, *Works* 2:189–90; *Puritan Manifestoes* 5.

100   Emotional reaction to the Danish occupation was still palpable in Elizabethan England, as evidenced by pageants on the subject presented to the queen on progress (F. J. Furnivall, ed., *Robert Laneham's Letter* [London: Kegan Paul, Trench, Trübner and Co., 1887], xii, 26–27, 31–32) and by references in Foxe and Holinshed, each of whom includes the story of the confrontation on the bridge (Foxe, *Acts* 2:75–76, 82; Raphael Holinshed, *Chronicles of England, Scotland, and Ireland*, 6 vols. (London, 1807; reprint, New York: AMS Press, 1965), 1:709).

101   *Homilies* 238, 235. Quoting Jesus, the homily declares that "the hour cometh, when you shall worship the Father neither in this mountain nor at Hierusalem, but true worshippers shall worship the Father in spirit and truth" (239).

102   Luke's is also the only account that includes Christ's "bloudy sweat."

103   Montrose, "Of Gentlemen and Shepherds" 430. See chapter 5, "The Politics of Paradise," in Elaine Pagels, *Adam, Eve, and the Serpent* (New York: Random House, 1988), for a discussion of how the claim of the Fall's contagious effect was used in church history to support the power of autocratic political structures.

104   This shepherd, E.K. tells us, "bent hys mind" to his social responsibility (447).

105   Jewel, for example, cites the golden calf episode as an important instance of

Moses' priority: "Moses, a civil magistrate and chief guide of the people, both received from God and delivered to the people all the order for religion and sacrifices, and gave Aaron the bishop a vehement and sore rebuke for making the golden calf and for suffering the corruption of religion" (*An Apology of the Church of England*, ed. John E. Booty [Ithaca, N.Y.: Cornell University Press, 1963], 115).

106   See Exodus 19:3 and 20; 24:13; and 32:30–31.

107   Such conversation does not compromise reverence. Thomalin had previously praised "the first shepheard" (127) because, bringing sacrifices, he "lowted [bowed] . . . unto hys Lord" (137).

108   This tribe was marked by its unwillingness to fully participate in the affairs of the national community: "In the Song of Deborah, Dan is reprimanded because it did not show an interest in the common Israelite cause, but lingered with the ships as a stranger (Judges 5:17). . . . the autonomy of Dan was . . . felt to be a problem in the circle of the amphictyony"; *Interpreters Dictionary of the Bible*, vol. 1 (New York: Abingdon Press, 1962), 759.

109   See the *OED*. This meaning derives, like *lord*, from the Latin root *dominus*. The rhyme of *Dan* (51) with *Pan* (49) emphasizes this link.

110   E.K.'s gloss that the "brethren" are the twelve sons of Jacob (447) links the passage to Dan, who was one of those sons. The rhyme of *Pan* (144) with *Canaan* (142), the whole nation, underscores the point of community under God.

111   *Homilies* 111–12.

112   Foxe cites lightning a number of times as judgment (see Foxe, *Acts* 1:92–93, 145; and Thomas, *Religion and the Decline of Magic* 84, 88), and Whitgift intoned that "the punishment of God by thundering and lightning is more notorious and terrible, not by any help of man to be repelled" (*Works* 2:483).

113   The lightning strike was widely regarded as a sign of God's displeasure, though the precise target of that disapproval was variously attributed. See Patrick Collinson, *Archbishop Grindal, 1519–1583: The Struggle for a Reformed Church* (London: Jonathan Cape, 1979), 154–55; Alan F. Herr, *The Elizabethan Sermon: A Survey and a Bibliography* (Philadelphia: University of Pennsylvania Press, 1940; reprint, New York: Octagon Books, 1969), 44; Millar MacLure, *The Paul's Cross Sermons, 1534–1642* (Toronto: University of Toronto Press, 1958), 58. The association of lightning with divine judgment is found in classical writing as well. Meliboeus in Virgil's first eclogue refers to "the oaks struck down from heaven above" (Paul Alpers, *The Singer of the Eclogues: A Study of Virgilian Pastorals* [Berkeley: University of California Press, 1979], 11), and Horace uses the image to depict the fragility of high status, warning his readers away from "a place liable to excite envy," because "the highest peaks most often are struck by lightning" (*Odes* 2.10, in Horace, *The Complete Odes and Epodes*, trans. W. G. Shepherd [Harmondsworth, Eng.: Penguin Books, 1983], 114).

114   This usage went back at least as far as the 1543 "Acte for thadvauncement of true Religion," which allowed certain plays to be performed so long as they "meddle not with interpretacions of Scripture, contrarye to the doctryne set foorth or

to be sett forth by the Kinges Majestie" (quoted in Frank Fowell, *Censorship in England* [London: Frank Palmer, 1913; reprint, New York: Benjamin Blom, 1969], 9).

115 Nicholson, *Remains of Edmund Grindal* 384, 467. Participation by the people would also undermine the uniformity the regime held as the cornerstone of national security. The queen declared that the exercises "schismatically divided [the people] into a variety of dangerous opinions . . . and manifestly thereby encouraged [them] to the violation of our laws, and to the breach of common order" (467). The Privy Council supported the queen's suppression because of "the great divisions and sects" to which prophesyings contributed, fearing "that religion, which of his own nature should be uniform, would against his nature have proved milliform, yea, in continuance nulliform" (471).

116 Nicholson, *Remains of Edmund Grindal* 391. See Patrick Collinson, "The Downfall of Archbishop Grindal and Its Place in Elizabethan Political and Ecclesiastical History," in *The English Commonwealth, 1557–1640*, ed. P. Clark et al. (New York: Barnes and Noble, 1979), 45. Though it did bar the people by suppressing the prophesyings, the regime could not control their indirect influence in the conflict between the archbishop and the queen itself: Grindal, the focus of intense public attention, was so popular that the Crown's options for dealing with him were restricted. One nobleman cautioned the Privy Council against removing him from office, "the people addicted to the matter as they were" (Collinson, *Grindal* 289).

117 Whitgift, *Works* 3:406–7.

118 The likeness of the sayings is reflected in the parallel grammatical structure of the Latin phrases, as well as in the point-counterpoint of the shepherds' debate. I am grateful to Professor Francis Newton of the Duke University Classics Department for his assistance with the translation of the Latin in the emblems and gloss.

119 Bishop Thomas Cooper, in his Latin-English dictionary, *Thesaurus Linguae Romanae & Britannicae . . .* (1578), translates the phrase in this way in a number of passages.

120 Archbishop Parker frequently used the term *mediocrity* (e.g., John Bruce and Thomas Perowne, eds., *Correspondence of Matthew Parker* [Cambridge: Cambridge University Press, 1853], 173, 215). See also Norman L. Jones, "Elizabeth's First Year: The Conception and Birth of the Elizabethan Political World," in *The Reign of Elizabeth I*, ed. Christopher Haigh (Athens: University of Georgia Press), 47. Grindal referred to his *sequestration* himself in a letter to the Privy Council in November 1577 (Nicholson, *Remains of Edmund Grindal* 393).

121 For example, McLane, and several of those excerpted in the *Variorum* edition (Greenlaw et al., *Works of Edmund Spenser* 350–54).

122 A. L. Beier, "Vagrants and the Social Order in Elizabethan England," *Past and Present* 64 (1974): 24–25; Stone, *Crisis* 506; Edwin A. Greenlaw, "The Shepheardes Calender," *PMLA* 19 (1911): 425.

123 The Vagrancy Act of 1547 defines vagrants as those who "idelye wander," and

the 1572 act lumps a wide variety of persons (e.g., "Pedlars Tynkers and Comon Players") into the category of those who "wander abroade" without a license (14 Eliz. 1, c. 5; R. H. Tawney and Eileen Power, eds., *Tudor Economic Documents* [London: Longmans, Green and Co., 1924], 329]).

124 *Acts of the Privy Council of England* 7:116 (hereinafter *A.P.C.*); *Homilies* 552, 555–56; Harrison, *Description* 183; Edward Viles and F. J. Furnivall, eds., *The Rogues and Vagabonds of Shakespeare's Youth* (New York: Duffield and Co., 1907), 20.

125 Lawrence Manley, "Proverbs, Epigrams, and Urbanity in Renaissance London," *ELR* 15 (1985): 267; A. L. Beier, *Masterless Men: The Vagrancy Problem in England, 1560–1640* (London: Methuen, 1985), xix; Frank Aydelotte, *Elizabethan Rogues and Vagabonds* (Oxford: Clarendon, 1913), 3; A. L. Beier, "Social Problems in Elizabethan London," *Journal of Interdisciplinary History* 9 (1978): 204.

126 The 1563 Statute of Artificers prohibited laborers from traveling outside the locale of their employment without a license, on pain of whipping or punishment; Bland, Brown, and Tawney, *English Economic History* 327. Lawrence Manley notes "the official impulse to categorize" and "the various schemes to establish an articulate social order without margins," concluding: "The greatest challenge to such typifying schemes comes from the mobile characters who inhabit the ever-widening interstices of the social fabric. Marginal and mysterious, they resist proverbial labels, and so cannot be explicated or 'unfolded'; their relentless activity conforms to no one familiar model" ("Proverbs" 268).

127 Youings, *Sixteenth-Century England* 88; Privy Council quoted in Aydelotte, *Elizabethan Rogues* 157; comment on Acts 17:6 quoted in Christopher Hill, *The World Turned Upside Down: Radical Ideas During the English Revolution* (New York: Viking Press, 1972), 32; Paul Slack, "Poverty and Social Regulation in Elizabethan England," in Haigh, *Reign of Elizabeth* 226; Beier, *Masterless Men* 141. According to Youings, 1569 "inaugurated a very determined national effort to put down vagrancy" (*Sixteenth-Century England* 268). Roger B. Manning, *Village Revolts: Social Protest and Popular Disturbances in England, 1509–1640* (Oxford: Clarendon, 1988), 165; Speaker quoted in Paul Slack, "Poverty" 285, n. 3.

128 Harrison, for example, divides the poor between those who are "poor by impotency . . . [or] casualty . . . [and the] thriftless poor [mainly vagabonds]" (*Description* 180). The first two are "the true poor indeed . . . for whom the Word doth bind us to make some daily provision" (181). Harman also separates "the poore, nedy, impotent, and myserable creatures" from "vagarantes and sturdy vacabons" (Viles and Furnivall, *Rogues* 19).

129 *Homilies* 553. Though some provision was made in the 1576 act for relieving the vagabond's situation by giving work to the able-bodied, the primary impetus until late in Elizabeth's reign was to preserve public order by disciplining vagrants. Punishment was frequently exacted: "In the Middlesex sessions between 1572 and 1575, for example, forty-four vagabonds were sentenced to be branded, eight to be set to service, and five to be hanged"; John Pound, *Poverty*

and Vagrancy in Tudor England (London: Longman Group, 1971), 47. Harrison's claim that three or four hundred a year were hanged (*Description* 193) may be an exaggeration, but it does suggest widespread punishment.

130 Mary Dewar, introduction to *A Discourse of the Commonweal of This Realm of England*, attributed to Sir Thomas Smith, ed. Mary Dewar (Charlottesville: University Press of Virginia, 1969), ix–x; Williams, *Tudor Regime* 214. See also Stone, *Crisis* 139, 548–49.

131 See Lawrence Stone's introduction to R. H. Tawney, *The Agrarian Problem in the Sixteenth Century* (New York: Harper and Row, 1967), xi; Eric Kerridge, "The Movement of Rent, 1540–1640," *Economic History Review*, 2d ser., 6 (1953): 16–34; Harrison, *Description* 202; Beier, *Masterless Men* 21. "Although substantial farmers producing for the market could sustain the high burden of rent and still profit from rising prices, the subsistence farmer—the cottager or small husbandman—was often forced off the land in competition for holdings" (Williams, *Tudor Regime* 141).

132 Harrison, *Description* 181–82. See Joan Thirsk, *Tudor Enclosures* (London: Routledge and Kegan Paul, 1959), 5; Manning, *Village Revolts* 4–5, 20. Harrison described this "notable and grievous . . . inconvenience," which was "growing . . . by encroaching and joining of house to house and laying land to land, whereby the inhabitants of many places of our country are devoured and their houses either altogether pulled down or suffered to decay little by little" (216).

133 Thirsk, *Agricultural Change* 55; Manning, *Village Revolts* 6, 3, 55. See *A.P.C.* 7:137; 8:195, 240–41, 243–45, 313; 9:160, 167, 323–24, 382; 10:155, 374, 399–400, 412; 11:95–96, 99, 103, 106, 110, 111, 129, 154, 178–79, 191–92, 320. See also *Calendar of State Papers, Domestic* 7:367, 1:554 (hereinafter *Cal. S.P. Dom.*); and F. G. Emmison, *Elizabethan Life: Disorder* (Chelmsford: Essex City Council, 1970), 101f.

134 Elizabeth's first Parliament, reenacting a Marian statute, made collective action destroying enclosures a felony punishable by death (1 Eliz. 1, c. 16).

135 Fletcher, *Tudor Rebellions* 64, 142. The loss of community could be at least symbolically rectified by tearing down the hedge that constituted that enclosure: "By destroying an enclosing hedge, the dispossessed restored, if only momentarily, a sense of community and dramatized their own sense of justice" (Manning, *Village Revolts* 27).

136 *Cal. S.P. Dom.* 7:465. See Hughes and Larkin, *Proclamations* 2:310.

137 Williams, *Tudor Regime* 336. He notes that the violations uncovered by government commissions "seldom led to any remedy" (184). See also Tawney, *Agrarian Problem* 327–29.

138 According to Stone, "Under Elizabeth the court was more useful to magnates wishing to punish poachers on their deer-parks than it was to gentry or lesser men seeking protection against the tyranny of their superiors" (*Crisis* 235).

139 Williams, *Tudor Regime* 336.

140 Manning, *Village Revolts* 69–70; Williams, *Tudor Regime* 183; *A.P.C.* 11: 191–92.

141 Thirsk, *Tudor Enclosures* 7; Manning, *Village Revolts* 77–79.

142 "The outbreak of popular disturbances usually reflected a deterioration in the quality of justice dispensed" (Manning, *Village Revolts* 1).

143 For example, "Ket and his men . . . claimed to be enforcing government policy where the commissions had failed" (Williams, *Tudor Regime* 336). The relationship such rioters saw between their action and failed legal procedures is emphasized by "the rituals of protest employed by demonstrators, [which] frequently mimicked judicial ceremonies" (Manning, *Village Revolts* 1).

144 Stone, *Crisis* 330; Furnivall, *Phillip Stubbes's Anatomy of the Abuses* 1:105; Tilley, *Dictionary* 99.

145 See Christopher Hill, "The Many-Headed Monster," in Hill, *Change and Continuity in Seventeenth-Century England* (Cambridge: Harvard University Press, 1975), 181–204.

146 Tilley, *Dictionary* 203; *OED*, s.v. "lick" 1.b. Diggon's phrase nicely reverses Harrison's image of vagrants exploiting others by "lick[ing] the sweat from the true laborers' brows" (*Description* 183).

147 See Amos 4:1: "Heare this word, ye kine of Bashan . . . which oppresse the poore, *and* destroy the nedie." The gloss in the Geneva Bible identifies the "kine" as "princes and governors."

148 There may also be a specific reference to enclosures in the phrase "brace hem about" (124), echoing the "compassing" and "closing about" of the psalm. Obviously, enclosures did not encircle those who suffered because of them, but in both the biblical passage and Diggon's statement, the action of enclosing was the means and sign of oppression. Further, many enclosures were erected to create pasture for fattening cattle. Bashan itself was "a fertile region east of the Jordan famous for its cattle and sheep"; Mitchell Dahood, ed., *The Anchor Bible*, vol. 16 (Garden City, N.Y.: Doubleday, 1966), 140. Harrison describes those owners who, "still desirous to enlarge those grounds . . . for the breed and feeding of cattle, do not let daily to take in more, not sparing the very commons whereupon many townships now and then do live" (*Description* 256).

149 A similar motif is central to *Colin Clouts Come Home Againe*. See also Hume, *Edmund Spenser* 33–34.

150 Harvey later repeats this image, referring to the court as "the only mart of prefaerment and honour" (quoted in Weimann, *Shakespeare and the Popular Tradition* 168).

151 The same impulse lies behind E.K.'s effort in his argument to confine the eclogue's interpretation to the "loose living of Popish prelates" (452).

152 See Michael G. Brennan, "Foxes and Wolves in Elizabethan Episcopal Propaganda," *Cahiers Elizabethains*, no. 29 (1986): 83–86. The Puritans themselves used the wolf image to refer not only to Catholics but also to courtiers who preyed on church property (Higginson, *Spenser's "Shepheardes Calender"* 82).

153 Bromyard, in Owst, *Literature and Pulpit* 303; Robert Crowley, *The way to wealth* . . . (London, 1550), A.4v.

154 Though such searches became more frequent after the rebellions of 1569 and 1570, they had been conducted in the 1560s as well (Beier, *Masterless Men* 156).

155 *Pert* here means "open" or "unconcealed."

156 William Harrison refers to "the mastiffe, tie dog, or bandog, so called bicause many of them are tied up in chaines . . . for doing hurt abroad" (*Description* 343). These animals would be considered most dangerous during the "dog days" in late summer, a four- to six-week period between July and early September when dogs were thought to go mad (*Book of Common Prayer* 390). In 1617 a pamphleteer named William Fennor complained about law enforcement officers as a "brace of bandogs"; Sandra Clark, *The Elizabethan Pamphleteers: Popular Moralistic Pamphlets, 1580–1640* (Rutherford, N.J.: Farleigh Dickinson University Press, 1983), 165.

157 Lindsay Boynton, "The Tudor Provost-Marshal," *Economic History Review* 77 (1982): 439. In 1570 the first peacetime provost-marshal was appointed in London "to clear the city of rogues, vagrants and maimed soldiers" (442).

158 Harrison, *Description* 185. See Lindsay Boynton, *The Elizabethan Militia, 1558–1638* (London: Routledge and Kegan Paul, 1967), 11, 13. Musters were frequently held at Michaelmas in September (Boynton 19, 93). One of the early firearms was called a dog (*OED*, s.v. "dog" I.9).

159 The trained bands were a fallback for the Crown after a "uniformly hostile reaction" killed its proposal for a corps of harquebusiers paid for by local taxes (Boynton, *Elizabethan Militia* 60–62, 89).

160 Quoted in Youings, *Sixteenth-Century England* 220. Crowley may have been referring to the same danger when he inveighed against "leaving with everye flocke a dogge that woulde rather worye a shepe then drive away the woulfe" (*Way to wealth* A.5).

161 Barnaby Rich's pamphlet *Allarme to England* (London, 1578) proclaimed the virtues of military prowess for the health and security of the nation. Barnaby Googe declares in his prose introduction to Rich's work: "For according to the opinion of a late learned writer . . . The onely strength of every commonwealth is, To have skilfull and well trayned souldiers: so shall they live in happiness, being free from all kinde of terrour and tumult" (4v).

    See Roy Strong, *Gloriana: The Portraits of Queen Elizabeth I* (New York: Thames and Hudson, 1987), 139.

162 In contrast, he identifies the literary sources of the fables in February, May, and July.

163 Sir John Harington, *A Supplie or Addicion to the Catalogue of Bishops to the Yeare 1608*, ed. R. H. Miller (Potomac, Md.: José Porrúa Turanzas S.A., 1979), 142; Hill, *Economic Problems* 26–27; C. J. Kitching, "The Quest for Concealed Lands in the Reign of Elizabeth I," *Transactions of the Royal Historical Society*, 5th ser., 24 (1974): 74. Such "concealed" property was an important source of patronage during Elizabeth's reign, "an asset which the queen might use to satisfy faithful servants, or the land-market at large, without drawing on good lands"; Kitching, "Quest" 66. It was not only the land itself but the authority to search for concealment that was valuable: "By the end of the 1560's licenses to seek concealments as a reward for service were well established" (68). Further, "the initiative [for these commissions] came from the courtiers seeking lands" (66). They were often rewarded with either a favorable purchase price for land

they uncovered or title in fee-farm (69; see also Williams, *Tudor Regime* 419).

164   *Encyclopaedia Britannica* 5:345–46; A. C. Judson, *Biographical Sketch of John Young, Bishop of Rochester, with Emphasis on His Relations with Edmund Spenser*, (Bloomington: Indiana University Press, 1934), 25.

165   Strype, *Annals*, vol. 2, pt. 2, pp. 272–73. McLane refers to this episode but, following E. K.'s lead, rejects it in favor of Protestant-Catholic conflict as the proper context for the eclogue (*Spenser's "Shepheardes Calender"* 162–63). It is worth noting that Archbishop of York Edmund Grindal also complained to Cecil about the conduct of royal commissioners pursuing concealment in his diocese (John Strype, *The History of the Life and Acts of . . . Edmund Grindal* [Oxford: Clarendon, 1821], 264–65. The same year he opposed an enclosure in his jurisdiction because of the hardship to the poor inhabitants in the neighborhood (270–71). He also interceded to save a hospital victimized by "unreasonable leases and grants" (274–75).

166   His disguises even suggest the name given to those who prosecuted claims of concealment: *concealers*. See the *OED*, which cites an early seventeenth-century legal dictionary. Though the dictionary's editors describe this account of the word's meaning as "absurd," both Strype and Kitching use it in this way.

167   John 10, taken from *The Book of Common Prayer* 173.

168   Aegremont Ratcliffe, trans., *Politique Discourses . . .* (London, 1578), A.2, A.3v–A.4; *Homilies* 326.

169   Hobbinol's own acknowledgment that human agency is responsible for social conditions—"Such il, as is forced" (139)—deprives those conditions of religious sanction. The decision about whether to change them then becomes, as it did for the peasants who decided to "leave of" (134), a pragmatic calculation whose outcome is far less predictable and stable than it would have been had religion conferred on those conditions transcendent prestige.

170   John Frederick Nims, ed., *Ovid's Metamorphoses: The Arthur Golding Translation, 1567* (New York: Macmillan, 1965), 3.598.

171   The scales had this meaning in classical, biblical, and popular lore. See Burton Stevenson, ed., *Home Book of Proverbs, Maxims, and Familiar Phrases* (New York: Macmillan, 1948), 1286–87; Daniel 5:27; and H. Oskar Sommer, ed., *The Kalender of Shepherdes*, 3 vols. (London: Kegan Paul, Trench, Trübner and Co., 1892), 3:91, 134.

6 "Rurall Musick Scorned": Poetry in the Poem

1   Nancy Jo Hoffman, *Spenser's Pastorals: "The Shepheardes Calender" and "Colin Cloute"* (Baltimore: Johns Hopkins University Press, 1977), 62.

2   Balthazzar Castiglione, *The Book of the Courtier*, trans. Sir Thomas Hoby (London: E. Arnold, 1900), 123; George Puttenham, *The Arte of English Poesie*, in *Elizabethan Critical Essays*, ed. G. Gregory Smith, 2 vols. (Oxford: Clarendon,

1904), 2:191, 183. Unless otherwise noted, all passages from Puttenham are from this volume.

3   George Puttenham, *The Arte of English Poesie*, ed. Gladys Doidge Willcock and Alice Walker (Cambridge: Cambridge University Press, 1936), 186.

4   Puttenham, *Arte* 18. See Louis Montrose, "Of Gentlemen and Shepherds: The Politics of Elizabethan Pastoral Form," *ELH* 50 (1983): 438, and David Norbrook, *Poetry and Politics in the English Renaissance* (London: Routledge and Kegan Paul, 1984), 77. Montrose (433f.), Daniel Javitch (*Poetry and Courtliness in Renaissance England* [Princeton, N.J.: Princeton University Press, 1978], chap. 2), and Gary Waller (*English Poetry of the Sixteenth Century* [London: Longman Group, 1986]) each discuss Puttenham's *Arte* in the context of courtiership.

5   Puttenham, *Arte* 160–61, 191. His emphasis on decorum, for example, grows from the conviction that it is the wellspring of "every thing which pleaseth the mind or sences," particularly, as one chapter title puts it, "What . . . Generally Makes Our Speach Well Pleasing & Commendable" (173). Unlike others who preferred quantitative meter to "barbarous rime," Puttenham preferred rhyme because of the enjoyment it gave the audience, "the eare taking pleasure to heare the like tune reported and to feel his returne" (80). It should therefore be constructed "as may best serve the eare for delight" (88).

6   Puttenham, *Arte* 56, 64–65, 33–34 (my emphasis). In his *Partheniades* Puttenham eschews the writing of "churlishe satire" (in *Ballads from Manuscripts*, ed. W. A. Morfill [Hertford, Eng.: Stephen Austin and Sons, 1973], 74).

7   In addition to the discussions by Montrose, Javitch, and Waller, Puttenham is the subject of Jonathan Crewe's "The Hegemonic Theater of George Puttenham," *ELR* 16 (1986): 71–85.

8   Stephen Gosson saw poetry as the first step on the slippery slope leading, through pleasure, to the devil (*The School of Abuse*, ed. Edward A. Arber [Westminster: A. Constable and Co., 1895], 24). Though Sidney shapes his poetics from classical and Continental sources, while Spenser in the *Calender*, as we have seen, draws much more heavily on the vernacular literary tradition, each is antagonistic to important elements of court poetics.

9   Katherine Duncan-Jones and Jan van Dorsten, eds., *Miscellaneous Prose of Sir Philip Sidney* (Oxford: Clarendon, 1973), 81, 92; hereinafter cited as Sidney, *Prose*.

10 Louis Montrose, "Celebration and Insinuation: Sir Philip Sidney and the Motives of Elizabethan Courtship," *Renaissance Drama*, n.s., 8 (1977): 14; Sidney, "A Letter Written by Sir Philip Sidney to Queen Elizabeth Touching Her Marriage with Monsieur," in Sidney, *Prose* 46, 53; *Defence*, in Sidney, *Prose* 94.

11 This work was not published until 1595, but it may have been written as early as 1591, after Spenser made a trip to England with Sir Walter Ralegh in 1589–90.

12 In July Morrell echoes Palinode, accusing Thomalin of antipathy to delight. Like Palinode, he uses religion to enhance pleasure's moral status, associating its loss with the Fall: "sithens [the Fall] shepheardes bene foresayd / from places of de-

light: / For thy I weene thou be affrayd, / to clime this hilles height" (69–72). The rhyme of *delight* and *height* is particularly emphatic in aligning superior social status with pleasure.

13 See Edwin A. Greenlaw et al., eds., *The Works of Edmund Spenser: A Variorum Edition* 11 vols. (Baltimore: Johns Hopkins University Press, 1932–57), vol. 7, pt. 1, pp. 310–11, 315, 321. Thomas H. Cain, the editor of *The Shepheardes Calender* in *The Yale Edition of the Shorter Poems of Edmund Spenser,* ed. William A. Oram et al. (New Haven: Yale University Press, 1989), mistakenly identifies the figure in the woodcut gesturing toward the castle as Colin (108), misreading Hobbinol's invitation to Colin to come to court and ignoring the broken pipe at the feet of the poet figure. See Ruth Samson Luborsky, "The Illustrations to *The Shepheardes Calender,*" *SSt* 2 (1981): 26, 35.

14 Puttenham, *Arte* 26. Calliope's name is glossed in both eclogues, June's referring back to April's.

15 See Louis Montrose, " 'The perfecte paterne of a Poete': The Poetics of Courtship in *The Shepheardes Calender,*" *TSLL* 21 (1979): 34.

16 Both "garlands" (*OED* 4) and "dight" (*OED* II. 6 and 7) refer to literary work, the latter recalling Colin's song in April as "trimly dight" (29).

17 Louis Montrose, " 'Eliza, Queene of shepheardes,' and the Pastoral of Power," *ELR* 10 (1980): 168. For discussion of Petrarchism, see Arthur Marotti's classic essay " 'Love Is Not Love': Elizabethan Sonnet Sequences and the Social Order," *ELH* 49 (1982): 396–428; Ann Jones and Peter Stallybrass, "The Politics of *Astrophil and Stella,*" *SEL* 24 (1984): 53–68; Montrose, "Of Gentlemen and Shepherds" 440–48; Leonard Forster, *The Icy Fire: Five Studies in European Petrarchism* (Cambridge: Harvard University Press, 1969), chap. 4; and Leonard Tennenhouse, "Sir Walter Ralegh and the Literature of Clientage," in *Patronage in the Renaissance,* ed. Guy Fitch Lytle and Stephen Orgel (Princeton, N.J.: Princeton University Press, 1981), 235–58.

18 John Frederick Nims, ed., *Ovid's Metamorphoses: The Arthur Golding Translation, 1567* (New York: Macmillan, 1965), 11.191.

19 Paul Alpers, "Pastoral and the Domain of Lyric in Spenser's *Shepheardes Calender,*" *Representations* 12 (1985): 96.

20 Puttenham, *Arte* 87, 65. Skelton affirms the plain style in his own poetry: "For though my ryme be ragged, / Tattered and jagged, / Rudely rayne-beaten, / Rusty and mothe-eaten, / Yf ye take well therwith, / It hath in it some pyth" (*Colin Clout,* ll. 53–58 from John Skelton, *The Complete English Poems,* ed. John Scattergood [New Haven: Yale University Press, 1983]).

21 See Greenlaw et al., *Works of Edmund Spenser,* vol. 7, pt. 1, pp. 651–55.

22 Translated by Paul Alpers, in Alpers, *The Singer of the Eclogues: A Study of Virgilian Pastoral* (Berkeley: University of California Press, 1979), eclogue 3, ll. 25–27.

23 Ovid *Met.* 11. 181, 187.

24 This is in sharp contrast to the monarch celebrated with "grace" five times in April.

25 Greenlaw et al., *Works of Edmund Spenser*, vol. 7, pt. 1, p. 367; John King, "Spenser's *Shepheardes Calender* and Protestant Pastoral Satire," in *Renaissance Genres: Essays on Theory, History, and Interpretation*, ed. Barbara Kiefer Lewalski (Cambridge: Harvard University Press, 1986), 397; Fletcher in Greenlaw et al., *Works of Edmund Spenser*, vol. 7, pt. 1, p. 368; Waller, *English Poetry* 46. According to King, in the eclogue "Spenser . . . evolves a Protestant theory of poetry" that incorporates "neoplatonic views of poetry as a divine gift and a poetic rapture" (397).

26 Even those critics who give some account of the conflict in the eclogue describe that conflict in abstract psychological or philosophical terms rather than in social ones. For example, de Sélincourt internalizes the conflict "in the poet's own nature" between "the practical—eager for fame, and inclined to value poetry at its market price, as a means to further his worldly ambitions—and the ideal, expressed in a passion for an art which, as he had learned from his master Plato, 'was a divine gift and heavenly instinct' "; J. C. Smith and E. de Sélincourt, eds., *Spenser: Poetical Works* (London: Oxford University Press, 1912), xvi–xvii, quoting E. K. Patrick Cullen echoes this approach, casting the debate as a "dramatic conflict of pastoral perspectives," a philosophical conflict that, significantly, pits social engagement against the transcendent integrity of the self: "How and to what extent can a man participate in the world and yet preserve himself and his eternal responsibility from being tainted?" (*Spenser, Marvell, and Renaissance Pastoral* [Cambridge: Harvard University Press, 1970], 69).

27 William Webbe, *A Discourse of English Poetrie*, in Smith, *Elizabethan Critical Essays* 1:230.

28 See Kenneth R. R. Gros Louis, "The Triumph and Death of Orpheus in the English Renaissance," *SEL* 9 (1969): 63–80. Thomas Lodge, responding to the charge of poetry's "wantoness," exemplifies these allusions: "The holy spokesman of the Gods, / Which heave[n]ly Orpheus hight, / Did drive the savage men from wods, / And made them live aright" (*A Defence of Poetry*, in *Elizabethan Critical Essays* 1:74). Puttenham declared that "he brought the rude and savage people to a more civill and orderly life" (*Arte* 6). See Webbe's similar paean (*Discourse* 234) and Sidney's references in his *Defence* (*Prose* 74, 80) and his "Third Song" in *Astrophel and Stella*.

29 In Ovid some of Argus's eyes continually "duly watch and warde, / And of the charge they tooke in hande had ever good regarde" (*Met.* 1.777–78). This model was invoked to praise Roffyn in September (203) and to exemplify the qualities of the good shepherd in July (154).

30 In Ovid, Mercury "pyped . . . upon an Oten Reede" (*Met.* 1.842), using pastoral itself to accomplish his treachery.

31 Lawrence Stone, *The Crisis of the Aristocracy, 1558–1641* (Oxford: Clarendon, 1979), 266.

32 His own transformation (*corruption* is not too strong a word), culminating in his later use of the phrase "pierlesse Poesye" (79), reinforces the idea, as I noted earlier, of the vulnerability of poetry to the court's prestige and power.

33   In Theocritus' idyll 16, which E.K. cites as the model for this eclogue, the poet bids for patronage from Hiero II of Syracuse ("I seek of mortals one / to whom I may come, not unwelcome, bringing my Muses" [66–67]), relying on the same claim E.K. invokes: that poets generate fame. See Anna Rist, trans., *The Poems of Theocritus*, (Chapel Hill: University of North Carolina Press, 1978).

34   See *OED*, s.v. "fain" v.¹ 2, 3.

35   Lodge, *Defence* 76. Among its other meanings, *ribald* referred to someone of the lower class, specifically a vagabond (*OED* A.2.).

36   The Yale edition, for example, describes Tom Piper as a "generic name for an ignorant rustic rhymster" (174), ignoring the character by that name in the popular Morris dance.

37   The Yale edition's editor here, too, reverses the two figures (167) but does not explain why the figure wearing poetic laurels should be Piers rather than "the perfecte paterne of a Poete," Cuddie. See Luborsky, "Illustrations" 36–39.

38   Thomas Elyot, *The Boke Named the Governour* (London: J.M. Dent and Co., 1907), 57; Lodge, *Defence*, 64, 75.

39   *Vaunted* echoes the *vaunting* of line 69, referring to a poetry of celebration. These are the only times the word is used in the *Calender*.

40   Richard McCoy, "Gascoigne's '*Poëmata castrata*': The Wages of Courtly Success," *Criticism* 27 (1985): 30.

41   H. Oskar Sommer, ed., *The Kalender of Shepherdes* (London: Kegan Paul, Trench, Trübner and Co., 1892), 3:19; Edwin Miller, *The Professional Writer in Elizabethan England* (Cambridge: Harvard University Press, 1959), 16. Webbe, for example, cites the imbibing of those who wrote "Ale-house" songs: "Every one that can frame a Book in Ryme, though for want of matter it be but in commendations of Copper noses or Bottle Ale, wyll catch at the Garlande due to Poets; whose potticall, poeticall (I should say), heades I would wyshe at their worshipfull comencements might in steede of Lawrell be gorgiously garnished with fayre greene Barley, in token of their good affection to our Englishe Malt" (*Discourse* 246). See also Richard Stanyhurst's criticism of Ennius, who wrote "but when hee were haulfe tipsye" (Smith, *Elizabethan Critical Essays* [1:137]). "It became the tradition that [the ballad writer] Elderton 'armed himself with ale when he ballated, as old father Ennius did with wine'"; C.H. Firth, "Ballads and Broadsides," in *Shakespeare's England*, vol. 2 (Oxford: Clarendon, 1932), 512, quoting William Fulwood's "Supplication" addressed to Elderton.

42   Puttenham refers to the "lofty stage" and "buskins" of tragedy (*Arte* 35).

43   Though tragedy's subject is the politically powerful (portrayed on its "stately stage"), its orientation is altogether different, warning present rulers by rebuking past ones; in Sidney's words, it "maketh kings fear to be tyrants" (*Prose* 96). Puttenham tried to sap tragedy of this critical potential.

Epilogue: Inventing Society

1 Edward Dering, *A Sermon preached before the Quenes Magistie . . . the 25 day of February . . . 1569* in *M. Derings Workes* (London, 1597; reprint, Amsterdam: Theatrum Orbis Terrarum, 1972), fol. 27.

2 T. E. Hartley, ed., *Proceedings in the Parliaments of Queen Elizabeth I*, vol. 1, (1558–1581) (Wilmington, Del.: Michael Glazier, 1981), 426, 453.

3 Elizabeth's sensitivity on this issue was well known. The Spanish ambassador reported that "the Queen [became] very angry at the gossip that was going about Alençon's coming, and . . . formally ordered that the matter should not be spoken of" (*Calender of State Papers, Spanish, Elizabeth, 1568–1579* 692). Her anger led to the arrest of two of her ladies, the countess of Derby and the earl of Bedford's daughter, and others felt the brunt of her disapproval: Francis Knollys and Christopher Hatton were sharply rebuked, and Walsingham and Leicester were driven to leave court for months (Leicester's secret marriage was another factor in his exile). This was not a new tactic: the queen had earlier "banished several leading nobles from court because they supported the Parliamentary succession campaign"; Michael A. R. Graves, *The Tudor Parliaments: Crown, Lords and Commons, 1485–1603* (London: Longman Group, 1985), 26.

4 Sir Philip Sidney, *Prose Works*, vol. 3, ed. A. Feuillerat (Cambridge: Cambridge University Press, 1962), 129.

5 The lawyer was committed to the Tower, and the judge was so severely rebuked that he resigned. See James A. Froude, *History of England from the Fall of Wolsey to the Defeat of the Spanish Armada*, 12 vols. (London: Longmans, Green and Co., 1902), 10, 501–2; John Stubbs, *Gaping Gulf*, ed. Lloyd E. Berry (Charlottesville: University Press of Virginia, 1968), xxxiv, quoting Camden; and H. J. Byrom, "Edward Spenser's First Printer, Hugh Singleton," *Library*, 4th ser., 14 (1933): 140.

6 Stubbs, *Gaping Gulf* xxxvi–vii. Stubbs was then returned to prison, where he remained until 1581.

7 Carlo Ginzburg uses these terms to measure the adequacy of historical accounts. See Roger Chartier, *Cultural History: Between Practices and Representations*, trans. Lydia G. Cochrane (Ithaca, N.Y.: Cornell University Press, 1988), 66.

8 See, for example, Stephen Greenblatt, "Invisible Bullets: Renaissance Authority and Its Subversion, *Henry IV* and *Henry V*," in *Political Shakespeare: New Essays in Cultural Materialism*, ed. Jonathan Dollimore and Alan Sinfield (Ithaca, N.Y.: Cornell University Press, 1985), 18–47. The "cultural distance" between the two exemplars underwrites the tacit claim that only a "pattern," a characteristic fundamental to the society as a whole, could account for the similarity.

9 Pertinent here is Lee Patterson's warning against the use of "the exemplary instance" as an avenue back "to the expressive unity of *Geistesgeschichte*" through synecdochic logic (introduction to *Literary Practice and Social Change in Britain, 1380–1530*, ed. Lee Patterson [Berkeley: University of California Press, 1990], 9).

10 Lee Patterson, *Negotiating the Past: The Historical Understanding of Medieval Literature* (Madison: University of Wisconsin Press, 1987), 62.

11 See Alan Liu, "Local Transcendence: Cultural Criticism, Postmodernism, and the Romanticism of Detail," *Representations* 32 (1990): 75–113.

12 See Marilyn Butler, "Against Tradition: The Case for a Particularized Historical Method," in *Historical Studies and Literary Criticism*, ed. Jerome J. McGann (Madison: University of Wisconsin Press, 1985), 28–30.

13 Sir Walter Ralegh, *The History of the World*, 2 vols., ed. C. A. Patrides (Philadelphia: Temple University Press, 1971), 1:80.

14 It is not "furthest fro the marke" to suggest, for example, that the supposed absence of class in contemporary American society weighs on our capacity to recognize it elsewhere.

15 Greenblatt, "Invisible Bullets" 45. Greenblatt's declaration also derives in large measure from the antifoundationalist maxim that you cannot see, much less challenge, the ground on which you stand. Whatever the validity of this premise in its original context, the psychology of a single consciousness, it is simply inapt when applied by analogy to the dynamics of a society that is, by definition, composed of plural minds, shaped by diverse experiences, and moved by often clashing interests. It is the equation of mental operation with social interaction that gives some antifoundationalist (and new historicist) discussion of society its monolithic cast.

16 *Spin* is the term for one political variant of this practice. See Hannah Arendt's provocative reflection on the consequences of elevating the practice to the level of policy, in "Lying in Politics: Reflections on the Pentagon Papers," in Arendt, *Crises of the Republic* (New York: Harcourt Brace Jovanovich, 1972), 1–47.

Index

Elizabeth I (*continued*)
(nn. 115, 116), 229 (n. 3); royal
progresses, 11, 197 (n. 100), 215 (n.
72), 217 (n. 100); cult of, 16–26
passim, 53, 136, 142, 143, 182 (nn. 9,
12, 13), 183 (nn. 21, 22); as mother of
England, 18, 32, 101–14 passim, 214
(nn. 64, 66); Accession Day, 26, 183
(n. 23), 185 (n. 45). *See also* Court, the
Elizabethan; Monarchy, Elizabethan
Elton, Geoffrey, 94
Elyot, Thomas, 164
Emblem books, 45, 117
Enclosures, 2, 135–39, 141, 221 (nn. 132,
134, 137), 222 (n. 48); litigation over,
136–37, 139, 221 (n. 138), 222 (nn.
142, 143), 224 (n. 165); protests
against, 136–37, 141, 221 (n. 135), 222
(n. 142)
England's Helicon, 17
Epigrams, 149–50
Erasmus, 54
Essentialist perspective in literary
criticism, 3–6, 10, 11, 12, 177 (n. 6),
178 (nn. 9, 15), 203 (n. 41)
Ezekiel, 81

Fables, 11, 39, 41–42, 43, 54, 89, 193 (n.
66), 194 (n. 81); of Aesop, 41–42, 63,
69; of the eagle and the shellfish
(Algrind), 62, 72, 115, 128–30; of the
oak and the brier, 68, 90–101, 140,
143, 151–52, 211 (nn. 26, 32); of the
fox and the ape, 69; of the goat, kid,
and fox, 82, 101–14, 143, 211 (n. 33),
215 (n. 73); of the mother ape, 112–13.
See also Aesop
Family of Love, 199 (n. 6)
February eclogue, 13, 42, 43, 62, 68, 69,
89–101, 140, 143, 151, 171, 183 (n.
29), 193 (n. 64), 194 (n. 81), 207 (nn.
38, 42), 211 (nn. 26, 32), 223 (n. 162).
See also Patronage
Field, John, 59
Fletcher, Anthony, 52, 96
Fletcher, J. B., 158

Foxe, John, 29, 44, 46, 47, 65, 76, 92, 186
(n. 9), 211 (n. 32), 218 (n. 112)
Friedland, Louis, 45

Gaping Gulf, 33, 59, 109. *See also*
Stubbs, John
Gascoigne, George, 84
Geneva Bible, 81, 134, 186 (n. 10), 187 (n.
13), 213 (n. 48)
Goldberg, Jonathan, 67
Golden Age, 76–77, 205 (n. 18). *See also*
Ball, John; Egalitarianism;
Primitivism
Golding, Arthur, 18, 65, 66, 70–71
Googe, Barnaby, 117
Gosson, Stephen: *School of Abuse*
(1579), 150
Gower, John, 39
Greenblatt, Stephen, 174, 179 (n. 21),
230 (n. 15)
Greenwich, 110
Grindal, Edmund, archbishop of
Canterbury, 26, 60–61, 62, 74, 97, 98,
100, 112, 125, 129–30, 131, 168–69,
173, 219 (n. 116), 224 (n. 165)
Gundolf, bishop of Rochester, 144

Hall, Vernon, 49–50
Harman, William: *A Caveat or Warning
for Commen Cursetors . . . etc.*, 133
Harrison, William, 28, 47, 110, 111, 133,
135, 142, 217 (nn. 93, 98), 220 (n. 128),
221 (n. 148)
Harvey, Gabriel, 77. See also
Shepheardes Calender: letter to
Gabriel Harvey
Hayward, John, 109
Heal, Felicity, 95
Heisch, Alison, 109
Helen, 20, 183 (n. 26), 215 (n. 77)
Helgerson, Richard, 191 (n. 45)
Henry VII, 98, 101
Henry VIII, 46, 52, 66, 92, 94, 96, 101,
216 (n. 92)
Henryson, Robert, 193 (n. 66)
Heraldry, 52, 116–17

Hierarchy, 13, 38, 43, 51, 60, 78–80, 98, 139, 187 (nn. 16, 18, 19), 188 (n. 21), 215 (n. 80); ideology of, 28–35, 89, 114–31, 133–34, 145–46, 188 (n. 26); cultural, 35–38, 45–46, 53–54, 153, 163, 165, 166, 170, 181 (n. 36), 192 (nn. 51, 52, 57), 196 (n. 94). *See also* Class relations

"High" social status. *See* Class relations; Elite; Hierarchy

Hilton, Rodney, 88

Historicism (in literary criticism), 6–9, 11, 49–50, 170–75, 178 (n. 7), 179 (nn. 19, 25), 180 (n. 36); nonliterary materials in, 171–73, 174; particular and general in, 172–73, 178 (n. 7), 179 (n. 25); importance of institutions in, 173–74; role of imagination in, 173–74. *See also* History

History, 3, 4, 5, 201 (n. 14); and society, 6, 171–75; and antiquarianism, 173; contemporary bearing of, 173–75, 178 (n. 7). *See also* Historicism (in literary criticism)

Hobbinol: in the September eclogue, 12, 62, 72, 133, 140–47, 181 (n. 31), 224 (n. 169); in the April eclogue, 20; in the June eclogue, 21, 152–55, 161, 165, 226 (n. 13)

Hobsbawm, E. J., 76

Hoffman, Nancy Jo, 4–5, 12, 148–49

Holinshed, Raphael, 15, 37

Homer, 164

Homilies, 29, 30–31, 32, 33, 34, 57–58, 112, 126, 134–35, 146, 188 (n. 27), 190 (n. 36), 215 (n. 80), 216 (nn. 88, 92)

Horace, 218 (n. 113)

Hospitality, 138

Howard, Henry, earl of Surrey, 84

Humanities, 6

Husbandry, metaphor of, 92–93, 171

Ideology, 10, 13, 28–29, 74, 75, 89. *See also* Hierarchy

Idolatry, 123

Inflation, 135

Inspiration. *See* Poetry: sanction for

Institutions of Elizabethan society, 11, 66, 77, 89–90, 101, 168–72, 174. *See also* Agrarian economy; Church of England; Class relations; Monarchy, Elizabethan; Patronage

Instruction as aim of poetry, 149–52, 159–60. *See also* Pleasure as aim of poetry

Isaiah, 137

January eclogue, 156–57, 167, 185 (n. 46)

Jeremiah, 87

Jonson, Ben, 192 (n. 59)

Judgment: exercise of, by the nonelite, 33, 45–46, 189 (n. 31)

July eclogue, 13, 43, 62, 66, 69, 70, 72, 73, 80, 81, 82, 83, 89, 114–31, 132, 207 (n. 42), 223 (n. 162), 225 (n. 12), 227 (n. 29)

June eclogue, 13, 21, 148–58, 159, 161, 165, 167, 207 (nn. 38, 39), 226 (nn. 13, 14)

Kalender of Shepherdes, 25, 43, 44, 99

Kantorowicz, Ernst, 184 (nn. 37, 39)

Kelso, Ruth, 79

Kenilworth, 20

Kett's Rebellion (1549), 81, 136, 197 (n. 105), 208 (n. 52), 222 (n. 143)

King, John, 158

Kinsman, Robert, 40

Labor, manual, 79, 119–20, 124, 217 (n. 93). *See also* Class relations; Nonelite in Elizabethan society

Langland, William: *Piers Plowman*, 39, 84, 86, 88, 150, 153, 156, 208 (nn. 46, 51, 53), 212 (n. 35)

Language: of poetry, 36–37, 39; standard English, 36–37, 40. *See also* Dialect; Vernacular, use of

Laslett, Peter, 49

Latimer, Hugh, 87

Leicester, earl of. *See* Dudley, Robert, earl of Leicester